DAILY LIFE SERIES NO. 2

DAILY LIFE IN FLORENCE

DAILY LIFE SERIES

by the same author

RESTORATION AND THE JULY MONARCHY
(Heineman, 1929)

THE BORGIAS
(Staples Press, 1954)

Cosimo de' Medici I, surrounded by artists, architects and engineers
(*clockwise*: Tribolo, Tasso, Vasari, Ammanati, Bandinelli and Cellini)
Fresco by Vasari in the Palazzo Vecchio, Florence

J. LUCAS-DUBRETON

DAILY LIFE
IN FLORENCE
In the Time of the Medici

TRANSLATED FROM THE FRENCH BY
A. LYTTON SELLS

Ruskin House
GEORGE ALLEN & UNWIN LTD
MUSEUM STREET LONDON

Translated from

LA VIE QUOTIDIENNE A FLORENCE
AU TEMPS DES MEDICIS

© *Librairie Hachette,* Paris, 1959

PRINTED IN GREAT BRITAIN
in 12 pt Fournier type by
T. & A. CONSTABLE LTD, EDINBURGH

FOREWORD

Although Florence ruled over the territories surrounding her, she was not a State in the true sense of the term, but a City; and this alone profoundly modified the daily life of her inhabitants. Her boundaries were limited, but not the ideas she gave birth to. And because she was a city of intellect and also of passions, rich in every kind of possibility, the events of history echoed here more loudly than elsewhere.

Whereas in great States such events are so to speak diluted and usually affect only certain classes of the population, they were so much more powerfully concentrated in the case of Florence, in as much as the Florentines all more or less shared in public life, a kind of equality prevailing among them. The nobleman did not reside in his distant castle as in other States, but in the town; the peasant was also a citizen; and there was a perpetual two-way traffic between town and country.

It follows that Florence has been perpetually marked and moulded by history, that history is the very life of 'the City of the Flower', and cannot be separated from it. To neglect history would be to risk distorting our picture of the life of the place, an incomparable life, constantly in motion and with few parallels in the annals of mankind.

CONTENTS

ILLUSTRATIONS

CHAPTER I

A CITY DIVIDED AGAINST ITSELF

Guelphs and Ghibellines – The origins of Florence – The
medieval city – Party strife – The 'Tumulto dei Ciompi' –
Condottieri and 'Caballeria'

Two German lords, one named Guelf and the other Gibelin, were close
friends, but one day when returning from the hunt they quarrelled about a
bitch and became mortal enemies, so that the barons and lords of Germany
were also divided, some siding with Guelf and others with Gibelin. Now,
as the latter felt they were the weaker party, they appealed to the Emperor
Henry I; their adversaries then appealed to Pope Honorius III, who was at
odds with the Emperor; and that is why the Holy See is Guelph and the
Empire Ghibelline, and all because of a wretched bitch.

Now it came to pass in the year 1215 that this evil strife invaded Italy, and
in the following manner. There dwelt in the house of the Buondelmonti in
Florence a wealthy and valiant knight who had pledged his troth to a
daughter of the Amidei. As he was passing the house of the Donati one day,
a lady called to him and said:

'Messer, I am astonished that you should have a leaning for one who
would be scarce fit to unloose your shoes. I had been reserving my daughter
for you. I desire that you see her.'

And she forthwith called the girl, whose name was Ciulla, fairer and more
pleasant than any other maiden in Florence. 'Here', she said, 'is the bride
I reserved for you.'

Buondelmonte fell in love at first sight.

'Madam, I am ready to do as you wish.' And before leaving he chose
Ciulla for wife and gave her his ring.

When they heard that Buondelmonte had taken a different wife, the
Amidei and their friends swore to take vengeance. Each man was giving
his opinion when one said: 'Cosa fatta è fatta', which means that 'a dead man
never makes war'.

On Easter morning Buondelmonte was on his way back from breakfast
on the far bank of the Arno. Wearing a white gown and mounted on a
snow-white palfrey, he was at the lower end of the Ponte Vecchio by the
statue of Mars which the Florentines used to worship when they were
pagans and where fish is sold now, when a band of men rushed out, pulled
him from his horse and killed him.

Florence was in an uproar, and this man's death led to a cleavage among the nobility: the Buondelmonti became leaders of the Guelphs and the Amidei of the Ghibellines. Next, the seeds of evil faction were sown all over Italy, and lords and peoples separated into two camps. Thus the Guelph and Ghibelline parties sprang up in Germany on account of a bitch and in Italy on account of a woman.[1]

THIS narrative, which reads like a philosophical tale, we owe to a *novelliere* of the fourteenth century, Ser Giovanni Fiorentino, a man famous among his compatriots, who were naturally enthusiastic for a city so exceptional and passionately interested in its remote origins and in the dramas so numerous throughout its history. The story has at least the merit of explaining in a concise and artistic form the origin of the factions with which the life of Florence was so often to be rent.

* * * *

How did the name of the city first arise? Was it from Fiorinus, one of Caesar's generals? Or from the vast number of flowers that grow in that region? The former view was held by Benvenuto Cellini, the sculptor and goldsmith who lived for a time in the Petit-Nesle in Paris. He rejected the etymology which made Florence derive from *Fluentia* on the ground that the Arno 'flows' ('flue') through the city. This, he asserted, is utterly improbable, because the Tiber does the same in Rome and the Seine in Paris. 'We therefore believe and maintain that we are descended from a man of valour.' The artist adventurer held, then, for Fiorinus.

On the other hand Benedetto Varchi, that distinguished historian of the sixteenth century who was better qualified to have an opinion, favoured the floral etymology. Flowers and lilies grew abundantly in the plain of the Arno, hence the name of *Floria*, the city built among flowers. Supported by a passage in Dante, Varchi also informs us that the first occupants of the

---

[1] This classification was not destined to remain rigid. In the course of time and under the pressure of circumstances, it was to break down. Sometimes there were Guelphs who favoured the Emperors and Ghibellines who sided with the Pope.

country came down from the hill of Fiesole to establish warehouses in the plain, where they built cabins and later houses,
because here they found it easier to market their produce.
Florence was presumably founded, then, by merchants of Fiesole,
and so it is no matter for surprise that the Florentines have
'always remained great merchants'. In the twelfth century they
threw off the yoke of Fiesole and annexed its territory. They were
great warriors in those days, but they were to get over it.

The present view of scholars is this[1]: Florence, which was no
doubt an old Etruscan city and was certainly a Roman Camp
divided into four quarters and having a capital and forum, was
so called because of the abundance of wild flowers.

Animated by the youthful energy which arose for some mysterious reason during the twilight of the Feudal Era, the Florentines
established a Commune. It was the product of an economic
revival of which they were literally the artisans. Thanks to a
privileged situation, a new social group had been slowly making
its appearance, a group utterly different from the '*Società delle
torri*', the men 'of the towers', nobles, more or less, of Germanic
origin, who were connected by birth and lived close together
under the shelter of their fortified towers. It was, as we shall see,
by means of a professional organization associated with an 'art'
that the people were able to force their way upward. This 'art'
was the dressing or finishing, and the dyeing, of woollen fabrics;
and when the corporations in question had attained their full
development, a clash with the nobility would be inevitable—the
beginnings of the class-war, for which Florence gave the signal,
as she did for so many other things.

In the twelfth century, however, the infant Commune appears
to have been relatively quiet. If we are to believe Dante, whose
testimony is rather suspect, since exile had inspired in him a
certain nostalgia for the past, 'she remained sober and modest
within the circle of her ancient walls'. From this high moral tone
the declension seems to have been rapid. Political intrigues sprang
up like a crop of toadstools, and the tribe of rhetoricians, whose

[1] Antonio Panella, *Storia di Firenze* (1949).

appearance was inevitable in an age which was beginning to honour the ancient world, were learning how to call together in some public square the disinherited classes and those who aspired to better material conditions. This was the 'call to parliament', another innovation, and one which was to be fruitful. Here the régime was transformed, constitutions were elaborated, magistrates and officials appointed. Disorder became the rule, and the quarrel between Guelphs and Ghibellines was ill calculated to pacify it.

We must now note a few stages of this internecine struggle which throws so much light on the future, on the years of Medici domination.

The year 1250 saw the victory of the Guelphs, the adoption of the Constitution of the *Primo popolo* and the appointment of the *Capitano del popolo*, entrusted with the protection of the people's interests. Ten years later the Tuscan Guelphs were defeated at Montaperti by the Ghibellines of Siena, and Florence which was on the brink of destruction was saved only by a patriotic Ghibelline. Then the wheel of fortune took another turn, and the *Parte Guelfa* gained the upper hand.

But what is exceptional in all this is that, in spite of faction fights and sanguinary rivalries, the handicrafts, industries and commerce of Florence continued to develop. Florentine banks outstripped all others, entering into closer and closer relations with France, the Papacy and Southern Italy. This marked the advent of capitalism and of a new social class which was equally opposed to the nobles and the common people—namely, the wealthy merchants or, if you like, the aristocracy of the counter.

The year 1293 marks an important step in the evolution of Florentine politics. This year saw the promulgation of the *Ordinamenti della Guistizia*, by virtue of which every citizen was obliged to enroll in a guild, or *arte*. He who did not enroll became a *scioperato*, a second-class plebeian. The noble was not exempt, far from it. The regulation was directed against him. If he did not enroll, he remained indeed a noble but had no right to the title of citizen, was excluded from government and had no vote in the Council. To degrade a man, Florence left him his social rank.

If Florence became the home of a higher culture, she owed it to the Republican spirit and still more to the existence of this mercantile 'aristocracy' which was so different from the others. The Venetian aristocracy was like a clique of conspirators, standing aloof from the populace who trembled in face of a 'mysterious and invisible' police-state. The Neapolitan noble was an idler for whom honour consisted in *far niente*. The Papal States harboured another kind of nobility, pastoral and agricultural—men who would refuse to soil their hands in trade. In Florence, on the other hand, the democracy aimed at disparaging the old nobility and at the same time at absorbing it.

This is how men of letters speak of the feudal lords: 'To pretend to keep up the virtue of one's ancestors only by maintaining hordes of dogs, falcons and horses, and by riding through woods and forests, is to seek nobility among animals. . . . Enthusiasm for hawking or hunting savours no more of nobility than birds' nests, or the lairs of wild animals, smell of a rosebower.' Petrarch says: 'One is not born noble, one becomes noble.' The Florentine Palmieri writes: 'The man who seeks glory by reference to his ancestors' virtue, exempts himself from personal merit. To give an example by one's own efforts, not by one's family's, is to merit honour.' Thus the real noble is the child of his own achievements.

This was the creed of a true citizen: work is the law, and a consequence of the increasing share in public life taken by the *arti* or guilds was to oblige the noble to carry the label of commerce, even if he despised it. By reason of its organization which was founded on the crafts, the *Parte Guelfa* now dominated the Republic. It was not a state within the State, but the State itself; and its aim was to level the classes, a task rendered easier by the fact that, unlike his fellows in France, the lord did not live in an isolated castle but in the city, in the *Società delle torri*.

This process of levelling was not at all of a nature to promote peace. The 'arts' were divided in their outlook and their policies.

Thus the major arts, namely the wool carders and the bankers, were not averse to financing a war if it was likely to open up foreign markets and facilitate trade; whereas the minor arts, those of the stone-mason, the blacksmith, the innkeeper and so on, were desirous only of peace, which favoured their trades; and soon a struggle was to begin between the *popolo grasso* and the *popolo minuto* , the 'fat' and the 'lean'.

But this was not all. Behind the 'lean people' thronged the horde of real plebeians, illiterate labourers, 'idiots',[1] who also wanted to force their way into the Republic and share in its deliberations and offices. Democracy has been defined as 'the soul of the citizens united in the common will'. This is good patter for the orator; but if the idea is pushed to its limits it will lead to unending conflict.

And on all this was grafted a new occasion of discord in which the protagonists were now the upper middle-class whose wealth was founded on trade and, on the other side, the feudal patricians.

In May 1300 in the *Piazza della Trinità* the ladies were celebrating amid games and dances the return of summer. Festivity, and not tragedy, was in the air, when, of a sudden, a band of Donati (patricians) rode into the square with the clear intent to provoke a riot, and began to hustle the onlookers. A few members of the Cerchi family (wealthy burghers) were violently jostled and took the intrusion for an affront. Swords were drawn, blood flowed and the crowd fled in panic. Several people lay wounded in the square, including one of the Cerchi whose nose had been cut off.

These hostilities were duplicated by a war of factions, which broke out in the subject-town of Pistoia, between the *Bianchi* and the *Neri*. The former were backed by the Cerchi, the latter by the Donati, there was more fighting and each side in turn banished its adversaries. Dante was the most celebrated of the exiles. The Donati finally had the upper hand, but not for long. Their leader was accused of aspiring to be tyrant and was killed in 1308.

[1] From Greek *idiotés*, Latin *idiota*, originally a private individual, and later a vulgar or unskilled person.   (Translator)

In a city rocked with such convulsions there were times when men were overcome with fatigue and incapable of either attack or defence. They would then forget the Republic and fall into the power of a foreign prince or soldier of fortune. But such interludes usually brought the dictator to a bad end, and Florence would then return to her succession of political contrivances and short-lived constitutions. After the plague of 1358 she added a new weapon to her armoury in the form of an admonition, of which the object was to prevent anyone suspected of being a Ghibelline from accepting or filling a public office; the Ghibelline being always regarded as the enemy. This admonition was equivalent to proscription, since men's minds were now so imbued with the idea of public life that to be excluded from it seemed to reduce one to a mere cipher.

But if one was excluded from office or usually outvoted, there was still a means of possible redress: one could appeal to the *Consiglio del popolo*.

It was a dangerous expedient. A wealthy merchant and demagogue, Salvestro de' Medici, had recourse to it, and this led to the first plebeian insurrection. The small artisans who were not organized in guilds rose up against the classes in power, destroyed the old Republic, cancelled the burghers' privileges and proclaimed a new republic of the poor. They set up the gallows in the Piazza della Signoria; and, as a symbol and occasion for merriment, hanged the *bargello* or chief of police. They next threatened the members of the government, who had shut themselves up in the *palazzo*, that they would kill their wives and children if they did not surrender; and the 'lords' (*signori*)[1] then hastened out one by one, handing over the keys to the insurgents.

The latter were headed by a certain Michele di Lando, a real plebeian, a ragged and down-at-heels workman who carded wool in a textile factory and whose wife and mother sold vegetables near the *Stinche*, the town gaol. But Michele was no common rioter. He took possession of the *Gonfalon della Giustizia*, installed himself in the palace and issued orders. His first move was to

---

[1] Hence the 'Palazzo della Signoria'. (Translator)

establish three new minor *arti* or guilds, including that of the *Ciompi*, or companions, a name which became attached to this revolution.[1] The establishment of the minor arts liberated the plebs from the crushing patronage of the *Arte della lana*, or Wool Weavers' Guild. The registers of this guild were burned, and all the guilds were now placed on a footing of equality.

Unfortunately the *Ciompi* proved so brutal, incapable and absurd that Lando, whom they had raised to power, was overcome with disgust and assisted in their overthrow. The 'art' of the *Ciompi*, the lowest of all the guilds, was suppressed, and reaction followed. At the beginning of the fifteenth century the aristocracy and the major arts regained control of the government.

*   *   *   *

A stranger who once visited Florence was amazed to hear shouting and to see people running along the street with drawn swords.

'What is happening?' he asked.

"Oh, nothing serious. They are simply sharing out the magistratures and other public offices.'

Umori—that is, disturbances provoked by rival factions—were the daily bread of the city. They were so usual that most people paid no attention unless these *umori* took a dangerous turn. Government worked in a succession of jerks and starts. The party in power would banish its rivals and proceed to remodel the government to suit its own interests; while, from far away, the exiles strove to stir up discontent in the city. Pistoia, Prato and Arezzo, which were subject to Florence, jealous of her power and at the same time torn by faction within themselves, joined in these intrigues. Thus the Republic grew weaker and distrustful of itself. The notion of a confederation with other Republics, which would have increased her power and perhaps have made for stability, seemed quite inconceivable.

At the end of the fifteenth century we find three parties in being:

[1] The *Tumulto dei Ciompi*. (Translator)

the new nobility, founded on the major 'arts', an aristocracy of wealth into which the old territorial aristocracy was merging; the middle class: and the artisans proper.

'If she had no great parties, fair Italy would dominate the world.' This observation of a satiric poet of the Renaissance errs by reason of ambitious pride, but is true in the sense in which Italy—and first of all, Florence—dominated Europe by her commercial expansion and intellectual and artistic brilliance.

By 1338 Florence possessed more than two hundred factories producing annually eighty-thousand pieces of cloth; she was developing the silk industry, which had come from Sicily towards the thirteenth century, and the weaving of tapestry, an art introduced by French and Flemish workmen. Her merchants, who were better informed than anyone regarding the financial condition of the nations, travelled throughout Europe, visiting their warehouses and founding banks. The Florentine florin was the principal currency, the strongest and the most sought after. Florence in brief was become more than ever the seat of capitalism.

Meanwhile, unaffected by these practical and terrestrial interests, pure art continued to flourish. We shall explore this pleasaunce in a later chapter. Suffice it to refer here to the buildings of an urban or civic character, such as the *Loggie* of the Grano and the Bigallo (near the Campanile and the Baptistery), and especially the Loggia dei Lanzi, as we now call it, which incarnated 'the majesty of the Republic', as it was from there that the rulers harangued the people. Finally a college, the *Studio*, was founded in the year of Dante's exile; and the works of Dante himself were explained and commented on by Giovanni Boccaccio.

This prosperity, alas! had its drawbacks. The Florentine had found a marvellous vocation for the arts of peace and lost any vocation for the art of war. It was natural. War distracted him from his favourite pursuits, prevented him from attending to business and making money. The maxim that 'A shopkeeper cannot go and fight' was currently accepted, and the task of defending the country was entrusted to mercenaries.

These soldiers of fortune, who were often foreigners, served under a *condottiere*, a military leader and sometimes tyrant of one of the many Italian principalities. This man would hire out his *condotta*; and thus was organized a sort of nomadic despotism. Hence the relations between Florence and the *condottieri* took the form of a commercial deal. A military enterprise involved only two considerations: the expense of supporting the troops which had been hired, and the risk of being pillaged by the enemy. One purchased a mercenary band as one would buy any other commodity. When a king of Naples asked a Florentine envoy how Florence proposed to resist him, the envoy replied: 'With your own soldiers.' And it was in fact so.

But if soldiering meant nothing to them, the Florentines liked to pose as noble warriors. This little weakness is noted by Francesco Sacchetti, that racy news-writer. Look at all these workmen, he says, bakers, wool carders, odd fish of every description. They all want to be made knights, and not one of them has a horse or knows how to handle a weapon. Masters of smuggling who do exactly the opposite of what chivalry ordains. This is not *caballeria* but *cacaleria*!

No matter. The artisan and the bourgeois enjoy this warlike façade. Sunday tournaments are their delight. A seventy-year-old lawyer was to remain famous as the hero of one of these tourneys. The pastime was harmless enough, after all, since the jousters hardly dreamed of running each other through. But the serious part of it was that for these amateur warriors the power of the State rested more on its finances than on the courage of its citizens.

CHAPTER II

THE *SIGNORIA* AND FLORENTINE TRADE

The four quarters of Florence – The Gonfaloniere – The
Rage for Office – Commercial Organization and the
Hierarchy – Growth of Trade in the fifteenth century

He who would create a State in our day would find it easier to do so among
the men of the mountains where civilization does not yet exist than in the
cities where it is already corrupted. Thus a sculptor will more easily extract
a fair statue from a shapeless block than from a piece of marble roughly
shaped by a clumsy hand.

THIS observation of Machiavelli, the founder of political
science, applies exactly to his own country, which was
like a block of marble constantly chipped and broken and
which never managed to become a state with any chance of
stability, except in the hour of dictatorship.

Many countries, including France, have played at constitution-
making, but none has ever surpassed Florence at the game. Her
political character seems to have been congenitally deformed.

It would be painful for the reader to follow all the ups and
downs of these political schemes, which our own age has inured us
to, and in which some of our compatriots, such as Sieyès, took a
positive pleasure. In any event, it is easy to diagnose the case of
the Florentines. They were the first people, since the ancient
Greeks, to be infected with the mania for constitution-making—
a chronic disease. Such subjects as the relations between social
classes, the characteristics of various régimes, the rule of the
nobility, tyranny, middle-class versus lower-class, pure democracy, modified democracy, façade of democracy, government by
a ruling house, theocracy and so on—these were what excited
their interest and on these they founded doctrines, theories and
perilous experiments.

Florence was a sort of political laboratory, ill-kept and so encumbered with apparatus that we shall study only one of the durable forms of government which gives some notion of what can be produced by a marvellously intelligent people[1] when it loses itself among the ruts of political sophistry.

*   *   *   *

Florence was divided into four quarters: San Spirito (beyond the Arno), Santa Croce, Santa Maria Novella and San Giovanni; each quarter being in turn divided into four 'gonfalons' with individual names: the Ladder, the Shell, the Dragon, the Golden Lion, the Viper, the Unicorn, and so on. There was not a citizen but enrolled under one of these sixteen gonfalons, or banners, and in case of need had to repair to the Palazzo della Signoria to fight for the people's liberty. Thus the gonfalon was the civic unit.

The supreme magistracy at first belonged to eight *Priori*, two from each quarter, then to twelve *Buoni Uomini* (or *Buonomini*), three from each quarter, who acted as counsellors, and finally to the *Gonfaloniere della Giustizia*, a creation of the famous egalitarian ordinances of which we have already spoken.

Priors, 'good men', and *gonfalonieri*—such was the triumvirate which formed the Signoria. The *gonfaloniere* had to be at least forty-five years of age. On the morning when he entered on his duties, he received the banner with a red cross on a white ground, and this he kept in his room in the Palazzo della Signoria. If he rode out, everyone escorted him. A like ceremonial attended the appointment of the Priors. The shops closed, the people assembled in the square, received the outgoing Prior and accompanied him to his home.

During their term of office, these 'lords' were lodged in the palace, where they were excellently treated and waited on by a large body of servants in green livery, bearing the insignia of the Commune. The hall was hung with tapestries, the table covered with fair linen and silver plate, the food excellent—all thanks to a

[1] Conversely, Walter Bagehot argues that a certain degree of *stupidity* is needed in a nation if it is to have a good and stable government. (Translator)

monthly credit of three hundred gold florins. To add to the luxury there were singers, musicians and buffoons, in addition to a notary who recorded the proceedings and a chancellor who attended to the correspondence.

It was a lordly establishment, and one to be envied. Citizens took infinite pains to be elected, but it was not easy. If you aspired to office, it was necessary that your father or grandfather should himself have been invested with one or other of the three magistratures. In that case your name was *imborsato*, that is, placed in a purse, or urn, from which it might one day emerge. Then you would be either *seduto*, which meant that you were in possession of a public office; or *veduto*, a word reserved for a person who was eligible for office, but had not in fact exercised it.

All these refinements of red tape lent themselves to the shadiest schemings. A man would intrigue to be *imborsato* even if he could not fulfil the conditions, or if he wanted to keep out a rival. But if your name should indeed be drawn from the purse, what an honour! You donned the *lucco*, the gown of pink, violet or crimson; ushers and mercenary guardsmen with long bucklers escorted you to the palace, and here you received ambassadors and were a great man.

Although he was not paid, the lord did well out of his position. While maintaining his commercial activities, he exploited his temporary influence to favour his friends and bully or persecute his competitors; and he took precautions to reduce the number of the latter by means of the *specchio*, a book in which, for each quarter and gonfalon, the names of those who had not paid their taxes, or were otherwise debtors of the Commune, were inscribed. If your name was in the *specchio*, you were ineligible for office.

The *Signori*, being usually at odds, would fail to reach any decision and become bogged down in votes on contradictory motions or on the question when to use the beans placed before them, a black bean meaning yes, a white bean no. Once, towards midnight the story goes, the *Gonfaloniere della Giustizia* who was presiding called for the keys of the hall, sat on them, and swore that no one should leave if the meeting did not agree to what he desired; the members would be served with food in the hall itself until they had given in.

On another occasion, the *Gonfaloniere*—this time an easy-going big-wig—read out the proposal for discussion. The talking began and trailed on and on. . . . During all this time one of the lords, a remarkable politician named Niccolò Uzzano, whom we shall meet later on, slept like a log. After several hours, whether he had had his sleep out or had been awakened, he climbed heavily to the rostrum, said what he thought in a few words, and everyone agreed. It was the prototype of a Parliamentary meeting.

There existed, in addition to the *Signoria*, three important officials who were not Florentines: an arrangement designed to ensure their impartiality, at least in theory. These were the *Podestà*,[1] whose existence dated from an early period and who, with the assistance of notaries and doctors of law, supervised wills and dowries and looked after civil lawsuits; the *Capitano del Popolo*,[1] who was guardian of the city; and the 'Executor' whose business was to keep an eye on any intrigues on the part of the 'grandi' against the people, whether 'grasso' or 'minuto'. All three had to deal with persons condemned by the courts: exiles, homicides, thieves, forgers, etc.

Here, you might think, is a fairly ample sheaf of institutions. You can be reassured: there were others. The Priors deliberated in conjunction with other councils: the *Consiglio del Popolo* (ten members from each gonfalon), the 'Ten Counsellors of Liberty', who heard complaints relating to fraud, deceit or molestation; the 'Ten of the Balìa', who functioned in war-time; and the 'Eight of the Guard' who were the State Police. This was not all; but the main point is that this swarm of debating-clubs, these wheels within wheels that suggest some monstrous piece of machinery, clogged any efficiency in government. Six meetings were required

---

[1] By the Constitution of 1325 the *Podestà* presided over the *Consiglio del Comune*, which contained 125 nobles and 125 *popolani*. The *Capitano* presided over the *Consiglio del Popolo*.

to veto the smallest credit, to send a dying man to the hospital, or to have a wardrobe repaired. Red-tape—the plague of modern society, whether capitalist or not—has its letters of nobility.

Worse still, each member of the Signoria held office for only two months, which meant that elections were perpetually in progress. A candidate for the post of Prior would be feverishly canvassing, while the Prior in office was doing his best to exploit the last days of his greatness.

Add to all this the malady of minute controls. The exact amount of steel to be used in making a helmet, for example, was fixed; the objects a shopkeeper might sell were limited: one was not allowed to trespass on one's neighbour's specialities. Then, as they prepared to vote, the people would rebel in exasperation. It was a means of blowing off steam—*sfogarsi*. Men flew to arms, fought, killed and banished each other. Florence was like the sick man described by Dante as continually shifting his position in bed in order to escape pain.

* * * *

The cultured burgher felt little respect for a political system so absurd, and ended by despising democracy. 'The stupidity of appointing a cobbler to deliberate on the making of laws, the administration of the Republic and the conduct of war!' Do you know what the bell-ringer does when he wants to advise the government? He comes down into the square and sings. Oh, the folly of sacrificing rest and liberty in order to be preceded by trumpeters or to brandish a baton as you walk! Such men respect justice and honesty only so far as these bring them profit, they value 'know how' more than anything else, get in tow behind an influential citizen, join those sects or coteries that will assist their intrigues, in order 'to get their shop on the side of the men in power', so as to make money and find dowries for their daughters —and the Republic suffers. Riddled with corruption, it prevents men of wisdom and merit from making their way; or, if they do succeed, they are beset with so much jealousy and persecution that they rebel out of disgust, and either die or are driven out.

To cite a few examples of local politics that reveal the tenor of life in Florence:

A citizen of merit aspires to become *Gonfaloniere della Giustizia*. He receives promise of support from the most influential elector in his quarter; but a friend he has in another quarter puts him on guard. 'That man', he says, 'is deceiving you. It's he who moved for your exile, and the proposal will be put through in a fortnight. There's nothing to be done.' The good citizen was in fact banished, and simply because he was a capable man and his fellow citizens did not want him to outdistance them.

Then there was the case of Agnolo Acciaiuoli, a member of an old family, whose only fault was that he kept in touch with certain exiles. One of his kinsmen, on hearing that the Signoria held him in suspicion, galloped to his property, rushed into his office and threw into the fire all the papers he found there—very compromising papers which would have 'landed him into a sorry mess'. Hardly were the documents consumed when the mace-bearer of the Signoria arrived, searched the premises but drew a blank. As, owing to lack of proofs, it was impossible to prosecute Agnolo, he was banished to Cephalonia.

But as regards banishment the record was unquestionably held by Palla Strozzi, an eminent citizen, a distinguished Hellenist and a very handsome person. 'People had only to see him pass by, to exclaim: "There goes Messer Palla".' He had everything a man needs to be happy: a charming wife and thriving children. But for fiscal reasons (he was overburdened with taxes and found difficulty in paying) and political reasons (he favoured peace and was opposed to 'innovations'), the Signoria exiled him to Padua. Although he was then sixty-two—the age for repose at home, his biographer says—he accepted his misfortune philosophically, refusing to speak ill of Florence, or even to hear the city disparaged. After ten years, his exile was renewed; and ten years later it was again renewed. When he was informed of the Signoria's decision he merely observed that his good conduct had been of no use to him.

One of his sons was murdered, another died, then he lost his wife 'whom at his age he greatly needed'. The last of his children, who he had hoped would restore the fortunes of his house, died also. He had now himself only to await death, which came when he was over ninety-two, sound in body and mind. 'In the times of the Roman Republic, he would have been a great man.'

Examples of such dogged malice were not uncommon. Matteo Bandello, the great sixteenth-century *novelliere*, went as far as saying:

> I think that if all the people who have been driven from Florence, and all who have been miserably assassinated, were gathered together, they would populate a city far greater than Florence is today.

Whether by its own fault or its evil destiny, the Pearl of the Arno was 'marvellously subject to internal discord and division', owing to the frightfully complicated mechanism of its government, which was continually hatching new revolutions.

*   *   *   *

Florentine trade was saturated with politics, nor did it benefit from this, at least as regards simplicity. Let us inspect these corporations, where the seven major 'arts' confronted the fourteen minor 'arts', and not forget the Florentine maxim recorded by Boccaccio: 'He who has no possessions is regarded as a mere animal.'

The oldest, and the source of civic wealth, was the guild of Calimala, a name famous in Italy and derived perhaps from a street of ill repute, the *Calis malus* or *Via Mala*. Its object was to import raw or undressed cloths, which were put back on the looms and worked up into fine cloths. The Florentines obtained their raw material from Flanders, England and especially from France. They had branches or warehouses, as well as hostelries, in Paris, Caen, Rouen, Provins, Montpellier, Avignon, Marseille and Toulon; so that a considerable Italian colony, augmented by the influx of exiles, was installed in France under the direction of a Captain General. Note that to reach Avignon from Florence took fourteen days, Montpellier sixteen and Paris twenty-two.

The rough imported cloth was distributed among the corporations who undertook to full it, press and smooth, and finally cut
it. For the purpose of dyeing the fabric, they used *guado* (blue),
robbia (red) and *oricello* (crimson). With *oricello* and a little *robbia*
one obtained *scarlatto d'oricello*, a very fashionable colour. When
each piece of cloth had been prepared and marked with the seal of
the corporation and with a label, it was rolled into a bale of felt,
or coarse linen, doubled, and stamped with the arms of Calimala.

In view of the instability of civic government, this Guild of the
Cloth Merchants[1] very wisely governed itself. Its statutes, which
dated from the early fourteenth century, were a marvel of
minutiae. Every six months the merchants elected four consuls
and a chamberlain, and these representatives then appointed their
Prior. All had to be Guelphs and well affected to the Roman
Church. Each shop was protected like a private domain, no cloth
might be transferred, no street-display was allowed, business was
done inside, no games of chance (so injurious to good business)
might be played on the premises, and the opening and closing of
the cash-books were strictly controlled. A notary saw to it that the
statutes were duly observed, and enquiry was made if any companion, workman or apprentice appeared richer than he ought to
be. No companion could marry outside Florence without special
permission. The consuls were responsible for enforcing the
observance of Saints' Days, according to the rites of the Church
and the rules of Calimala. Finally, no cloth might be sold,
directly or indirectly—under penalty of a heavy fine—unless it
were of French, Flemish or English origin. One had to keep one's
customers. Thus the trading Republic operated within the frame-
work of the political Republic.

Calimala set the general pattern. In company with it, the Guild
of Manufacturers of Woollens[2] imported its raw material from
Spain, Portugal and England, and processed the wool from beginning to end. The Silk Manufacturers' Guild[3] had been prosperous

[1] '*Arte dei Mercanti di Calimala.*'   (Translator)
[2] *Arte della Lana.*   (Translator)
[3] *Arte della Seta.*   (Translator)

from the end of the thirteenth century. It also had its consuls and was distinguished for the splendid fabrics it produced for lords and great ladies; silken garments adorned with paintings, or spangles or filigree of gold.

As he prospered in trade, the Florentine, as Dante observed, naturally embarked on money-changing and banking. Hence a new major art,[1] that of the Banker, who sat in the *Mercato Nuovo*, in front of his office or *Banco*, beside a table covered with green cloth—the colour of administration—a purse and a ledger.

Since the letter of exchange had been invented, there was no more fear of theft. Money circulated invisibly all over Europe, thanks to the Florentines who had their branches and 'factors' everywhere, and dealt in a sound currency. Florence had become a great banking-house and its money was at a premium.

Calimala, wool-stapling, the silk trade and banking constituted the leading arts; while the judges and notaries were their legitimate offspring. 'If', as a Florentine proudly observed, 'Bologna is the nursery for doctors of the law, our city is the nursery for doctors in the profession of notary.'

After the jurists came the apothecaries and druggists, important because they dealt not only in drugs but in spices and other produce from the Levant, including precious stones. The fact that in 1295 Dante registered as a member of this guild is enough to indicate its prestige.

The furriers completed the group of the seven privileged 'arts'. Here too the regulations were detailed and meticulous, and delinquents were remorselessly prosecuted. A bankrupt had to repair to the *Mercato Nuovo*, and, to obtain his discharge, had, with his bare behind, to strike three times on the site of the *carroccio*, the symbolical chariot of the city. This was a circular space paved with marble flags, alternately white and black. In a merchant community the sanction for discharge had to be public.

Each major art of course had its banner: golden stars on a field azure for judges; a white sheep on a bright red field for wool-staplers; an *Agnus Dei* on a field azure for furriers.

[1] *Arte del Cambio.*   (Translator)

After the suppression of the *Ciompi* the minor arts had been reduced to fourteen. At the top came the butchers whose stalls were set up in the *Mercato Vecchio* (Piazza Vittorio-Emmanuele); then the blacksmiths, shoe-makers, carpenters, tavern-keepers, hotel-keepers, tanners, dealers in oil, salt and cheese ... and lastly the bakers, whose guild was the most despised because it was the easiest of access.

The democratic organization was a mere façade, and naturally so, since the conditions under which one could register were such that out of a population of about a hundred thousand, only three thousand five hundred were real citizens, eligible for public office. Power had to be kept respectable.

*   *   *   *

In the course of time the guilds were modified and concentrated. First now in the hierarchy came the judges and notaries, and they began to absorb each other. The wool-staplers ran 273 shops, the silk-weavers and mercers 84—a prosperous community. Banking became more and more concentrated. Of the 72 banks that existed in 1422, only 33 remained fifty years later, but they were sound and flourishing concerns.

The tentacles of commerce, meanwhile, were reaching out in every direction. Thus in 1421 twelve young men belonging to the best families set out for Alexandria to negotiate with the 'Soudan' and to found warehouses and banks. Florence was soon to outstrip the East in the manufacture of brocades and cloth of silver; and, along with Venice, to become the great depot for the supply of jewels, pearls and objects of finery. The Acciaiuoli installed themselves in Naples and even in Athens; the Scolari, who had once been banished, settled in Hungary.

But the country with which Florence maintained the steadiest commerce was France, Guelph sympathies had drawn them together of old, and when in 1452 ambassadors were sent to the court of Charles VII, they were instructed to remind the King of the close bonds which had united the two countries for centuries, and also to recall that Charlemagne had once delivered Florence

2. Panorama of Florence (1530) by Vasari showing the Prince of Orange's camp

(*above*) Matteo Franco and Luigi Pulci

3. Details from a fresco in the Chiesa de S. Trinita by Ghirlandajo:

(*right*) Lorenzo il Magnifico with three members of the Sassetti family.

from the Lombards. It is true that the social system beyond the Alps was very different. In France even in cities which had trade-guilds, there existed a large proportion of craftsmen who worked independently. And yet the opposite system, which Florence imposed, was not a source of inferiority.

The 'City of Flowers' was a great commercial establishment; and in her eyes Venice and Genoa were simply rivals to be supplanted. Even Dante, in the course of his wanderings through Hell and through Heaven, never loses sight of the florin[1] and, like others, dreads anything that might debase its value. Gradually and without at first realising it, the Florentine merchant was becoming a cosmopolitan, practical and experienced, enriching and polishing his personality by contact with other customs and ideas—a man who has breathed the sea-air and is the exact opposite of a narrow-minded fossil.

At the same time his aptitudes were widening, and we shall soon see him changed into a diplomatist. Diplomacy is after all a kind of trade, 'under fair and somewhat obvious colours', as Comines remarks. To maintain a nice balance between upright-ness and knavery, to preserve the outer appearance of an honest man and, once your reputation for honesty is established, to act as you please and tell lies when convenient—such was the good method which Machiavelli was to formulate. If it was not very satisfactory from the moral point of view, who was to blame? Why, those princes who, by deceiving your ambassadors, have compelled them to use the weapon of deceit.

There was one thing that the Florentine, whether merchant or politician, had a horror of, and that was to be a dupe.

[1] The Florentines had begun to coin florins in 1252, to commemorate the extension of their power in Tuscany, following their victory over Pisa and Siena.

B

CHAPTER III

VARIOUS ASPECTS OF THE FLORENTINE CHARACTER

Intellectual independence – L. B. Alberti, the complete Florentine – Some figurative expressions – The sense of the comic – Grace and refinement – Love of gambling – Astrologers and sorcerers – Religion and superstition – Some notable churchmen

OBSESSED as they were with politics and money-making, the Florentines might well appear as a most unattractive people, and there were writers—and Dante first of all—who did not spare them.

A conceited race of men, greedy and envious! Arrogance and love of quick profits have so corrupted them that 'virtue is treated as an enemy and driven out like a snake'. Fosterling of Lucifer; or, to quote the politicians, 'the well-steered bark'! And what of the Arno? a stream that rises where unclean swine wallow, then flows past the snarling curs of Arezzo, lingers long enough for the wolves of Florence to lap its waters, and finally descends to the foxes of Pisa!

This chaplet of anathemas, which Dante so liberally bestows on Tuscany as a whole, would prove (if proof were needed) to what extremes the Florentines let themselves be carried by partisan hatred. But Varchi shows us the other side of the picture:

The Florentines excel other nations in all they apply themselves to. Apart from commerce, which is the real foundation of their city, they are reputed to be great men and skilful; expert also in the arts of painting, sculpture and architecture, which they exercise at home and abroad. It was they who revived the study of Greek and Latin. I have always been very much surprised to see that in these men who have been accustomed from childhood to carry heavy bales of wool and baskets of silk and who spend all day and a large part of the night glued to their looms and spindles, there should dwell so great a spirit and such high and noble thoughts.

Varchi ascribes this privilege to the climate, Florence lying midway between the rarified atmosphere of Arezzo and the heavy air of Pisa. He adds that his countrymen are better fitted to rule than to obey, and that they are incapable of any kind of moderation. If fools, they are great fools, if clever extremely clever; but the intelligent outnumber the stupid, and it has been said that to destroy the world, you would have first to remove all the Florentines. At the time of the jubilee of 1300 Pope Boniface VIII had proclaimed that the Florentines constituted the fifth element. And their fame had gone on increasing. When Nicholas V, a highly cultured Pope of the fifteenth-century, was asked why he had no Italian servants, he replied: 'Because they are too lofty of spirit and always wish to climb higher; whereas a Frenchman or a German, whatever work you put him to, is satisfied with his task and does not look beyond it.'

The Florentine was not in fact a stick-in-the-mud. Whether *grasso* or *minuto*—'fat' or 'lean'—he would strive to become an *uomo singolare*, quite naturally, without false modesty or hypocrisy. He would make himself singular by his dress, if he had no other means. To follow the herd was abhorrent to him; he was no copy-cat. Emile Gebhart relates that on the occasion of a suspicious epidemic, at the end of the nineteenth century, the Italians set up furnaces on the frontiers and at the entrance to cities, to fumigate newcomers, and foreigners were more or less politely required to undergo this unpleasant ordeal. When on reaching Florence Gebhart smelt no whiff of the poison which the government had made him breathe at Milan and Bologna, he asked the strapping porter who was carrying his luggage: 'So you don't fumigate here?' 'Ah! Signor', was the reply. 'Here we are in Florence!'

Everything was summed up in these words. The Florentine prided himself on being exceptional, on initiating, inventing, creating his own world—a world not built according to the ordinary rules; and he had the requisite qualities for the task. He was sharp-witted, fundamentally inquisitive, with a passion for the novel, the rare and the beautiful; merry too and ever ready to amuse himself at the expense of others.

Chi ha a fare con Tosco non vuole esser losco, runs an old proverb. If you are to deal with a Tuscan, you can't afford to be one-eyed. A little caution is certainly helpful on such occasions, but he is so charming and good-humoured, and he has so keen and often so profound an understanding of the way of the world.

Here is a specimen of the complete Florentine, endowed with every gift—a man whom we encounter at the very moment when the Medici dynasty is about to take root.

Born at Genoa in 1404, but into a Florentine family which had been exiled, persecuted and decimated (three of his kinsmen had been executed, and assassins had been hired to dispose of others), Leone Battista Alberti spent his early years in poverty and hardship. On returning to Florence, however, he was protected by Cosimo de' Medici, who caused his property to be restored to him; and he now became a horse-tamer and a sort of athlete. Holding his feet together he could jump over the shoulders of ten men in succession, he was unmatched in fencing with a pike, he could pierce an iron breastplate with an arrow. Supporting his left foot against the wall of the Cathedral, he would throw an apple right over the dome. Sometimes, mounted on horseback and holding a slender rod in one hand, with the lower end placed on the ball of his foot, he would make his horse circle round without moving the rod. His feats made one think of a succession of ancient bas-reliefs.

This Alberti of the strong and youthful features was more than a gymnast. Musician, singer and organist, he had a vocation for the arts. He knew Latin, Greek and Law; he studied until he grew weak; then conceived disgust even for the letters of the alphabet which he likened to twisted scorpions, and decided for a life of gaiety; only to return before long to his studio.

A friend of Brunelleschi, Donatello and Luca della Robbia, he would disconcert them with his eccentricities; bearish and taciturn one day, amusing and witty on the morrow. But everyone admired his universal genius. 'Tell me', people said, 'what that man hasn't known about'. He wrote on the breeding of horses, on offences and punishments, on the secrets of women's clothing, on navigation and statistics. His book on painting may still be read with interest. 'There is no art', he wrote, 'of which the study or the practise, at any age, brings greater pleasure to those familiar with it, or unfamiliar'. He invented numerous recipes for pigments and instructed beginners in the theory of tonal values, for he was a painter himself. He was even more an architect. The Medici palace in the Via Larga was partly his work, and he was responsible for the Church of St Francis at Rimini— a pure Renaissance edifice.

He was liberal in giving the public the benefit of his ingenuity as he was tireless in every manner of invention. In his chamber of optical illusions you might see in succession, thanks to a contrivance of lights and shadows, vast landscapes; or the moon and stars shining above sombre mountains, or misty gulfs, or ships cleaving the waves. Such marvels, including a number of distorting mirrors, are explained in his treatise on mathematics for amusement. He painted a panorama of Rome, salvaged a Roman galley from the Lake of Nemi, composed a dialogue on home life, family management and female perversity. And he wrote only in Italian; he felt no respect for the pedantic theorists and smug admirers of classical Latin, because he wished to be readable and accessible to all men, and so, like Dante, he defended the Tuscan dialect, which he declared to be as clear and elegant as the language of the humanists. And here too, as we shall see, he was original.

While free from the superstitious cult of ancient art, he nevertheless admired all that was fair of form: a flower, a landscape, man, woman and animal. He had a rule, or 'canon', for understanding the beauties of nature, and was as much at ease in the open air as in his studio. Open to every kind of experience, curious and inventive, he was a true precursor of Leonardo da Vinci and one of the men who enable us to realize the greatness of Florence.

But Alberti was an exceptional being. What distinguished the average Florentine was the fact that he had ceased to regard the world in the medieval way, that is, as a place of exile for penitents, but as a source of joy which man should know how to make the most of. He was like the sundial: *Sine Sole Sileo*—'When there is no sun I am silent.' Gay parties he adored, parties where you could play, or sing, or gossip and tell stories in all freedom, and laugh at the specatacle of the human comedy. And so he tried to follow the advice of the poet of Ferrara: 'Let every man put his troubles in a box, and there lock up his sorrows and gloomy thoughts ... and then lose the key.'

Although violent on occasion, he was by nature cheerful and independent, and his language racy and picturesque.

When happy he would say: 'It's raining caresses.' When someone pleased him: *Mi va al pelo*—'He is good for my skin', or again, 'I carry him in the palm of my hand.' If he understands his wife's character, 'he knows the trot of his mare'. If hesitant: 'I hover on wings', or 'I am picking my brains.' If, like a good tradesman, he is afraid of losing his time: 'Don't think that I shall go away with my hands full of flies.' If angry, 'he puts his patience under his feet'.

To hate his neighbour is 'to tear out his tongue by the neck'; to bungle a business deal is 'to remain with dry teeth'; to complicate it is 'to look for five legs on a sheep'. To learn how to practise patience, he would repeat to himself: 'See that you don't spoil the pheasant's tail.' To do a useless job is 'to pound water in a mortar' or 'to wash bricks'. A long-faced, melancholy fellow seems to him 'to be holding back his soul with his teeth'; but a self-satisfied man is 'as heavy as macaroni water'.

His common sense is summed up in such maxims as: 'He who transacts his own business does not soil his hands' or 'A bird in the hand is worth two in the bush.'[1]

'Keen of eye and sharp of tongue' defined the Florentine. His rejoinders could be cutting. An irritable young woman once called her man an ass. 'If you were an ox instead of a cow', he

---

[1] Literally: 'A chaffinch in the hand is worth a thrush in the bush.' Some of the above expressions sound very odd in English; but to replace them with English idioms is to lose something of their flavour.   (Translator)

retorted, 'we should look well standing with the Holy Family by the manger.' And nothing delighted him more than *bons mots* and stories which he would take pride in repeating. Once when a woman was drowned and her husband was seen looking for her upstream, 'You should look for her downstream', a friend advised him.—'I should never find her', was the reply. 'When alive, she was so strange and contradictory that she can now only be moving against the current.' And here was another story that amused him: A priest who had found only bad pennies in the offertory and who responded by having sulphur burned in the censer, explained to the faithful, disgusted by the smell, that when he went to market he was given sulphur instead of incense just as they, the faithful, had given him bad pennies instead of good.

Some anecdotes, such as the following, are particularly instructive. A Duke of Milan was displaying his treasure to the ambassador of Florence with the idea of intimidating him. The piles of ducats, he thought, would demonstrate his ability to make war. The ambassador took up a few in his hand. 'Fine things.' he murmured, 'and all bearing the stamp of our city. You can imagine how many we have, as it's we who coin them.'

The Florentine also loved quaint stories and practical jokes. Mountebanks enchanted him. There was the story of one who, on the morrow of a drinking bout, rose at dawn to get a breath of fresh air. But he opened the wardrobe by mistake for the window, and seeing it was dark inside, crept back into bed. And then there was the adventure of the she-bear. One night the great bell of Santa Maria in Campo began to ring furiously, which brought people out of their beds, running hither and thither and asking where there was a fire. The parish priest ordered his clerk to light a sacred candle, in order to exorcise the evil spell, and to go to the church. With his hair standing on end, the poor fellow took two steps backward for everyone he took forward. Finally, having plucked up his courage, he approached the church exclaiming: '*In manus tuas, Domine!*—But, oh, father, the devil is in there.' All that was in the church was a tame she-bear that some practical jokers had fastened to the bell-rope. And the citizens remarked amid their laughter that it would not have happened if the clergy had been less negligent. The church door had remained open because they would not spend a mere five soldi on a bolt.

If we need proof of the artistic subtlety of the Florentines, we shall find it in their songs; for they were essentially singers, possessed no doubt of those fine voices we admire in their descendants. Here is the refrain of a dancing-song:

> An hundred, and yet one, are we;
>   In heart and will we're all united.
> Let every dancer jump for glee,
>   And he who will not dance, be blighted!

Or again, a song in praise of the fair:

> More white than mother's milk are you.
> More red than dragon's blood your hue.
> When at your casement you appear,
> 'The sun is risen', we declare.
> The sun is rising, the moon sinks lower,
>   (Say 'good morn' to your lover).
> The sun has risen, the moonlight goes
>   (Say 'good even' to your rose).

Or again:

> O rose that I plucked from the green bough,
> You were planted in a garden of love . . .

And:

> Consider my rosy lips
> And that my husband is stranger to them . . .

But the grace of these melodies can only be conveyed in the original.

These people know Dante's ballads. They even sing verses of the Divine Comedy—and sometimes murder them[1]. To vary the

---

[1] Once, when passing the forge of a blacksmith who was thus treating his verses, Dante walked in, seized the hammer and tongs, and threw them into the street. 'What the devil are you doing?' cried the blacksmith.—'And what are *you* doing?'—'Following my trade; and you are spoiling my tools.' —'If you don't want me to damage your trade, don't damage mine.'—

subject, they are expert in composing part-songs, accompanied by pantomime, on themes taken from everyday life. Now it is the townsman setting off to fish or hunt, or to see a house on fire; now, a girl going to gather flowers, or again, to get herself weighed by the miller. The tone here is less decent:

> 'How fat you are, my girl!'
> —'May Heaven blast you, churl!'

The Florentine also had a peculiar passion for games of chance, and, despite the veto of the Church and the lay authorities, he would play in the open street. The city was always in the vanguard of novelties. At the end of the fourteenth century a certain Buonaccorso Pitti inspired pride in his compatriots. He was a merchant, a traveller, a speculator, a diplomat and a professional gambler who won and lost sums so enormous that no one but princes from Savoy, Brabant or Bavaria would play with him—a frequenter of gambling dens long before Casanova.

This love of risk and the chance of gain brings us back to the trader, with his utilitarian morals. Here is a merchant's advice to his son:

It is wise to be inconspicuous in one's person, one's family and way of life. Never let people know more than half of what you own, and so never have your crops brought to the house, because the neighbours will say you have enough for six families. Send the produce straight to market. Never trust anyone. . . . One need not be afraid of lying, provided it harms no one; but one should lie only just enough to win a reputation for truthfulness.

'Happy the man who can steal most from the poor Commune', sighs another merchant, less scrupulous.

Bernardino of Siena, a famous preacher who was travelling round Italy about that time, was particularly severe on the merchants who traded on Sundays and feast-days, sold on credit, traded in

'What am I damaging?'—'You are singing from my book, but not as I composed it. I have no other trade, and you are spoiling it.'

On another occasion he met a peasant who, while singing the Divine Comedy, was crying: 'Gee up!' to his nag every few moments. 'I didn't write that word,' growled the poet, as he smote the man over the shoulders.

B*

Church or left their wives to seek a fortune abroad. He denounced the cunning of those who counted out change hurriedly so as to filch a part of it: 'See now, see now ... 1, 2, 3, 5, 7, 8, 10, 13, 14, 17, 19, 20!' He urged the draper not to stretch his tape-measure too tightly, and not to take advantage of the customer's ignorance.

You go and sell your wares in the public square. If a stranger asks: 'How much is that?' you reply: 'Thirty soldi'. But to a citizen you sell it for twenty.

Warming to his inspiration, Bernardino strives to inculcate charity in these skinflints. Their wives, he says, should take 'a little cooked food, a few small garments, to the poor'.

What did you take to those wretched prisoners? I ask you. A couple of vests, I'm told, and two pairs of drawers and a pair of old stockings full of holes. I think you'll die in the midst of your trading.

Yet these Florentines who are for ever conning their account-books, for ever bent on filthy lucre, are creatures of imagination, prone to believe in visions and accept fantastic rumours. They tremble when someone tells them that near Como, four thousand dogs have been seen running towards Germany; and after them a great herd of cattle, and after them a crowd of armed men on horse and on foot, some without heads, others with heads scarcely visible, and lastly a gigantic rider. They are terrified of ghosts, whom they consider maleficent. To exorcise an apparition, they will open the grave, quarter the body, burn the heart and cast the ashes to the four winds of heaven.

More and more, in these years, every class of society was becoming obsessed by anything fantastic or even absurd. Super-stition remained firmly anchored in their minds. A sceptic endowed with a wealth of Renaissance 'enlightenment', a man who affects to deride the supernatural or miraculous elements of religion, listens open-mouthed to tales of fairies and wizards, and remains the most credulous of mortals.

It was in vain that Dante had depicted a procession of sorcerers, in Hell, with their heads twisted so as to look only to the rear. They had wished to see the future and now their tears flow, not on to their breasts but into the hollow of their backs. And yet people admired and sought them out. The authorities might prosecute and punish those who 'call up spirits capable of doing harm'. They continued none the less to operate underground. People consulted them, and it was only in the early sixteenth century that they began to lose favour and to emigrate northward.

But astrologers exercised their 'mystery' in the open. They were scholars, university professors or state officials. It was all very well for Matteo Villani the chronicler to say: 'Astrology is a vice that the Florentines have inherited with other superstitions from their idolatrous Roman ancestors.' As early as the thirteenth century Florence had her municipal astrologer in the person of Guido Bonatto, whose business was to indicate the day most favourable for a great enterprise, such as war. Saturday was regarded as of ill omen.

In later times maestro Pagolo, who conferred with monks and led an ascetic life, tried to turn astrology into a moral science, and Cosimo de' Medici among others listened to him. Sceptics were few. A belief in the influence of the stars was general, especially among the exiles whose numbers were legion in an age of civil strife. Soon every family of consequence maintained an astrologer —a poor sort of devil, as a rule—who cast the children's horoscopes and advised the master of the house. But in this respect the Florentine was merely imitating the great ones of the earth, from the prince to the condottiere, who all kept 'planetaries' (as they were then called) among their retainers.[1]

Alchemy also had its adepts. One of the most famous was Cosimo Rosselli (1439-1506), a Florentine painter of great talent, whose passion for the 'science' was such that he squandered all his substance on it and fell from ease into poverty.

And lastly, in the lowest rank, came the practitioners of sorcery, an art with many adherents. Its principal centre was at Norcia, in the Duchy of Spoleto, among the high Apennines, but it had an important branch at Fiesole near Fontelucente. Here you might see strange beings coming to draw water: creatures with false eyes which they remove and put back as old men do with their

---

[1] Recall Scott's description of Louis XI's astrologer.   (Translator)

spectacles and false teeth, which they change as women change their frisons; they stroll about in the markets, and even in churches, and scrutinize you closely. Beware of the ghouls!

Here—to conclude this excursion into the fantastic—is the Tuscan *novelliere* Grazzini's portrait of a magician who is both astrologer and sorcerer. He is tall and handsome, with an imposing glance, a sombre countenance and a black beard that descends on to his breast. The quest of the philosopher's stone has ruined him. He possesses philtres, magic letters, phylacteries, alembics, furnaces, eyes of lynxes, the slaver of a mad dog, a dead man's bones, a cord that has hung a man, daggers that have been used by assassins, the collar-bone and knife of Solomon, plants and seeds gathered during the various phases of the moon. He understands astrology, physiognomony, chiromancy, and a hundred other sciences as subtle, firmly believes in old witches, calls up spirits and takes part in all witches' sabbaths.

As he has neither father nor mother, although he is otherwise fairly comfortable, he remains alone. No one dare approach him, and no servant will work for him. He is alone too when he goes out, and secretly congratulates himself on the fact. His beard is always matted; he never combs his hair, and is invariably dirty, and so, in the eyes of the populace, he passes for a great philosopher and necromancer.

When officiating, he takes a white alb, passes a red belt round his waist and puts on a helmet garlanded with artificial snakes that are extraordinarily lifelike. Then, holding a marble vase in his left hand and a sponge tied to a dead man's leg-bone in his right, he draws a book from under his cloak, mutters incantations, kneels, kisses the earth, dips the sponge into the vase which contains an infusion of Brasil wood and says: 'Let us now trace Pluto's circle with this dragon's blood. . . .' Then the spirits begin. . . .

If the portrait is colourful, one still discerns a shadow of fear behind the irony.

*   *   *   *

The following parable is to be found in the *Novellino*, an old collection of Italian tales.

A sultan in need of money sent for a rich Jew in order to plunder him, and began by asking which was the best of the religions. If the Jew answered: 'The Jewish', this would be an insult to the Sultan's faith; if 'The Saracen', this would be apostacy. Either would afford a pretext for confiscation. But the Israelite held in reserve a story (which had perhaps been invented in Babylon).

My Lord, once upon a time there was a father who had three sons and also a ring set with a precious stone, the finest on earth. Each of the sons asked his father to leave him the ring when he died. Now to satisfy them all, the father summoned a master-goldsmith and said: 'Master, make me two rings, like this one, and put in each a stone like this one.'

The goldsmith made the rings so alike that no one except the father could distinguish the genuine one. He then sent for each son separately and told each the secret, and each believed he was to receive the original ring, which only the father could distinguish. . . . This, my Lord, is the story of the three religions. Only the father, who has given them, knows which is the best, and each of his sons, that is ourselves, we each believe that we have the right one.

This parable pleased the Florentines, who, owing to their relations, cultural and commercial, with the Arab world and with Byzantium, were now imbued with the spirit of free enquiry and toleration. Add to all this their keen interest in the discovery of the ancient world, and it will be readily understood that on the banks of the Arno religious feeling was of a rather special variety. According to certain preachers, the young Florentine became a pagan more easily than a Christian; he knew more about Jupiter, Saturn, Venus and Cybele than about the Father, the Son and the Holy Ghost[1] and in consequence true faith was despised and virtue disregarded. Everyone thought of saving his body; no one his soul. A man in peril on the deep would rather have an inflated gourd to support him than the Gospel of Saint John.

Scholars and writers, on the other hand, were so far from opposing paganism to Christianity that they attempted to reconcile

[1] It is fair to say that the pagan gods had been Christianized and in a large measure assimilated, especially to our Lord and to the Virgin. See J.-J. Seznec, *La Survivance des dieux antiques*. (Translator)

them. They interpreted Plato as a forerunner of Jesus; and sound doctrine was not improved by all this.

The sense of sin, and of repentance, grew weaker by slow degrees; people ceased to worry about salvation. 'The worst that can happen to you', according to a character in Machiavelli's play, *The Mandragora*, 'is to die and go to Hell. But such multitudes have died before you, and in Hell there are so many nice people.' Such remarks did not scandalize the Florentine. He thought them witty—which was what counted—and left it to others to split hairs on questions of faith.[1]

He was not far from agreeing with the historian Guicciardini, that 'too much religion effeminates and damages society'. In any event, religious controversy did not interest him and he could be an unbeliever with impunity provided that he did not openly attack the Church. Notable cases of incredulity were however rare, down to the end of the fifteenth century, and no heresy ever established itself in Florence.[2]

Religion remained outwardly in honour. Walking along the streets you would come upon chapels and oratories at every turn. On the doorways were sacred images. Every guild had its church. At *Ave Maria* the workmen's fraternities sang a hymn; and at the hour of curfew everyone kneeled down. A miracle was sure to arouse enthusiasm, as witness the roses that bloomed in mid-winter on the grave of a saint, or the olive-branch which, during a

[1] Savonarola used to say: 'The Faith of my Florentines is like wax: a little heat is enough to melt it.'

[2] In the sixteenth century, a certain Antonio Bruciolo did not scruple to disparage the secular clergy and the monks. One of his enemies, an orthodox believer, used to say: 'The Bruciioli are fit only to be burned.' Bruciolo means a caterpillar. When people warned Antonio about his imprudence, he would answer: 'To speak the truth is to do no wrong.' But being suspect, he was summoned before the Council of Ten, who fined him fifty gold ducats. He pleaded that he hadn't a penny on him. 'We'll make you find the money!' shouted one of the judges. 'I beseech your lordships', was the reply, 'to make me find a hundred, because I need fifty more.' This humorist, who was accused of Lutheranism (he had travelled in Germany), was punished with banishment, a penalty which sensible Florentines thought altogether excessive. This took place in 1529.

procession, attached itself to the starry robe worn by the image of the Virgin, and which could not be torn off: this foretold an era of peace. People shed tears of emotion over an infant which one Good Friday refused to be suckled, so blessed was its soul. If war broke out, or the plague—the *moria*—yesterday's free-thinkers were carried away on a wave of piety, and rushed to hear the preacher who lavished his exhortations on them, such as this prescription 'of joy at becoming mad for the sake of Jesus':

Mix at least three ounces of hope with three of faith, six of love and two of tears, and set the mixture over the flames of fear.

Fear, most certainly. Terrified by the omens which everyone reported when times were bad, the Florentine would return to the traditional beliefs of his forefathers; for he had never ceased to read the admirable *Fioretti* of St Francis of Assisi, *il Poverello*; and now he would sing lauds like the following:

Behold Italy, a prey to war and great famine. God has sent the plague as a judgment on thee! Such are the fruits of thy blindness. O thou of little faith. Alas! Alas! Alas!

And the chorus would answer: 'Yes, indeed. Alas! Alas!'

Any kind of profanation inspired horror, especially when the city was in peril. One day a *marrane*, or Jewish convert, defiled several statues of the Madonna, including the one by the outer pilaster of Or San Michele. He threw dirt in her face, he scratched the eye of the Bambino and the eye of one of the saints. Seeing this, children began to throw stones at the Jew; after which, the men laid hands on him and finished him off with paving-blocks. Significant also is the fact that, in a sermon which he preached in Santa Maria del Fiore, the Franciscan Bernardino da Feltre persuaded the people to expel the Jews. Hastening to carry out the plan, a number of children made their way to the house of a certain Manollino, a money-lender who did business at the Sign of the Cow, near the Archbishop's Palace, in order to rob and murder him. But on this occasion the police (the 'Eight of the Guard' as they were called) intervened, threatened to hang the self-appointed executioners and so 'put out the fire'. Next day, the preacher was asked to leave the country, so as to obviate further trouble. This however, to a people 'who wished to live like Christians', seemed of evil omen. Bernardino was regarded as a saint. Moreover, the 'Eight' suffered misfortunes. One of them was thrown by his horse and broke his neck; another went mad.

The moral was, that you should show respect for those who preach the Word of God and inspire fear for His judgments. When, after preaching an eloquent sermon, a certain monk suddenly died 'of chest trouble', the congregation rushed forward to kiss his feet; and, to prevent a continuance of such frenzy, the body was buried in secret by night.

But when times were good, all this righteous talk was forgotten and the Florentine relapsed into the tepid Christianity that was natural to him. If a preacher began to speak of unlawful contracts, or irregular deals, or to recommend the restitution of ill-acquired wealth, the citizen would begin to murmur and even retort. Such questions did not concern the clergy; people should mind their own business. Only—to make sure of divine favour—the same citizen would return to his little pagan practices; he would, for example, go to the *Fallimagini*, in the Via dei Servi, to buy a wax doll, more or less like himself, and would suspend it in the Church of the Annunziata as a means of devoting himself to the protection of the Virgin.

*   *   *   *

It would however be a mistake to suppose that all the Florentines were either sceptics, unbelievers or merely conventional Christians. Florence also produced men of remarkable character, noble-minded ecclesiastics whose strong and practical faith greatly impressed the masses. The names of three in particular have been recorded by the bookseller Vespasiano Bisticci, whose journal is the more attractive for being that of an ingenuous witness.

The simple life of Cardinal Branda, an old friend of Pope Eugenius IV, inspires Bisticci with whole-hearted admiration.

Branda's servants were few in number and wore no livery. His meals, which he took in company with a bishop, were abstemious, while for diversion he perused religious texts or discussed theology with his companion. His supper consisted of bread and chicken broth. No costly hangings adorned his bed—only a curtain of blue cloth, embroidered with his coat-of-arms, and a single wax candle to give light. Nothing in his way of life to bespeak the splendour of Roman prelates.

Cardinal Cesarini, the child of a poor family, was charity incarnate. His manservant said to Bisticci: 'Don't be surprised if you see Monsignore walking to the palace without a cloak, for, by Heaven, he gives away what he has and even what he hasn't.' He was broad-minded, too. One day he said to Bisticci: 'Do you want to be a priest? If you do, I will help you to study, and then give you a benefice. Think about it and let me know in a fortnight.' At the end of this time Bisticci replied that he did not feel he had a vocation. 'If I can help you in any other way, I will do so', the Cardinal told him. Cesarini was to end up gloriously as Papal legate at the battle of Warna, against the Turks, in 1444.

But the churchman who about this time inspired more respect and even fear, than any other, was Antonino. He thought only of winning souls for Christ, of promoting peace in the city, of founding schools for handicapped children, and hospitals for the 'innocents', or illegitimate infants who had been abandoned by their parents. In times of famine he distributed bread in secret. When he appeared on foot or on his little mule, 'the only ornament of his household', everyone kneeled as he passed by.

Fearing to be made Archbishop, he fled with a *frate* to the woods. It was all in vain. A messenger sought him out and announced his elevation. As the messenger stood waiting for a gratuity, Antonino said, 'I couldn't have received worse news. And my companion and I haven't a *soldo* between us—only the robes we are wearing.'

But he could be terrible on occasion. In Santa Maria del Fiore he glared so sternly at the women and the young idlers, the *scioperati*, who were whispering together, that they all slipped away without waiting for more. Once, when he saw some game-sters under the Loggia of the Buondelmonti, he bore down on them and overturned their tables. 'Gambling in public! What a horrible example!' And the offenders did not dare to show them-selves again. The political morals of the Signoria also displeased him, and he censured so roughly the trading in votes that a number of citizens threatened to have him removed from his office.

'Do so, by God', he retorted. 'I shall be greatly obliged to you, and you will relieve me of a heavy burden. I shall return to my cell in San Marco; the key hangs here at my girdle; and then I shall dwell in holy quietness. I could not receive a greater pleasure.'

What hold had one over a man who, when sounded as to whether he would accept a Cardinal's hat, refused point-blank; observing that he could hardly attain this dignity without peril to his soul?

With all this, he was a man of culture who wrote in simple language and ended by forcing the admiration of the 'archi-mandrites of fine writing'. His poverty was truly apostolic, for all he had to bequeath at his death was a few kitchen utensils and the little mule that carried him about.

CHAPTER IV

COSIMO DE' MEDICI AND THE ADVENT
OF THE BANKERS

The 'men of figures' – Giovanni de' Bicci – Cosimo the big
merchant – His exile – The business world and the world of
politics – A Rothschild of the fifteenth century – A patron
of the arts – Piero de' Medici

I N the meantime the rhythm of life in Florence pursued its
habitual course, which was one of civil discord. At the
beginning of the fifteenth century, power was in the hands of
an oligarchy headed by the Albizzi and supported by the major
'arts'. Some people were beginning to think that stability could
only be assured by a government more and more limited in its
membership; the example of Venice, controlled by a handful of
citizens, was most instructive in this respect. In Florence, however,
the régime was acquiring an increasingly monarchical appearance.
A small faction now held the reins of power. Decisions were
taken in secret council, often over a meal, and all that the Signoria
and its associated councils had to do was to confirm what had
already been decided.

The system did not please everyone. The minor 'arts', the
multitude of the *popolo minuto*, found it hard to endure the
insolence of their present masters. 'In this bad world of ours,
nine hundred out of every thousand are living like sheep, with
their eyes bent on the ground and their minds full of folly and
evil thoughts.' Thus wrote a Florentine who dreamed of leaving
his city and its wicked ways, and of going 'to live with the birds
or the fishes who neither do evil nor speak it'.

This discontent on the part of the plebeians was surreptitiously
encouraged by a family which had come down, about the year
1200, from the valley of Mugello, to the north of the city.
They were of peasant origin, but they now owned large estates

and a country house with battlemented towers, known as Cafaggiolo.

We have already, in 1378, encountered a certain Salvestro de' Medici, who had played the principal part, albeit off-stage, in the revolt of the *Ciompi*. Since that time the family had continued to enjoy popular favour, and had been opposed to the oligarchy of the rich. At the beginning of the fifteenth century it was represented by Giovanni de' Medici, or 'de' Bicci' as he was called, who belonged to a different branch of the clan from Salvestro's. He was a big dark-faced fellow, more of a humorist than his melancholy countenance suggested; a good sort of country squire who concealed, under a mask of innocence, a deep fund of knavery and astuteness.

It was in vain that the Albizzi had stripped him and the other partisans of the poor of their possessions. Giovanni de' Bicci repaired his fortunes by commerce, banking and foreign exchange, and before long he was nearly the richest man in Florence. He provided dowries for respectable girls who could not otherwise have got married; he was benevolent and increasingly popular. At critical moments he lent large sums to the Republic; he became banker to Pope Martin V; and it was he who commissioned Brunelleschi to build the sacristy of San Lorenzo.

This prudent Florentine avoided political coteries and refrained as much as possible from appearing in the Palazzo della Signoria. A little before his death, in 1429, he left the following advice to his children:

Never hold an opinion contrary to the will of the people, even if this same people should prefer something that is perfectly useless. Do not speak with the air of giving counsel, but prefer rather to discuss matters gently and benevolently. Do not turn the palace into a shop; on the contrary, wait for the palace to invite you ...[1] Try to maintain the people in a state of peace, and to promote trade. Be as inconspicuous as possible.

These lessons were not to be lost on Giovanni's children; but

[1] Meaning, presumably: Do not seek public office, with a view to making money out of it; but wait until you are urged to take office.   (Translator)

he had already cleared the ground and laid the foundations of the house of Medici.

The Florentines are regarded as having a natural bent for expressing in figures everything that relates to daily life, whether household or business affairs, estate-management or even politics. The Medici were no exceptions to this rule: they too dealt with figures. They were such prudent business-men and bankers that they contrived in the course of time to be princes while remaining private individuals, and to govern without appearing to give orders. Thanks to this skill, they were to become 'the hereditary counsellors of the Florentine people', the interpreters and executors of public opinion, and all this without title or mandate. Wealth was their only visible weapon, but their active and secret instrument was a gift for inspiring confidence. 'Only their successes', says Herman Grimm, 'were seen in the light of day; the means to their success remained in shadow.'

When Giovanni de' Bicci died, his son Cosimo was more than forty. He had never been young or handsome, and had no taste for wine and women; he detested mountebanks and buffoons. A business-man from his youth upward, he was expert in the art of persuasion, saying very little, coming to the point without flowery preamble, answering questions in a word or two. He was fairly cultured, knew more Latin 'than was fitting in a business-man', even a little Greek, and was a constant reader of the Scriptures. By the age of twenty-five his fame was such as to provoke jealousy. He therefore travelled in France and Germany for two years; and as, on his return home, he was warned that his enemies were still hostile and that he was in danger of death or banishment, he engaged a number of 'men of mean condition' as bodyguard, and shut himself up in his town-house in the Via Larga—the Palazzo Riccardi. His kinsfolk had lived more modestly by the Mercato Vecchio.

Although he did not appear to covet honours—although the name of Medici figures much less often in the list of officials than the names of ambitious families like the Pitti and the Pazzi—he continued to grow in power. His bank was now paying 428

florins a year in taxes, whereas on his personal budget he paid
only 44. This made his competitors anxious, especially as a war
with Lucca was going badly and costing a great deal. On the
initiative of Rinaldo Albizzi, a plot was formed. Among the
citizens registered in the *Specchio*, that is excluded from public
office for not having paid their taxes, was a certain Guadagni.
Albizzi cancelled his debts, had him appointed Gonfaloniere, in
return for which Guadagni promised him the head of Cosimo and
a reform of the Constitution.

It was a risky move, even, as Niccolò Uzzano frankly admitted,
a stupid one. 'The Medici party is united and in agreement', he
pointed out. 'The people are behind it. Whereas our party is
divided, and divided by nature more than by chance.'

No one listened to him. On September 7, 1433, Cosimo was
summoned to the palace.[1] When one of his kinsmen met him near
Or San Michele and besought him to return home, Cosimo
replied: 'No matter what happens, I mean to obey my lords.' On
reaching the palace he was asked to go up to the higher floor,
where the Captain of the Guard arrested him and confined him in
a dark cell hollowed out of the massive wall of the tower, a cell
which was facetiously known as the *Alberghettino*, the little inn,
and which Cosimo called the *Barberia*.

Now that the Medici was caged, Albizzi and his friends
summoned the people 'to parliament', which meant a public
meeting in the piazza where, under the eye of armed men who
kept them well in hand, the people voted by acclamation any
measure that was proposed. A revolutionary practice which, in
the words of the ever-wise Uzzano, boded no good for the State.
'The first man who summoned a parliament dug his own grave.'[2]

Power was now assumed by two hundred citizens who had
been chosen by Albizzi. The Medici were officially stigmatized
as 'very cruel and truculent enemies, incendiaries, authors of

[1] The 'palace', unless otherwise specified, apparently refers to the Palazzo
della Signoria. (Translator)

[2] Later on, this proverbial saying became current: *Chi disse parlamento
disse guastamento.*

disaster and every kind of devastation, and yet in spite of their diabolical character tolerated by the singular benignity of the people of Florence'. At the same time an attempt was made to poison Cosimo.

But Cosimo had been warned by the Captain of the Guard, who was his companion at meals. A little later he told a friend, who had been allowed to pass the time with him, to go to Santa Maria Nuova and take a thousand ducats from a sum he had on deposit there. These thousand ducats went into Guadagni's pocket, the Gonfaloniere now selling himself to Cosimo as he had previously done to Albizzi. And Cosimo afterwards observed that his persecutors were not very clever, as they might have extracted ten thousand ducats or more from him, so anxious was he to get clear.

In any event, he had saved his life. On September 29, 1433, he was banished to Padua for ten years on the charge, which was absolutely unjust, of having advocated the war with Lucca. When the first emotion had passed away, he appeared very calmly before the Signoria; and his departure had something of the air of a triumph. As he mounted the hillside at Pistoia, the natives offered him the presents of honey which were customary at the passage of ambassadors.

It was a gilded exile, worthy of a great lord. In Padua he was surrounded by a kind of court. In Venice, where there was a branch of his bank, he lived in the monastery of San Gregorio and had the library decorated at his expense. Everywhere he was treated with deference, and never a word did he breathe against his enemies.

Meanwhile, however, in Florence his partisans were using the methods their adversaries had previously employed, and now Uzzano's prediction was accomplished. On September 29, 1434, there was a new summons 'to parliament'. This time the wind was blowing from the opposite quarter. Cosimo's exile was cancelled by acclamation, Rinaldo Albizzi was banished and his kinsmen and descendants *posti a sedere*—'sent to sit down'—that is excluded from public office. The exile reappeared in October.

Cleverly abstaining from a triumphal return, he lodged at the inn, and awaited the moment for vengeance.

For Cosimo was no saint. He temporized at first, but once he felt himself firmly in the saddle he struck ruthlessly—by the hand of intermediaries. The Signoria obeyed him without question. Great numbers of citizens, including Palla Strozzi, were exiled, and it was at this time that many Florentine businesses were founded in France, especially at Lyons. Hangings were frequent. After these executions a painting was made of the victim, suspended by his feet and with his names in large letters, and this was displayed on the front of the Podestà's palace. A poet was then employed to compose verses that would blacken his memory; and if anyone hinted to Cosimo that he was going too far and that such measures of repression were depriving the city of men of honour, the response was dry and laconic: 'Better a city devastated than a city ruined.' The fox had turned into a tiger.

The image of the new prince survives in the portraits and medals of his age. He is of middle height, rather lean, with a wrinkled and olive-coloured face, a long nose broad round the nostrils, and strongly-marked lips. An air of benevolence concealing a deep malignity bespeaks the crafty politician who likes to seem gentle. Wearing his characteristic headgear, he makes one think of a clerk who has grown old in harness, or a cashier behind his counter.

Like his ancestors he loved the country and made frequent sojourns at one or other of his estates, especially when there was an outbreak of plague in the city. At such times, he said, one should leave all business and save one's skin. This man whom you might see in peasant's clothing, digging in the garden or pruning his vines or grafting a fruit tree, was one day to be addressed as follows by the Pope: 'You are the arbiter of peace, of war, of the laws. Of kingship you have everything but the name.'

A great deal has been written about the Medici dictatorship, which so deeply modified the daily life of Florence. Some historians hold it up to execration, others extol it. One must simply recognize that the family could only conserve its wealth

through control of the State. Lorenzo, the son of Piero, says this
in so many words. Thus for the Medici, the control of the Signoria,
that is the Lordship of Florence, was perhaps not the outcome of
ambition, but a matter of vital necessity. 'They became lords',
someone has written, 'as a measure of legitimate self-defence.'

But whether this has anything to do with morality is another
question. Cosimo made use of the populace in order to crush his
rivals; but once this was done he set about extending his domination over every class in the community; and Florence, harassed as
she was by faction and discord, meekly accepted the yoke. In
return for this she gained several decades of comparative tranquillity, a fact that one should not forget when contemplating the
effigy of the grim old merchant.

He lost no opportunity of pleasing the Florentines. He offered
them fine shows, assemblies of notables, flattering ceremonies.
In 1439 he arranged for the Council which was to proclaim the
union of the Greek and Catholic Churches to meet in Santa Maria
del Fiore, and did his best to make the meeting particularly
splendid. On the side where the Gospel was read were seated
Eugenius IV in his pontifical robes, the Cardinals in their copes,
and the Bishops wearing mitres of white damask; on the side where
the Epistle was read, the Emperor of Constantinople, a handsome
bearded personage wearing a very rich doublet of damascened
brocade, in the Greek manner, and a small pointed hat adorned
with a splendid jewel; around him, the Greek Bishops were
arrayed in silken robes. The Pope sang a solemn mass, after
which 'the privileges of the Greek union' were read with great
ceremony. A vast multitude attended this solemn act, and the
Florentines observed that the vestments of the foreign prelates
were much more dignified than those of the Roman. As to the
spiritual bearing of the union, this interested them less than the
costumes of the ecclesiastics.

The foundation of the first public library, the first meetings of
the Platonic Academy which was open to all men of culture and
which helped to give the Florentines intellectual ease and freedom,
were other means by which Cosimo showed his fellow-citizens

that they were in the van of civilization. No wonder that he was admired and respected. People collected and repeated the sayings of this uncrowned monarch.

The Albizzi in exile sent word to him: 'We are not asleep.' Cosimo replied. 'I believe you. I have deprived you of sleep.' When they again warned him that 'the hen is brooding', he answered: 'The hen cannot brood away from her nest.'

His experience enabled him to become an adviser of princes. 'Take good care of your lands and revenues. That is what confers real strength in this world of ours.' Dreamers and idealists he held in very low esteem. 'You are pursuing the infinite, I the finite. You raise your ladders towards heaven, I set mine on the ground, so as not to fly so high that I risk a fall.'

He now refused any open fight with his enemies. 'You and I are like big dogs who sniff at each other and then, as we both have teeth, return to our own affairs. Go about yours and I will go about mine.' He also observed that there is in gardens a plant which one ought to leave dry, although most people water it. It is the weed called envy.

This sententious countryman, whose dwellings were of royal splendour, 'never himself departed from the modesty befitting an ordinary citizen', never had an escort or bodyguard and feigned to live on an equal footing with everyone else. Yet he was a great builder, and not merely in Florence. He built a palace in Milan, an Italian College in Paris; he restored the Church of the Holy Ghost in Jerusalem and the Badia at Fiesole; he enlarged the monastery of San Marco. If he was a free-thinker, he gave no appearance of it. 'Never', he declared in his mercantile idiom, 'never shall I be able to give God enough to set him down in my books as a debtor.'

But he nourished no illusions about humanity. 'I know the men of this city. Fifty years will not pass before we are driven out; but our buildings will remain.' For that reason, for the sake of glory, and sometimes also to salve his conscience on account of money dishonestly acquired, he spent without counting the cost: 400,000 florins, much of it in charity.

But not a soldo was ever wasted. He kept a firm grip on his debtors and never lent unless he was sure of his man. When asked for a loan of 100 ducats on behalf of a poor monk named Tommaso Parentucelli, he agreed at once. The money was well placed. Tommaso became Pope Nicholas V, and Cosimo was his banker.

So the House of Medici prospered; it had banks everywhere; crowned heads, like Edward IV of England, were among its customers. Comines, a stateman whom no one could tax with credulity, greatly admired the head of the house, 'a man worthy of being named the very great. And his house, which was a trading establishment, was I believe the greatest that has ever existed in this world; and its servants enjoy such credit from the name of Medici that you would marvel to hear what I have seen of it in France and England.' And he commends princes for 'keeping on good terms with these merchants, and dealing honestly with them, for they know not in what hour they may have need of them. . . . A little money is sometimes of great service.'

But it was not enough for Cosimo to be the Rothschild of the fifteenth century, he was also its Maecenas. Thanks to an unfailing memory, he could converse with anyone; he had the 'matter', literary or theological, at his disposal. So all the thinkers and writers were on his side, the artists, too, from Brunelleschi to Donatello, and including L.-B. Alberti. To assemble a library he had recourse to the good Bisticci, allowing him an unlimited credit on the Medici bank; and in less than two years, with the help of forty-five scribes, Bisticci collected two hundred volumes, including the Holy Scriptures, various Fathers of the Church, and works of Aristotle and Aquinas.

To keep Florence peaceful, or at least docile, the programme was a simple one. The structure of the Commune was left intact, but Cosimo so arranged matters that all the key-posts were in the hands of his partisans. The selection of citizens who were *imborsati*, that is eligible for office—'placed in the purse' or urn— was entrusted to *accoppiatori*, 'assemblers', who saw to it that only the names of reliable men were drawn from the 'purse'. To preserve an appearance of democracy, a 'Council of the Hundred' was established—all hand-picked men—and the Priors of the Arts became 'Priors of Liberty' at the very moment when liberty was disappearing. The government was, in brief, a government by a clientèle, dominated by a single man and supported by the people who, without sharing actively in the conduct of affairs, knew that they were protected and defended. And if a burgher attempted to resist the master, the latter had a sure means of bringing him to heel. He overwhelmed him with taxes, employing the fiscal cudgel, a weapon perfectly adapted to a trading community.

So Cosimo could take his ease now. On the banks of a mountain stream that flowed by his villa at Careggi, under the shady trees, he would converse with scholars and writers. Once, when a member of the circle suggested that they should discuss the advantages or disadvantages of providing amusements for the populace, Cosimo, before replying, prudently arranged that the peasants who had come to consult him about farming should be taken away. After this the company talked and talked until it was time for dinner, when the menu was choice though not sumptuous, the menu of a Platonic banquet.

In July 1464 the man who was to be called 'Pater patriae' felt that his end was near. One evening at dusk, when his young protégé, Marsilio Ficino, was with him, he began to speak of death. He declared it to be a benefit. 'That also was the opinion of Xenocrates, a disciple of Plato', observed Ficino. 'Then bring me a copy of Xenocrates, and read to me', said Cosimo.

Taking to his bed, he remained in a state of 'suspension' and silence, and as this astonished his wife, Contessina de'Bardi (who belonged to one of the reputedly noblest families), 'When you are going into the country,' he said, 'you spend a fortnight in preparations. Doesn't it seem to you that I, who must journey from this world into the next, should meditate awhile?' After which, being a business-man after all, he made a little parting speech to Contessina and his son Piero. He reviewed the pattern of his life from the time of his accession to power, his commercial and political doings, he expressed regrets, offered a great deal of advice and ended by giving minute directions for his funeral at San Lorenzo, at which there were to be neither display nor demonstrations, and no more candles than at an ordinary burial.

His family were amazed by a mind that remained absolutely clear. When the moment for the last parting approached, he kept his eyes obstinately closed. 'Why do you close your eyes like that, Father?' asked Caterina, who was watching at his bedside. 'Daughter,' he replied, 'it is to accustom myself to not opening them any more.'

On August 1, 1464, the merchant-prince made his final exit. He was seventy-five.

*   *   *   *

His son Piero, who was more subject than Cosimo to gout and rheumatism, was far from being a mediocrity. He loved old books and befriended men of letters; he supported Alberti's campaign on behalf of the Italian tongue and favoured the literary competitions in which the winner received a crown of wild olive. Botticelli, then a poor young artist, received help and protection from him, and it was he who employed Benozzo Gozzoli to paint the wonderful frescoes in the Medici palace.

For business he was less gifted. He followed bad advice when he announced that he was retiring, temporarily, from trade and demanded repayment of the loans his father had advanced. This step provoked a general outcry and violent protests, even bankruptcies. Once again the city was riven by faction. One party was led by Lucca Pitti, a former creature of Cosimo, and very wealthy—the man who had built the great palace on the hillside beyond the Arno. This was the faction of the *Poggio*, or hill; the faction of the *Piano*, or plain, remained devoted to the Medici.

The two parties watched each other like china dogs, each ready to bite the other. One day when Piero was being carried from Careggi in a litter to Florence, hired assassins lay in wait for him by the roadside; and he would have been murdered had not his son Lorenzo, then a boy of seventeen, told them that his

father was following him and would soon be there. . . . Piero
meanwhile made his way into Florence by another road. The
Pitti next had recourse to the Gonfaloniere Niccolò Soderini,
but the latter did not know how to set about the task. And when
the people were summoned 'to Parliament' they acclaimed Piero
and invested him with power for ten years (September 1466).
His enemies were banished, and Lucca Pitti died in obscurity.
Thus the Medici were victorious. Piero, more gouty and stiff-
jointed (except as regards his tongue) than ever, emerged from the
ordeal with even greater powers than Cosimo had enjoyed. It
was he who added three golden lilies, emblems of his friendship
for France, to the *palle*, or balls, on his coat-of-arms—the famous
balls which showed, according to humorists, that the family's
ancestor had been an apothecary.[1]

As to the revolt, there had been no long period of repression,
Piero judging that the best way to reduce his enemies was 'to
force them to lick rather than bite'. His wife Lucrezia Tornabuoni,
whose family was associated with the Medici bank, encouraged a
policy of benevolence.

Lucrezia was a remarkable person. She was the mother of
Lorenzo and Giuliano de' Medici, and grandmother of Popes
Leo X and Clement VII. Of her beauty we can judge from the
Saint Elizabeth—for whom she was the model—in Ghirlandajo's
fresco at Santa Maria Novella. She was shrewd in the direction of
her house, which she maintained in a state of splendour, 'taking
pleasure', we read, 'in the quiet joys of the family circle, in the
innocent pleasures of life, the study of literature and poetry'. For
she was a poetess herself, not in the manner of the neo-Platonists
or the Humanists, who wrote only in Greek or Latin, but in the
medieval vein. She composed lauds, Hymns to the Virgin, and
translations of the Bible; her *History of the chaste Susannah* is not
without charm. 'The garden-door being shut, Susannah stepped
down into the fountain in all her naked loveliness.' She had
character, too, and was a good observer of men and affairs. When

[1] The name of Medici of course suggests something of the kind.   (Translator)

arranging a marriage between her son Lorenzo and the Roman maiden, Clarice Orsini, she sent her husband the following description of the bride: 'She has a pleasing figure, a fair complexion, a gentle manner if not as gentle as ours. She is shy, but tall and slim. . . . On the whole, much better than the average, but not comparable to our maidens.' Obviously, a Roman could not hold a candle to a Florentine.

Piero held the reins of state from his bed, and at the same time superintended the education of Lorenzo. At the age of eighteen the boy was sent to the princely courts of Bologna, Ferrara, Milan, Naples and Venice. 'Take heed', his father told him, 'to be old before your time; to behave as a man and not as a boy.' But Piero's own days were numbered. Towards the end, according to Machiavelli, he severely admonished his fellow-countrymen:

You strip your neighbour of his goods, you haggle over matters of justice, you evade the law and you oppress peaceable citizens. . . . I don't think that the whole of Italy offers as many examples of violence and rapacity as Florence. Did your city give birth to you so that you might murder her?

After thus prophesying the fall of the principate, which was to be caused by the excesses of the aristocrats, Piero departed this life on December 2, 1469.

CHAPTER V

LORENZO THE MAGNIFICENT: AN ERA OF CULTURE AND VIOLENCE

A princely marriage – The Florentines' 'darling' – A gay and
polished society – The strong hand – The affair of Volterra –
The conspiracy of the Pazzi – Reprisals

PIERO, before dying, had seen his son married; which was
wise, because the democrats looked greatly askance on this
union with the daughter of a Roman prince, and efforts had
been made in advance to placate them with fêtes and rejoicings.
Thus on February 7, 1469, the sons of the greatest families
assembled in the Piazza Santa Croce for a magnificent *giostra*, or
tourney.[1] Lorenzo and his younger brother Giuliano bore as their
device the lilies of France covered with gold, silver and precious
stones. Each knight was escorted by pages and trumpeters, and
brandished a banner on which appeared the likeness of his lady.
One, clad all in white, held a crown of oak-leaves in one hand
while a captive leopard crouched at her feet. Another, in a purple
gown, was throwing arrows of love into a meadow. Lorenzo's
lady, bathed in sunbeams and arrayed in a bright-blue dress of
Alexandrian fabric, was weaving a laurel-wreath (by allusion to
Lorenzo), and on the standard bore three French words: '*Le
temps revient*'. Everyone knew and admired this lady, the beautiful
Lucrezia Donati, the young prince's mistress.

Although scarcely inured to weapons and hard blows, as he
admits himself, Lorenzo received the prize of valour from the
hands of Lucrezia, amid the plaudits of the multitude. It was a
helmet adorned with silver, and bearing an image of Mars as its
crest.

[1] This *giostra* is the subject of one of Poliziano's most brilliant poems.
(Translator)

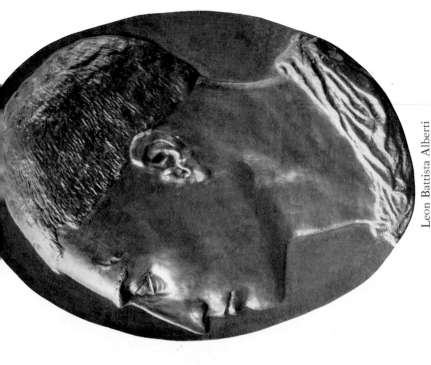

Leon Battista Alberti
bronze by Matteo de' Pasti (Louvre)

4: Piero de' Medici by Botticelli (Uffizi, Florence)

5. Detail from Gozzoli's 'Journey of the Magi' in the Palazzo Riccardi, showing camels, mules and leopards, as well as contemporary Florentine dress

The wedding was celebrated in the following June. One hundred and fifty calves and two thousand brace of capons had been brought in, together with great casks of Tuscan and foreign wines. Then, amid fanfares of trumpets and musical instruments the red-haired Clarice Orsini rode on horseback into the palace in the Via Larga. Olive-boughs had been placed in all the windows as a symbol of the happy event.

The Medici did the thing well. In the Loggia and gardens of the palace five banquets were given in the course of three days. Fifty young 'dancing ladies' sat at the bride's table, while the older ladies were seated at another table under the presidency of Lorenzo's mother, Lucrezia Tornabuoni. Other tables accommodated the young 'dancing men' and the older men. When the bride attended the wedding Mass at San Lorenzo, it was observed that she was holding 'a little book of our Lady, a marvellous book, written in letters of gold on ultramarine paper, and covered with crystal and graven silver'.

Thus was the daughter of a great Roman family transplanted into the mercantile, if splendid, court of the Medici. She was to have some difficulty in adapting herself. The scepticism and the care-free, egalitarian gaiety of the Florentines shocked a person who was naturally haughty, rigid and pious. She was obliged, however, to tolerate them and try to become easy-going.

Two days after Piero's death, certain of the notables asked that Lorenzo, who was then twenty-one, and Giuliano, who was sixteen, should direct the government and be heads of the Republic as their father and grandfather had been. Lorenzo hesitated, pleaded his youth and the perils he would incur, but accepted in the end in order to preserve his fortune; because he knew that in a city like Florence it was difficult to remain rich unless one was in control of the government.

This succession of Medici rulers, after Cosimo, Piero, and after Piero, Lorenzo and Giuliano—seemed a scandalous novelty to Lucca Pitti's old friends, to all who, when on bad terms with the law or the Signoria, had once found refuge in the palace beyond the Arno. Yet there were no disturbances. Six hundred supporters

C

of Lorenzo swore loyalty to the family. The dictatorship of Cosimo was turning into a dynasty.

Lorenzo, who had not forgotten his father's last words against the nobility, strove to humble all those citizens who were distinguished by birth, wealth or reputation; and those whom he did not altogether exclude from public life but admitted to certain councils were always outnumbered by men of mean condition, partisans of the Medici who really controlled the government.

This was to bring Cosimo's policy to perfection. Instead of openly wielding the rod, Lorenzo had become a kind of invisible tyrant who governed by means of his clientèle. The old constitution continued to survive; the number of councils was even augmented by the addition of a *Consiglio Maggiore* of two hundred members who exercised sovereign power in the name of the people. But these two hundred deputies were nominated by a group of forty, and the forty were selected by ten *accoppiatori* or 'assemblers', themselves appointed by Lorenzo, the head *accoppiatore*; and so the trick was done. The tyrant sat on the top of the pyramid and below were his creatures who were supposed to represent the people.

Thus was democracy engulfed in darkness, thus did the last feeble flame of liberty go out.

*   *   *   *

Truly strange was the figure of the new prince. His lean, hollow-cheeked and deeply furrowed mask seemed to be set in a perpetual grimace; and all this, with a snub nose, big round eyes, a jutting lower jaw, an olive complexion like his grandfather's, and long black hair, lent something simian to his appearance. His voice was harsh and disagreeable; he liked singing and sang out of tune. For the rest, he was tall and strong; very short-sighted and with no sense of smell. And yet this man, who looked like a plebeian, completely devoid of kindness or gentleness, was the most refined and intelligent man in the world, 'the most Florentine of the Florentines'.

'You are our darling', cried the poet Luigi Pulci, one of his familiars.

The darling, young as he was, had seen and learned a great deal, and was well acquainted with men and affairs. He had received a princely education under the best masters, and knew Latin and Greek without however letting himself be obsessed, like so many others, with the cult of the ancient world. An even rarer gift was his sense of poetry; and his verses, which are in Italian and not in Latin, are especially charming when he speaks of the country, of flowers and of woman:

> How purple is thy bloom, fresh violet.
> And oh! how white the hand that gathered thee!

While the fêtes he organized were splendid, his own way of life remained simple. In winter he wore a purple cloak and hood, in summer the *lucco*, a short Florentine jacket; his son-in-law Franceschetto Cibo was to be astonished later on at the modesty of his ways. There was no court in the palace of the Via Larga, but only a family and friends for whom the door was always open and the table laid. In the street Lorenzo stepped aside in deference to older persons, and he advised his son to behave in the same way, reminding him that he was a private citizen of Florence.

He would listen to people's opinions, as it was 'a marvellous means of enriching one's brains by the brains of others'; but he talked little for his own part, and then only in concise language. 'When my mind is busied with an affair, I have no time to think of anything else.' He liked to be understood merely by a gesture. 'Before he begins to speak,' wrote the Venetian ambassador, 'his eyes speak for him.'

He liked the open air and the country-life at his villas and castles, at Careggi, Cafaggiolo and Poggio a Caiano, which last he had just had built. There he talked in dialect with the peasants, and laughed over the adventures of Piovano Arlotto, who, when setting out in search of the thirst which had abandoned him, carried at his belt bags of salt-meat, herrings, sardines and sausages.

Angelo Poliziano, a poor devil of a Greek scholar, in frayed doublet and down-at-heel shoes, whom Lorenzo had sheltered and made his companion, tells us of a stroll which he and his patron and his patron's friends took one day outside Florence. As far as San Miniato, they sang or reasoned on 'sacred topics' so as not to forget that the season was Lent; then they stopped to drink a *zappolino*; they read a little from St Augustine, and ended the day with music. What more could one desire? 'Under Lorenzo's shadow,' wrote Poliziano, 'Florence can repose in peace and joy.'

And indeed there now reigned in the Arno valley such calm as had not been known for centuries; some people imagined that in the future more poems would be written about the battle between the dogs and the birds than about battles between men. Life was very good, thought the intellectuals; paeans of praise rose to heaven, and men thanked God for being born in an age which had produced more genius and brighter wits than had been seen for a thousand years. Florence was the meeting-place for men perfect in all the arts, for criticism was not only permitted but encouraged; to pass muster, one had to prove oneself ingenious; and the very air one breathed inspired in every profession 'a thirst for glory and honour'.

Lorenzo conducted this orchestra with remarkable tact and skill. He was an open-handed Maecenas. He employed such artists as Antonio Pollajuolo, Baldovinetti and Ghirlandajo, and they responded by portraying him in their pictures and frescoes. In the garden of San Marco he founded a school of sculpture which was placed under the direction of a pupil of Donatello's, and where the young Michelangelo was to receive his first lessons and to be treated as a son by Lorenzo. Here, as in the Platonic Academy, there were no formalities or ceremonial. The newcomer took his seat beside the prince, while the latter was examining busts and medals. All topics were freely debated—aesthetics, philosophy, poetry, even politics. What men generally considered excellent was now subjected to the closest scrutiny; the critical genius, a speciality of Florence, enjoyed every freedom; and the most daring opinions caused no scandal whatever. For these subtle minds art was 'as necessary as salt and bread'.

It was a polished but in no way pedantic society, as one might judge from Luigi Pulci (known as Gigi), who occupied a prominent place in it. This favourite of Lorenzo, after going into exile to escape his creditors, had led a wandering life, trading in cloth and bricks. He was burdened with many children and was a poet into the bargain. To amuse his patrons, he was encouraged by none other than the pious Lucrezia Tornabuoni to compose a mock-heroic poem on the theme of Roland, a piece of buffoonery in which the giant Morgante, who used a big bell-clapper as his weapon and a fir-tree for a tooth-pick, vies with the cunning dwarf Margute in deeds of prowess.

The *Morgante Maggiore* is a sort of fairy tale told in a succession of fantastic episodes; the verses rush along in glittering cascades, deliberately absurd for all their clarity.[1] But at least the author has the merit of having freed himself from the pedantic discourses in vogue among the humanists who, with their Aristotle, appeared to him to be 'studying on the top of a large melon'. For the rest, he took singular liberties with exegesis; he wrote that 'the soul enters the body like jam which you put into a sandwich of bread fresh from the oven'; but again, no one was scandalized.

Lorenzo, though married to the strait-laced Clarice, was no more ascetic than his contemporaries. Deaf to the advice of his old tutor who had urged 'moderation in amorous enterprise', he had an extraordinary weakness for the sex and was a frequent night-rover. And yet, 'while committing follies to make you blush', he remained much attached to Lucrezia Donati, his titular mistress. He even became her troubadour:

> Was the sky bright or clouded when we met?
> No matter. Summer dwells beneath those eyes,
> And that fair face creates a paradise.

[1] This poem, and the subsequent work of Casti, were the first great models of burlesque poetry in Europe. Byron, during his sojourn in Italy, was fascinated by them, and they inspired, both as to manner and metre, his *Beppo* and his *Don Juan*. (Translator)

When it came to organizing a fête, Lorenzo was an altogether remarkable impresario, or *festaiuolo*. To share in the nocturnal 'triumphs', the populace was provided with appropriate costumes and marched torch in hand beside the carriages that were escorted by masked cavaliers. Then the songs would begin, first with one voice, then four, and then in chorus. Lorenzo had arranged the procession, written the verses that set the key for the rejoicing; and his carnival songs have remained famous.

Particularly memorable was the tourney held on January 28, 1475, in honour of Simonetta Cattaneo, wife of Marco Vespucci (a cousin of the 'discoverer' of America) and mistress of Giuliano de' Medici.[1] Lorenzo paid homage in verse to the beauty of this young Genoese, and one can well understand it when, in the Chantilly museum, one sees her portrait, attributed to Pollajuolo. The still childish profile is silhouetted against a purple cloud: a delicate nose like Roxelana's, a long flexible neck, a breast of dazzling whiteness set off by the dark coils of a snake-like pendent, the hair set with precious stones and surmounted by a *brocchetta*, which Robert de la Sizeranne calls a kind of lightning-conductor. Alas! the lightning-conductor was no defence against destiny. In the spring of 1476 the fair Simonetta died of consumption. They carried her to the grave with face exposed. 'As she lay dead,' it is recorded, 'you would have thought her as lovely and graceful as when living.'

Even death seem'd fair upon so fair a face, as Petrarch had once written.

*   *   *   *

To describe Lorenzo the Magnificent (as he was called) as a good-natured prince would be a complete error. His was, on occasion, the iron hand in the steel glove. If in need of money, he had a particular way of devaluing the currency. The State would only accept the old money after deducting a fifth of the nominal value; but the State's own payments were always made *at the*

---

[1] She is supposed to figure as one of the Graces in Botticelli's *Primavera*—the one with head turned towards the youth (Giuliano?) who is reaching up to pluck an apple from the tree.   (Translator)

nominal value; and the people paid the expenses of this ingenious operation. If, however, the Medici was in serious straits, he taxed them without scruple. We shall meet with further examples of his fiscal inventiveness.

His major anxiety, however, was to prevent the rise of other great families. More and more he put the curb on them. Even their marriages had to be licensed by the State; otherwise they might be too profitable to the contracting parties. If his personal security was in peril, Lorenzo struck ruthlessly. Thus, soon after his accession, the plot of a certain Bardo Nazi came to light in Prato. The Florentines made no move, but, as the conspiracy might have put ideas into their heads, Bardo and eighteen of his accomplices were hanged with their feet in the air.

And when trade, that sacrosanct thing, was threatened, the repression was still more severe. Florence had always been the rival of Siena, which blocked the road to Rome, and of Pisa, which blocked access to the sea. But in Lorenza's time it was the subject-city of Volterra that caused trouble. Volterra possessed mines of alum, a mineral indispensable for drapers, and Florence had taken these mines on lease. When the lease fell due for renewal, the Volterrans asked for a higher rent, which led to disputes and finally to a withdrawal of the concession. Lorenzo would tolerate no such solution; and on Volterra's rebelling, he let loose a *condottiere* who, despite his relative mildness, was unable to prevent the sack of the town. There were murders and hangings, and houses burned to the ground. The rebels had to be thoroughly frightened. A strong fortress, of which the keep still survives, was built at Volterra, and the alum mines continued to enrich Florence.

Yet this affair was a herald of calamity. The sky now began to darken over Florence, and threatening clouds appeared on the southern horizon. Sixtus IV, first of the bellicose Popes, wished to buy for his nephew, Girolamo Riario, the city of Imola which belonged to the Duke of Milan. Riario was to become a prince. But Lorenzo feared to see the Pope in possession of a place which stood on the confines of Florentine territory; and so he asked his colleague, the banker Francesco Pazzi, a very ugly and violent-tempered little man who lived in Rome, not to lend the Pope the forty thousand florins that were required for the purchase of Imola. Pazzi, however, was jealous of Lorenzo and anxious to win the favour of Sixtus. He therefore advised the latter of Lorenzo's move, whereupon Sixtus withdrew from the Medici the office of Comptrollers of the Papal Finances, and gave it to the Pazzi. Hostilities had begun.

The Pope next appointed Francesco Salviati as Archbishop of Pisa, to replace a Medici. Lorenzo refused to recognize the new Archbishop, and in 1478 there was open war. The Pope and his nephew were supported by Naples and Siena, while Florence had the backing of Venice and Milan: such coalitions were constantly arising throughout the course of Italian history.

Riario, who was now lord of Imola, saw in Lorenzo and the Venetians an obstacle to his ambitions in Romagna. If his uncle should die, he would be caught as in a vice between Florence and Venice. It was necessary that Lorenzo be removed.

Francesco Pazzi the banker now declared himself ready to help Riario, who found another ally in Salviati, the nominal Arch-bishop of Pisa. The three got in touch with a sort of bravo named Montesecco; and although the aged and wealthy Jacopo, who was head of the Pazzi clan, thought the enterprise was folly, a con-spiracy was hatched.

Riario, Salviati and Montesecco now had an audience with the Pope. Their plan was approved, on condition that no one should be killed; simply, the Constitution was to be changed. 'Holy Father,' said Salviati, as they were going out, 'leave us to manage the boat. We will steer it with a sure hand.'

Jacopo Pazzi had ended by joining in the plot. At Montughi, his country-house near Florence, active participants were now enrolled: Bandini and Francezi, young hotheads; Bracciolini, a poor devil in need of funds; and two priests, Antonio da Volterra, who hated Lorenzo for having destroyed his city, and Stefano, a tutor in the Pazzi household. Troops were posted round Florence ready to invade the city once the plan had succeeded, for, despite the Pope's verbal injunction, it was understood that both Lorenzo and Giuliano should be killed, as otherwise the survivor might take vengeance. But how find an opportunity for the deed?

Sixtus IV provided one. He gave a Cardinal's hat to Raffaelle Riario, a boy of twenty—a nephew of Girolamo—and made him Legate to Perugia. On his way to that city he would pass through Florence, and there would be a reception and a fête. The scheme looked excellent. The new Cardinal invited the Medici brothers to dinner at a villa belonging to the Pazzi. But Giuliano was unwell and did not come. In the following week Lorenzo held a reception at Fiesole in honour of the young Cardinal, but again Giuliano was absent. This was ill luck indeed! To bring the thing to a head, Salviati instructed Raffaelle Riario to express a desire to hear Mass in Santa Maria del Fiore on the morning of April 6, 1478, before going to dine in state at the Medici Palace, where great preparations were in hand. Lorenzo and Giuliano would escort him to the Cathedral, and afterwards take him back with them.

The elevation of the Host was to be the signal. The bells would then ring, and this would be the cue for Salviati and Bracciolini to seize the Palazzo della Signoria. Montesecco would kill Lorenzo, while Francesco Pazzi and Bandini dealt with Giuliano. But Montesecco, who had been kindly received by Lorenzo and who also was averse to shedding blood in church, drew out. He was replaced by the priests Antonio and Stefano, who had no such scruples.

Lorenzo arrived, Giuliano was late. Pazzi and Bandini, 'assigned for the murder', went in search of him. They amused him with jests, and, under pretence of caressing him, felt him with their arms and hands to make sure he had no breastplate or hidden weapon. The victims were now 'ready'.

In the church there was a vast concourse. At the moment of the elevation the two brothers were walking round the outside of the choir, when the bells began to ring. Francesco Pazzi and Bandini, who were still accompanying Giuliano, drew their daggers; and

c*

Bandini struck Giuliano so violently in the side that the latter recoiled several paces before he fell. The two then rushed upon him with such fury that Pazzi wounded himself in the leg.

At the same time Antonio and Stefano were attacking Lorenzo. A friend covered him with his body and was killed, but this gave Lorenzo time to draw his weapon and defend himself, so that he received only a slight wound in the neck. Pazzi and Bandini now came up; but Lorenzo had already had time to jump over into the choir. He ran across in front of the altar and reached the sacristy. Someone pushed him in, and the bronze door closed upon him.

Panic and howls of terror broke out in the Cathedral. Some people ran home; others sought arms to defend Lorenzo. Suddenly cries arose outside the sacristy: 'Come out, come out!' Were they friends? A young man who was with Lorenzo climbed up to the *cantoria* of the organ, and returned with the news that friends had arrived.

And so, after remaining an hour in the sacristy, Lorenzo now emerged under a strong escort. A friend had asked to suck the wound on his neck, as it was feared that the weapon had been poisoned; a scarf had then been used to bandage him, and he was taken to his home. As to Cardinal Raffaelle, he had remained trembling before the altar until the priests took him in charge. He was provided with a guard and confined in the Palazzo.

On hearing the bell, Archbishop Salviati had left the church, stating that he was going to see his mother. He took with him some thirty men, including his brother and Bracciolini and a number of exiles from Perugia, and made his way to the Palazzo della Signoria. Half his company he took into the courtyard and told them to hide in the Chancellery; and the conspirators prudently closed the door behind them, not realizing that they had imprisoned themselves. The door could only be opened from outside.

Salviati, in the meantime, went up the stairway and asked to see Cesare Petrucci, the Gonfaloniere, who was required by regulation never to leave the palace, and who at this moment was at breakfast. Petrucci was a man of humble birth who owed everything to the

Medici. He was amazed as he listened to the Archbishop stammer-
ing and confusedly explaining some mission with which the Pope
had entrusted him. There was nothing clear about it, and, besides,
the visitor was constantly turning towards the door as if to make
a sign to people outside.

The Gonfaloniere, who had some experience of these affairs,
called to his men-at-arms. On Bracciolini's suddenly appearing, he
seized him by the hair, swung him round and threw him to the
guards. The Priors meanwhile ran to the kitchen and armed
themselves with spits and larding-pins, while the guards searched
the building and discovered Salviati's friends in the Chancellery.
The wretches were brought out one by one, stabbed in succession
and thrown out of the window on to the paving-stones of the
Piazza.

Suddenly there was a great clatter. It was old Jacopo Pazzi, who
appeared on horseback in front of the palace, followed by a
hundred armed men all shouting: 'Liberty!' The word had ceased
to mean anything—the cry was soon drowned in the howl of the
Mediceans: 'Palle! Palle!'[1] And although the Pazzi now attacked
the palace, the defenders hurled down on their heads a hail of
stones with which the place was always well provided, and so
forced Jacopo to retreat. He saw that the game was up, had one
of the city-gates opened, and fled with his followers towards
Romagna.

News of the outrage quickly spread through the city. Giuliano
had been killed, with fifteen dagger-wounds. His elegance, his
love of games, his beautiful mistress, had made him the idol of the
younger generation, and Florence was seized with a frenzy for
revenge.

On the order of Petrucci and the Priors, Archbishop Salviati
was forthwith hanged from a window of the palace. His purple-
stockinged legs, dangling below his cassock, looked like the
clappers of a bell. His brother and Bracciolini were dispatched
in the same way. The others were butchered, after which their
bodies were let down over the Piazza, where the people cut them

[1] 'The balls'—badge of the Medici family.

in pieces and carried the fragments in triumph on the end of staves. A priest who had been in Salviati's service had his head and legs severed, and 'quarters of his body with one arm' were paraded through the streets amid cries of 'Death to the traitors!' The apothecary Landucci witnessed this spectacle.

Twenty-six men were thus disposed of like butcher's meat. When one body, which had been hanged, fell to the ground, the soldiers quarrelled over the hose and other garments. Only one man escaped, crouching for four days under a wood-pile. When discovered, nearly dead of hunger, he was pardoned.

The Florentines meanwhile had rushed to the Medici palace. The multitude filled the street, acclaiming Lorenzo, who had to show himself, with his neck bandaged. But victims were still needed. Led by the prince's bravoes, the crowd invaded the Pazzi mansions. In one of them they found Francesco, lying wounded on his bed. Despite his small stature, he drew himself up courageously and defied his executioners, while they insulted and spat on him. Finally they dragged him to the Palazzo and displayed him as a trophy at a window on the first floor. From here he could see a stiff corpse, wearing a cassock that had been pulled up above the thighs. It was the Archbishop. Other bodies were hanging head downwards. A cord was then passed round Francesco's neck, they pushed him out, his body swayed, he struck the Archbishop's, moved his legs and opened his eyes for the last time without hearing the obscene cries of the multitude.

And the Pazzi continued to be hunted down. One of them, disguised as a woman, had hidden in a corner of the Church of Santa Croce. He and another were taken and led to the Palazzo. The Signoria had, in the meantime, sent out riders to capture or get news of any who had managed to escape. Three of the Pazzi, who were picked up in this way, joined the chaplet of hanging bodies, and the populace never wearied of disembowelling the corpses. Another, Renato Pazzi, was surprised just as he was leaving the city disguised as a peasant. He was hanged on the spot, although he had disapproved of the conspiracy and taken no part in it.

Old Jacopo was still at large. On the eve of the attempted *coup d'état*, he had paid all his debts and handed back the merchandise which he had been handling for the customs, so that, in the event of failure, no one should suffer. He was now galloping over the mountain roads. But the Signoria's horsemen came up with him and brought him back in a litter to the Palazzo. He had begged the mountaineers to kill him on the way—in vain. He ended like his kinsfolk.

He was buried in Santa Croce. But a rumour arose that before being hanged, he had given his soul to the Devil, and the proof was that continual rain was now threatening to destroy the crops. Why have buried this blasphemer, this gambler, in holy ground? A band of men, chiefly peasants, stole the body from the church; whereupon the sky cleared, the rain stopped and the sun came out—'an obvious sign that *Vox populi* was *Vox Dei*'.

Jacopo was again buried, this time outside the walls in unconsecrated ground. But he did not rest long there. On May 17th, under the guidance of brutal men, a number of children dug up the body, fastened a cord round its neck and dragged it through the streets. They would stop at intervals to tie it to door-bells, and call out: 'Knock at the door! Open to messer Jacopo di Pazzi!' This was amazing, wrote Landucci, for children are usually afraid of death, and just think how, from April 27th to May 17th, he must have been stinking! These horrors went on until the Signoria had the body thrown from the Rubaconte bridge into the Arno, then swollen with the spring rains, while the children cried out: 'Messer Jacopo goes off in the Arno.' But downstream a little later, other children fished out the body, hung it on a willow-tree, flogged it and then threw it back. People were said to have seen it floating down under the bridges at Pisa.

Antonio and Stefano, who had been the first to assault Lorenzo, had already been executed, after their noses and ears had been first cut off. Seventy corpses, slashed and hacked by the populace, were now lying in the Piazza. Montesecco, the hired 'agent' who had cried off at the last moment, let himself be taken. After being questioned at length, he made a written confession and was then beheaded. Francezi and Bandini had managed to escape. The former enlisted in the Neapolitan army, and was to die a year later; the latter took refuge in Constantinople, but he was arrested by order of the Sultan at the request of the all-powerful Lorenzo, and was hanged as soon as he reached Florence. For Lorenzo did not mean one of his brother's murderers to survive.

And the reprisals continued. Those of the Pazzi who were still alive were imprisoned in the fort at Volterra, save only one who, being related to Lorenzo, was permitted to go into exile. The conspirators were depicted on the walls of the Bargello, hanging head downwards, and Lorenzo himself is said to have written Bandini's epitaph, which ran as follows: 'I was another Judas, a traitor, a murderer in Church.' Finally, a medal was struck in commemoration of the crime, and bearing the words: 'Public Mourning.' On it the conspirators were depicted as they were stabbing Giuliano.

The name of Pazzi was deleted from the registers, and those who still bore it were obliged to adopt another. Everything that recalled the name was now cancelled: armorial bearings, devices and escutcheons. The crossroads known as the *Canto dei Pazzi* was renamed. Anyone who should take a wife among the descendants of the Pazzi, or give his daughter to one of them, was to be *ammonito*, excluded from public office. The family was abolished.

Two hundred and seventy victims—such was the outcome of this clumsy conspiracy, undertaken without assurance of popular support. Giuliano's youth and popularity, together with the fact that he had been murdered in church at the moment of the elevation, inspired pity and horror. Later on, people were to extol a bastard he had had by a girl of the Gorini family. The child was born after its father's death, was brought up with Lorenzo's children, and became in due course Pope Clement VII.

CHAPTER VI

THE LAST DAYS OF LORENZO:
A TURNING-POINT IN THE DAILY
LIFE OF FLORENCE

Courage and skill of Lorenzo – Pomp and dictatorship –
The 'Bel Vivere' – Prosperity – Omens of misfortune

T HE failure of the conspiracy infuriated Pope Sixtus. In a
brief of June 1, 1478, he excommunicated Lorenzo, that
'son of iniquity', together with the Priors, 'possessed by
the Devil, carried away with the frenzy of mad dogs', who had
actually dared to hang an Archbishop in public at the gates of
their palace! Of the outrage in a church there was not a word.

Lorenzo was not much impressed. He had Montesecco's confession, which proved that the Pope and the Archbishop were
implicated. On June 5th, however, he set Raffaelle Riario at
liberty. According to a chronicler the young Cardinal reached
Siena more dead than alive, after the mortal terror he had passed
through. He still imagined he could feel a rope round his neck.
But the Vatican was not satisfied with this single act of grace, and
on July 7th a Papal herald arrived in Florence with a declaration
of war, in which it was stated that His Holiness bore no ill will to
the Florentines but only to the tyrant, and that if the latter were
driven out, everything could be settled.

Lorenzo cleverly—as usual—offered to sacrifice himself. He
was told that his life was inseparable from that of the Republic,
and he was given a bodyguard as a mark of sovereignty. Whereupon Rome hurled a bull of interdict against the city: there were
to be no more masses or sacraments or bell-ringing. But
the citizens showed no repentance and reacted violently. A
pamphleteer insulted the Pope, treated him as vicar of the Devil,
and appealed to a General Council of the Church.

Yet Lorenzo's situation was by no means comfortable, threatened as he was by Rome, Siena and Naples. After weighing up the pros and cons, he now, with a resolution that did credit to his political genius, decided to throw himself on the mercy of one of his enemies, that old scoundrel Ferrante of Naples. He first sent a wealthy merchant, Filippo Strozzi, as ambassador, and meanwhile he addressed the Florentine notables as follows:

> My enemies maintain that they have no hatred for the city, but only for me. I have therefore deemed fit to go personally to Naples. It will be a useful journey. If my enemies desire my person, they will get me; but if they desire public harmony, one can make terms. I know I am placing myself in peril: yet I am disposed to prefer the public weal to my own. I recommend my house and family to your care.

This noble attitude inspired the most compassionate sympathy. Everyone remembered the fate of the condottiere Piccinino who, in 1465, had trusted to the good faith of Ferrante, and who had been coolly assassinated. But Lorenzo was made of other stuff. After arriving in Naples he kept a watch on the secretive Ferrante, studied his mind and character, impressed him by his own skill as a political analyst, and after five months got him to sign a favourable treaty. He then, with the treaty in his pocket, returned quietly home, paying no heed to the Pope who had intended to force Lorenzo to seek pardon on his knees. The Florentines welcomed him back as a saviour; and Sixtus, being now without the support of Naples, raised the excommunication and the interdict. Everything was settled, though not as the Pope had hoped.

*   *   *   *

Never had Lorenzo's fortunes stood so high. The King of France called him his dear brother and treated him as a friend. The Sultan of Egypt sent him 'a giraffe, very tall, fair and pleasant, gentle as a lamb'; a big tame lion, and strange goats and sheep, all of which were greatly admired. And yet, since the conspiracy, the atmosphere had seemed less clean. In the street, the prince was escorted by ten armed and cloaked attendants, one of whom, a man of Pistoia named Salvalaglio, marched in front of him holding a naked sword. It was a Pretorian Guard. More than ever now Lorenzo kept an eye on the great families; he had spies at every party and assembly; he maintained secret relations with every group, without any one suspecting what another was doing. He had an eye to everything—his friends, his interests, the very attitude of the citizens. Distrust was the order of the day.

Not only State business but his private affairs were a source of anxiety. It appeared from the *Monte*, the great ledger in which were recorded the banking and commercial debts of the Medici house, that there was not enough money to pay the creditors. The various branches of the Bank, and notably the one at Bruges, had suffered heavy losses. Lorenzo then coolly drew from the public funds. Why feel any embarrassment? Taking advantage of his popularity and the peace he had negotiated, he had established a new régime. The various councils had been replaced by a single council of seventy members, all Mediceans, and they appointed the commissioners of the Signoria: the eight who dealt with foreign affairs, the procurators who attended to home affairs, and the eight officers who controlled the police. Officially, the Republic still subsisted; in reality nothing was done save by the will of Lorenzo, and he was now far more than a 'lord with a rod': he was a genuine dictator.

The slightest rumour was a pretext for severity. On one occasion a youth who had killed a favourite of the Signoria's was handed over to the *bargello*. He was an attractive-looking fellow and the crowd which had collected cried out to him: 'Clear off! clear off!' Some of the notables interceded for him with Lorenzo. The latter gave them fair words, and had the young man hanged. Four of the people who had told the youth to make off received each four lashes of the whip and were exiled. And Lorenzo did not leave the Piazza until calm had been restored.

In September 1480 a pilgrim who had called at Poggio a Caiano, Lorenzo's country-house, was arrested under suspicion of intending to assassinate the prince. Men were detailed to scrape the soles of his feet and then to roast them until the fat flowed out; he was then made to walk over a bed of coarse salt. The poor wretch died without having been proved guilty. Lorenzo had descended to the level of the other Italian tyrants.

On the other hand he retained popular support by the spectacles and festivities he organized; and he was still the Maecenas, adored and flattered by artists and writers. His house was a museum, a school, a meeting-place for great minds.

Let us look over this house, the palace in the Via Larga. Here is the chapel, and the bright frescoes by Gozzoli, and here the bedroom, the great bed of inlaid wood with its green canopy, its embroidered coverlets and velvet, gold-bedizened cushions. On the wall are illuminated brackets supporting a figure of Christ between the two thieves, and a women's head—though whether it is our Lady, or the Muse of Poetry, one can hardly be sure. Then there are crests and helmets, gilded spears, Byzantine mirrors, bronze cherubs, coffers adorned with scenes from Roman history in relief, and Hercules triumphing over Antaeus. The austere Clarice finds it hard to accept this intrusion of paganism. She would like her children to be brought up in a more Christian atmosphere and not in the doctrines of the Greek and Roman writers whom their masters prefer. This Poliziano, for example, says so many horrid things! But she was a voice crying in the wilderness, and her strictures on Florentine life left her husband completely cold.

Apart from politics Lorenzo was at this time obsessed with his passion for a married woman, Bartolommea de' Nasi, hardly beautiful but amiable and graceful. He was so much in love that when she was living in the city and he in the country, he would go by night to see her and return—with an escort—before daybreak. But this kind of life was exhausting him. To gout, which was hereditary, was now added severe stomach trouble. He sought relief at the hot springs at Vignone, in Siennese territory, where Saint Catherine tried scalding herself in order to have a foretaste of Purgatory.

Life in Florence at this time was not perfectly serene. The

moria, or plague, was raging and tradesmen left their shops and withdrew to the country. There was famine too, and war in Lombardy. Whole families were seen emigrating southwards, dragging after them 'their wretched cooking pots, stoves and other poor utensils, tied to the back of a donkey'.

Sometimes also the severity of the Signoria provoked a murmur, though scarcely more. On Midsummer Day 1488—a national festival—a Bolognese was detected slitting people's belt-tags when the offertory was being taken, with no regard for the solemnity of the occasion. He was hanged from the window of the *Capitano del Popolo* and remained there until the evening, when there arose such a storm of rain and hail as had never been seen the like of. The tents which had been pitched on the Piazza were torn to shreds, all on account of this act of homicide. It was true that in the previous week the men of Bologna had burned straw lions (the arms of Florence) in derision. But after this, everything settled down and the sun shone again.

It was in a tranquil setting that the Magnifico—a term of courtesy and admiration—ended his days. His last care was to set up his son in an established position. This Giovanni de' Medici was a little snub-nosed fellow, quite without charm; his mouth, with its jutting lower lip, was usually half-open. But he had been a good student at Pisa, and as he was destined for the Church, his father was hunting for benefices with such importunity that Innocent III, the reigning Pope, called him a 'hunter of flies'. But Innocent was a timid and irresolute man, he was afraid of Naples, he needed Lorenzo and entrusted himself entirely to that prince.

The latter exploited his advantage. Once more he became banker to the Holy See and, *ipso facto*, counsellor to the Vatican. He petted Innocent, sent him bottles of exquisite Trebbiano, delicate cheeses and Florentine cloth of the finest texture. And he reaped his reward. His daughter, the amiable Maddalena, was married to Franceschetto Cibo, the Pope's 'nephew' (really his son); and Giovanni de' Medici was made a Cardinal. 'You are', wrote his father, 'not only the youngest of the Cardinals now living, but of all those who have ever lived.' And Machiavelli was to comment: 'This business was a ladder by which the Medici climbed up into heaven.'

The list of his successes was thus complete. At the age of forty-four he was a decrepit old man. Feeling that his end was near, he sent for Savonarola, a terrible Dominican who was hostile to those 'pagans', the Medici, and made him presents to conciliate him; but the monk remained haughtily unbending. 'It's he who will depart', he said. 'I shall remain.' And again: 'When you throw a piece of meat to a watch-dog, he puts his teeth into it and is quiet for a little; but he soon drops it and barks still more loudly against the brigands and oppressors.'

Did the watch-dog refuse absolution to the oppressor? This was probably a legend invented by Savonarola's followers with a view to Republican propaganda. In any case, the Magnifico's death was accompanied by sinister omens. A furious hurricane began to blow, bringing torrents of rain; the Medici escutcheon was shattered; a lion, in the den at the Signoria, was devoured by the others; and an ox breathing fire through its nostrils was seen pursuing a woman. All this, the experts explained *sub rosa*, was because the Magnifico had freed a spirit which had been kept for years imprisoned in a ring and which he had let out on falling sick.

In the villa at Careggi where he was dying, Lorenzo heard that the cupola of Santa Maria del Fiore had been struck by lightning. 'On which side?' he asked. They told him. 'Well then, I'm done for', he replied. 'It fell on the side towards my house.' It was in vain that his doctor, Pier Leoni of Spoleto, administered a beverage containing powdered diamonds—the normal remedy for a great financier. He died on April 8, 1492.

It was a national calamity. The whole population attended his burial, which was conducted without pomp. Everyone feared there would be new misfortunes. The doctor's body was discovered at the bottom of a well near San Giovanni: had he been murdered or committed suicide? No one knew. Preachers, astrologers, men of letters and philosophers all shared in the general alarm, and praise of the departed rose on every hand. What would happen after him? Landucci wrote as follows in his journal:

This man was in the eyes of the world the most glorious and wealthy you could find, the man of greatest estate and reputation. Everyone said that it was he who governed Italy, and truly he was a wise man. All his designs prospered, and he realized what no citizen had ever managed to accomplish, by raising his young son to the rank of Cardinal and by ennobling not only his house but the whole of our city.

The inscription, which had been engraved in 1490 under Ghirlandajo's fresco in Santa Maria Novella, seemed to be true: 'Florence fair and noble through her victories, her great works, her crafts and houses, enjoys abundance, health and tranquillity.' Under Lorenzo, in fact, culture and the 'bel vivere' had flourished. 'The Florentines have marvellously augmented their state', cried Landucci. 'They have learned how to build more decently and more sumptuously than other nations, and how to esteem the most excellent artists, and this redounds to their incomparable glory.' Ariosto was likewise to extol Florence. 'If all your scattered palaces', he said, 'were gathered together within one circle of walls and under one name, two Romes would not be your equal.'

The Florentines being well fed did not think of complaining; for 'the city was crammed with food and every kind of trade was flourishing'. Did not this people enjoy peace, pleasure and renown? They seemed to have forgotten their former liberty and the passion for politics that had once possessed them, as also the rough jolts which had followed the conspiracy of the Pazzi. They were united for once, in servitude no doubt, but could they have desired 'a better or more agreeable master'? Would they, subtle and refined as they were, have endured a coarse and uncultured tyrant?

* * * *

Cruel when he thought it necessary, but courtly in his behaviour and very much of a lady's man, a poet and artist too, Lorenzo de' Medici represents the most finished type of the Renaisssance Italian. His skill and courage enabled him to maintain a balance of power among the Italian States, and he was himself 'the needle of the balance'. He tried to constitute a league of these States which would, if acting in concert, oppose any attempt at foreign invasion. The future seemed clear to him: he foresaw the irruption of the 'barbarians'. And while he consolidated the position of his country, he did not, like the good merchant that-he was by tradition, forget the greatness of his own house. One could measure now the ground which had been covered from the time when Salvestro, who had first brought the name of Medici into notice, had supported the revolt of the plebeians against the wealthy classes, of the 'magri' against the 'grassi'.[1]

Once Lorenzo had gone, the balance was upset, political confusion followed, party feeling reawakened, the preachers thundered from their pulpits, and the old apostles of liberty raised their heads. A whole epoch was sinking into the grave. Machiavelli understood this when he concluded his *Istorie fiorentine* with the following words: 'Immediately after the death of Lorenzo, those evil seeds began to sprout which, a little later, in the absence of a man who could have cleared them away, ruined and are still ruining Italy.'

[1] The 'Popolo grasso' was, strictly speaking, the name given to the members of the 'Arti maggiori'.   (Translator)

CHAPTER VII

A TOUR OF THE CITY AND
THE COUNTRYSIDE

*Ramparts and suburbs – Bridges and gates – Convents,
churches and palaces – Markets – Streets – Middle-class
houses, shops and country-villas – Valuation of an estate –
Peasants and their relations with city-folk*

A FLORENTINE who had been captured by Turkish
pirates and was planning his escape spoke as follows to
a fair Moslem whom he wished to fly with him to Italy:
'Under the most temperate sky is seated Florence, my very dear
home, which—I may say without disparagement of other cities—
is unquestionably the most beautiful in the world. There you will
see temples, palaces, private houses, broad streets and noble
squares: and, all around, gardens and villages in abundance, each
of which will seem to you a paradise.'

Was this the voice of an exile boasting of his home? or a fine
story for dancing-girls? Let us see what Florence was really like.

Since the Middle Ages the City of the Flower had grown con-
tinuously. Its suburbs now stretched out beyond the Arno. It had
overflowed from the ancient walls, which had been replaced by a
second wall at the end of the twelfth century, and by a third, of
which remnants still survive, in 1284.

In the fifteenth century the city's appearance was as follows.
Some sixty square towers rose from crenellated ramparts which
were more than two leagues all round. There were as many inside
the walls. Seen from a distance, the city was shaped like a spindle,
narrow at the ends, very broad in the middle. Along the walls,
at intervals of about three hundred and twenty-seven yards, there
was a tower; but when from time to time the constitution was
changed and the Republic was gradually replaced by the principate
these old towers, which were the pride of the city, were broken

down and turned into dwelling-houses. A contemporary noted all this with sorrow. 'One can picture the fine effect they made when one sees the campaniles of the Signoria, the Podestà, the Badia, of Santa Maria Novella and of Giotto's campanile at Santa Maria del Fiore', he observed. Owing therefore to the distrust of her tyrants, Florence lost the great crown of towers which had once stood out in jagged silhouette; and anyone who is curious as to the appearance of the medieval city, must now take a look at San Gimignano.

On the other hand, four fine stone bridges spanned the Arno. Starting from the east, there was the Rubaconte bridge, named after a Milanese Podestà, Rubaconte da Mandello, who had had it built in 1237. Six massive piles supported houses, shops and a little chapel. Later on, it was to be renamed the Ponte alle Grazie. The Ponte Vecchio had been rebuilt in 1345. It was longer and broader than the others and was covered with shops and houses. The Ponte Santa Trinità, dating from 1250, was very handsome: it was occupied only by a small hospice for monks and a stone sundial. Finally the Ponte alla Carraja, so called from the name of an ancient city gate, had no houses on it. This bridge commemorated a disaster. On May 1, 1304, it had collapsed under the weight of the spectators who had assembled for a 'representation of Hell', presented on a platform of boats and rafts in the river.

In the sixteenth century Benedetto Varchi conceived the happy notion of describing the city. The streets, says this famous historian, are 'fairly wide', and nearly all paved with flagstones, thanks to the active Rubaconte. On each side was a footpath, and a gutter to carry rain-water down to the Arno, so that the streets remained dry and free from the mud and slime which you found elsewhere in winter. In summer, on the other hand, the flagstones radiated the heat, and from noon until evening one could only remain cool in the usually spacious ground-floor rooms of the houses.

Varchi next takes us on a visit to the gates and fortified barbicans. There were six on this side of Florence, and five on the far side. Beginning from the east, you had the Porta della Giustizia, so called because malefactors were executed there; then the Porta alla Croce, with a great suburb covered with shops and a vast hostelry. It was by this gate that you left the city to go to the monastery of Vallombrosa or to Pontassieve in the Casentino. The Porta di Fiesole led you along the convent of the Camaldoli and beside a marvellous garden to the famous Badia, which had been built at great cost by Cosimo de' Medici. There, you could see Fiesole 'making eyes' at her old rival: Fiesole which, men said, had been built by Atlas under the sign of a star so favourable that it assured the Fiesolans of peace of mind, rest of body and a joyful heart.

Further on stood the Port' a San Gallo, and beside it an Augustinian convent founded by Lorenzo de' Medici, and one of the finest hostelries where the citizens came for relaxation and amusement. When business took them to Romagna, the citizens left by the Port' a Faenza. In this direction lay many territories subject to Florence, such as Pistoia and Montemurlo of which we shall speak later.

Lastly, there was the Porta al Prato, beyond which were playgrounds and the stadium. Here they practised jumping, and played at *palla al calcio*, or football. This was also the starting-point for the horse-races, the course running through the entire length of the city to the Porta Santa Croce. And it was through this gate that the Medici passed when they went to rest at their villa of Poggio a Caiano—a villa so rich that when the Emperor Charles V saw it in 1535 he said it could not be the villa of a private citizen.

Let us now cross the Arno. If you wanted to go to Pisa, over forty miles away, you would leave by the Porta San Friano, where there was a monastery and a suburb, and away beyond, very agreeable villas including the *Selve*, or 'woodlands', belonging to Messer Filippo Strozzi. If you went out by the Porta San Pietro Gattolini, you saw a great number of villas, palaces, gardens and fountains, and these commanded a superb view of Florence. The Porta San Giorgio, standing on the highest ground, took you to the Piazza dei Giullari, so-called on account of the festivities and displays of jugglery of which it had formerly been the scene.

Further on, from the Porta San Miniato, you could see, silhouetted on the hilltop, the fortress-church raised to the glory of San Minias, one of the few Florentine saints; while the last gate on this side, the Porta San Niccolò, was a very busy one, because it led to the valley of Chianti, 'famous for the number of exquisite wines that were produced there, and worthy of admiration because it is harsh and rocky'.

* * * *

In their capacity as merchants the Florentines had for long been well versed in accountancy and statistics. Varchi tells us that seven or eight children, rather fewer girls than boys, were baptised every day at the Church of San Giovanni, where the civic register had been kept since 1450. Prior to that, people had been simply required to drop a black pea into a box for a boy and a white pea for a girl, to record births. Now counting the number of 'hearths', which was 10,000, and excluding the suburbs, the resident population was estimated at 70,000,[1] including the religious—monks and *frati*—who were continually increasing.

In spite of its libertines and free-thinkers, the city contained over a hundred convents, including forty-nine for women. Since the thirteenth century the Dominican and Franciscan orders had imparted a great impetus to monastic life. We have today, in witness of it, the Dominican church of Santa Maria Novella, the Franciscan church of Santa Croce, the Carmine founded by the Carmelites, and Santa Annunziata, founded by the new order of the Servi di Maria. Lastly, on the foundations of the old church of Santa Reparata had risen Santa Maria del Fiore, begun in 1296 by Arnolfo da Cambio. Giotto's campanile was added in the next century, and in the fifteenth, the cupola of Brunelleschi, that famous architect whose life every Florentine could relate to you.

His family lived opposite the present church of San Gaetano, beyond the Via Tornabuoni. He had learned drawing in a goldsmith's shop, and discovered a gift for architecture when helping

---

[1] Most authors regard this as an underestimate. Florence probably contained at least 90,000 or even 100,000 inhabitants.

to rebuild a kinsman's home at the Mercato Vecchio. For the offices of the Signoria he recommended arcaded openings in the antique manner, which created a sensation. To build the cupola of Santa Maria del Fiore he had to compete with Lorenzo Ghiberti, the famous sculptor who had carved the doors of the Baptistery. Furious at being obliged to work with him, he feigned sickness, and when people came to fetch him from his home: 'Go and talk to Lorenzo', he grumbled.—'But Lorenzo will do nothing without you.'—'Well, I can manage quite well without him,' he replied.

Ghiberti withdrew, for a consideration; and Brunelleschi completed the daring cupola, or dome, which is the pride of the Florentines and the glory of the great cathedral which Leone Battista Alberti was to extol.

This temple (he wrote) unites grace with majesty, a charming delicacy with the solid and the robust. Each of its parts seems to have been built to please the eye, everything to have been designed for eternity. Within, one breathes the perpetual freshness of spring. Outside there may be frost, fog or wind; but in this retreat, closed to every wind, the air is quiet and mild. What a pleasant refuge from the hot blasts of summer and autumn! And if it be true that delight resides where our senses receive all that they can demand of nature, how can one hesitate to call this temple a nest of delights? Here, wherever the eye comes to rest, images of joy and gladness present themselves. A delicate perfume fills the air; and, what I appreciate above all, is that when one hears the voices of the priests as they celebrate those rites which the Ancients called mysteries, one has a marvellous sensation of sweetness.

This peculiarly Florentine eulogy might almost have been written by a pagan.

Let us now consider the palaces, some of which had retained the aspect of a medieval fortress. Such was the palace of the Podestà begun in 1255; the palace of the Signoria which was taken in hand when the 'Arts' assumed power, in 1258; and the palace of the Guelph party with its battlements. But the great era of palace-building dates from the fifteenth century. Between 1450 and 1478 thirty new ones were raised, and the movement continued to grow in the years that followed. Varchi describes the residence of the Twenty-one Arts, with their sculptured arms, the admirable

Or San Michele, which had once been a storehouse for grain (*horreum*), and then an oratory where the archives of the Republic were housed on the upper floor; the Hall of the Pope, built in 1418 in the convent of Santa Maria Novella and reserved for the supreme pontiff when he visited Florence; and the Sapienza Vacchia, near the Church of the Nunziata—the *studio* where professors lectured 'in every faculty'.

One should add that the more distinguished families possessed, near their palaces, a *loggia* or *casolaro*, an open-air pleasaunce with an arbour and colonnades. Here citizens would come to converse, or arrange business-deals, or play games. Such was the Loggia dei Tornaquinci near the Palazzo Strozzi; and the Loggia of the Innocents. The most remarkable of these *loggie*, which still survives, is that of the Signoria, now called the Loggia dei Lanzi.

But Florence was particularly proud of its hospitals, where the invalids of both sexes were lodged and treated free of charge. The oldest and wealthiest, thanks to an accumulation of endowments, was the hospital of Santa Maria Nuova,[1] which controlled all the others. These included San Pagolo, near Santa Maria Novella, the hospital of the Incurables in the Via San Gallo, the small receiving-centres for poor folk and travellers, and especially the great hospital of the Innocents, with its gardens, where, 'through the hole of a little window', foundlings were taken in. There were over a thousand there, in Varchi's time.

*   *   *   *

The busiest centre remained where the Roman Forum had once stood, that is, in the Mercato Vecchio, now the Piazza della Repubblica. Here you might see the greengrocers with their movable booths, the butchers and their open stalls, the fishmongers and innkeepers. At each angle of the crowded square stands a church. Here and there barbers are shaving people in the open, except on Sundays when they have to remain in their shops (they are forbidden to shave at home). The din is like that of a poultry-

---

[1] Benvenuto Cellini lived near by, in the Via della Pergola.

yard; people hailing each other or quarrelling, and the barber threatening the apothecary whom he looks on as a competitor.

The Via Calimala is noisy with the shouts of apprentices. Here the first printing-press was founded. This street leads us to the Piazza Or San Michele, to the palace of the wool-merchants and thence by a sloping alley to the Mercato Nuovo. Here the murmur of voices is different. In shops or under awnings, the dealers in silk and other textiles ply their trade, while the money-changers sit gravely at their desks. No food may be sold here, for this is what we should call the Exchange. The Loggia bears the image of a wild boar. From here two streets, the Calimaluzza and the Canto di Vacchereccia, with its many goldsmiths' shops, take us to the Piazza della Signoria, another centre of commercial and political palavering, a birthplace for *combinazioni*. The Via Calzaiuoli—the Street of the Hosiers—well known to the modern tourist, was then divided into three portions: the Corso dei Amidei, the Via dei Pittori and the Via dei Formaggi.

In the course of time all these streets became more open and ornate. Buildings were replaced with a constant eye for beauty. Thanks to Brunelleschi and Alberti, the house in Renaissance style (there was no Gothic palace in Florence as there was in Siena) replaced the fortress-dwelling; a taste for elegance, luxury and comfort prevailed over notions of war and strife.

Florence already possessed open spaces, some fifty squares, or *piazze*, including those in front of the four churches of the four quarters,[1] as well as 138 gardens and vegetable plots. But there were sombre spots like the *Stinche*, the state-prison, 'a stinking gaol', according to Machiavelli, 'where the walls harbour vermin so huge and swollen that you might compare them to butterflies'. This was near the Badia, where the Podestà had charge of the city's banner. You felt as though a policeman was lurking at every corner.

The Florentine normally lived in the open. In good weather he would sit in the street which served as the outer room of his house, and there he would play at chess or dice. The bystanders

[1] Michelangelo lived in the Via Ghibellina, near the Piazza Santa Croce.

commented on every move, but, owing to the restricted space, the least untoward incident might occasion a panic. Thus one day Rinuccio di Nello's old horse, 'a sort of camel with a humped back, a head like a bell, and the crupper of a lean ox', suddenly materialized in pursuit of a mare. Rinuccio, who had been warned by a cobbler that his horse had broken loose, came running in pursuit. The Mercato Vecchio was, as usual, crowded. Alarmed by cries of 'St George! St George!' and thinking that there was a riot, the second-hand clothes-dealers closed their shops. Butchers' stalls were overturned, drapers hastily threw their rolls of cloth into the shelter of their booths. A hurricane seemed to be passing. Along the alley which led to Or San Michele, and where corn and grain were sold on open counters, the damage was terrible. A group of blind folk standing in front of the Oratory placed themselves on the defensive. And when at last the horse and its pursuers emerged on to the Piazza della Signoria, the magistrates thought a revolution had broken out. The doors of the palace were bolted, and the public executioner hid himself.

But visitors admired Florence. Rabelais, some years later, was to write: 'We were a right goodly company of studious folk, greedy to see the wonders of Italy; and so, with curious gaze, we contemplated the . . . beauty of Florence, the great building of the Duomo, and the sumptuous temples and stately palaces.' At the beginning of the nineteenth century Stendhal observed that in twenty different parts of the city, as for example if the visitor walked from the Ponte alla Trinità and past the Palazzo Strozzi, he might think himself back in 1500. 'How well one realizes', he remarks, 'from the solidity of these palaces, built of enormous blocks of stone undressed on the outer surface, that danger was often rife in these streets. It is the absence of danger in the streets that makes us so small and petty.'

What a privilege for Florence! 'The plant "man" is born there more robust than in other lands.'[1]

*   *   *   *

---

[1] 'La pianta uomo nasce più robusta in Italia che in qualunque altra terra'—a saying of Alfieri's, repeated by Byron and others.   (Translator)

The burgher's house, as compared with the palace, was still a very splendid residence. The home of a notable in the wool trade, for example, had a vaulted portico, two galleries paved with marble, and three floors. Beside it was the *Loggia* surrounded by colonnades. When the sun was hot, you took refuge on the first floor in a room with glass windows and curtains to hide you from the street. More modest houses also had their comforts—terraces, courtyards, stables, passages, antichambers and at least one well of fresh water. Better still, a fairly well-to-do Florentine owned a *casa*, or dwelling-house, a shop where he worked, and a villa or farm in the country.

In the Mugello, for example—the upper part of the valley of the Sieve, a tributary of the right bank of the Arno—the merchants had their country homes. Old dismantled castles had been turned into quiet residences, where the prosperous dealer in silk or woollens took his ease with his family. There were 800 of such houses in a space of twenty miles, surrounded by stone walls, and honoured with the name of palaces.

Thus the city stretched far beyond its walls. Florence, according to Alberti, 'is surrounded by innumerable villas where the air is pure as crystal, the landscape most pleasant, the views wonderful. In those parts there are no fogs or harmful winds. Everything is good, the very water is pure and wholesome.' Bird-songs and fresh verdure gladden the heart, 'the streams go leaping down or hide under tunnels of overhanging herbage'. You see 'the lamb trotting behind his mother. Another lamb has just been born. The good shepherd is carrying it in his arms, while the faithful dog keeps watch over them all.' A sort of pastoral poem!

This countryside was endowed with every blessing. In his country-farm the merchant cultivated cereals and vegetables; it also provided him with wine, oil, forage and wood. It supplied all his needs and he sold the surplus. 'Blessed villa', cried Alberti, 'sure home of good cheer, which rewards one with countless benefits: verdure in spring, fruit in autumn, a meeting-place for good men, an exquisite dwelling.'

Let us take the case of Agnolo Pandolfini, a cultured merchant whose ancestors had made a fortune in trade at Naples. He owns the fine villa of Signa, where he has everything a gentleman could desire: dogs, falcons and various kinds of nets for small game or fishes. He receives and lodges everyone; he even goes out into the road and invites the wayfarer in, gives him water to wash, seats him at his table, and when he has lunched, thanks him and sends him on his way, as he does not wish to embarrass him. He is a modern Lucullus. When hunting he is always accompanied by a score of cavaliers, apart from the kennel-men and whippers-in, and they kill hares and roebuck.

A philosopher into the bargain. Shortly before he died at the age of eighty-five—as keen-witted as if he had been only forty— Agnolo counselled his friends to give more thought to the welfare and prosperity of the city than to their private interests, though he added: 'And after all that, I know you will do nothing of what I am telling you.'

Here now is a countryman of another stamp, an official dismissed from his post in consequence of a political upheaval. Niccolò Machiavelli is now eking out a poor sort of existence in a modest house, the Albergaccio, not far from San Casciano. Rising before dawn, he makes ready his snares for birds and small game, or goes into his coverts to pass the time of day with the wood-cutters who always have a bone to pick among themselves or with the neighbours. Yet the slender resources that remain to him furnish him with many and many a good story.

While making the round of his traps he reads Dante, Petrarch or Ovid. On the public road he talks to wayfarers, listens to gossip, observes human nature; then, after a meagre supper, betakes himself to the inn where, with the host, the butcher, the miller and the lime-merchant, he loses caste—or at least lowers himself—by playing at cards or backgammon. The players squabble and hurl insults at each other, and the noise carries as far as San Casciano. Machiavelli plunges into such low life 'to preserve his brain from getting mouldy'; but then, on his return home, changes his clothes, dons his old court-dress and renews his mind and spirit by reading the ancient classics.

6. Horse race in the streets of Florence by Jacopo Franchi

7. (*above*) Details from a fresco by Ghirlandajo in the Chiesa di S. Maria Novella: (*left to right*) Ficino, Landino, Poliziano and G. de Becchi

(*below left*) Supposed self-portrait of Botticelli from his 'Adoration of the Magi' (Uffizi, Florence)

(*below right*) Ghirlandajo, from a fresco in the Chiesa S. Maria Novella

Yet he by no means loses his practical sense of business. We have a sort of survey and description he made of two country-houses which his friend Francesco Guicciardini—a shrewd official who had contrived to keep his job—thought of renting. The first house, Finocchieto,[1] is situated in a melancholy spot, a sort of Arabia Petraea. The house is poor, the rooms small, the windows high. In front is the beginning—or remnant—of a field, but the earth has been denuded and fresh soil will be needed, as otherwise only the 'bones' will remain. A hundred ducats would have to be expended in restoring the place, planting vineyards on the hill above the house, and making ditches.

The other property, the Colombaja,[2] looks better. The land seems good, and the place has all the conveniences usual for a villa near Florence, 'a church, a butcher's shop, a road and postal service'. As regards the house, you enter by a large courtyard; facing you is a loggia, with a balcony; to the right, an anteroom and bedroom; to the left, the hall with another room and ante-room. All these apartments are decent and fit to live in. Opening on the courtyard are the kitchen, the stables and the still-room. The poultry-yard is in a smaller court. Below are two wine-cellars; upstairs are three rooms which can be easily rendered habitable for 'a gentleman'. The roofs are neither good nor bad. By spending a hundred and fifty ducats in repairing the doors, gutters, drain-pipes and basement; in patching up the kitchen, and touching up the buildings to give them a brighter appearance, Guicciardini would be able to live there decently and agreeably, 'until the time comes for the last voyage'.[3]

This survey and valuation of property by a great writer gives one a vivid notion of the daily life of the times; the more so as it is quite without literary pretension.

*   *   *   *

[1] The Fennel-Farm.   (Translator)
[2] The Dovecote.   (Translator)
[3] Literally, 'for entering the great sea'—an old Florentine expression for death.

D

The peasant, or *contadino*, whom you meet can be recognized by his long grey garment without a cloak and often without trunk-hose, by a broad belt and a cape with flaps hanging down on each side. He is no ordinary peasant, tied to the soil, but ranks as a free man and is more comfortably off than the peasants of other lands.

There was no real barrier in Tuscany between the city and the village. Many small towns were inhabited by peasants who, on returning from the fields, called themselves citizens. A shepherd from the Mugello could leave his flock and join a trade-guild in Florence. There was constant communication between town and country; the contadino benefited from the prosperity of the merchant; and if he were a tenant he could by signing a contract with the proprietor become a free farmer. Peasants' revolts were unknown in Tuscany.

The countryman knew how to defend his rights. There is a story of one peasant who, seeing his parcel of land nibbled away, year after year, by a wealthy squire, had the funeral-knell sounded in his village. People rushed out in alarm.

'Why are they ringing the bell?'

'Because law is dead. They are ringing for the repose of the soul of law, which is dead.'

An original way of mobilizing public opinion! The Florentine was rarely at a loss.

No doubt as Pulci, Lorenzo's familiar, observes, the contadino understands nothing about the great 'debates regarding the soul, and as to where it enters the body and where it leaves it'. He does not trouble his head by wondering why the peach contains a stone, and people who discuss such problems strike him as having something wrong with their brains.

The cultured burgher, on the other hand, holds the peasant in low esteem or even regards him as a sink of corruption. According to Pandolfini, the squire of Signa of whom we have already spoken, the peasant gives his whole mind to cheating you. He never makes a mistake to his disadvantage and always tries to get the better in a bargain. Even if he had more money than the owner, he would complain more loudly. When the harvest is good, he keeps two-thirds of the best for himself; when the yield is poor, owing to storms or other mishaps, he always makes you pay for the loss. However, says Pandolfini, it would be a mistake to avoid contact with these cunning rustics who teach one how to contend with scheming townsmen and remain vigilant. They are professors of distrust, and in the end their tricks amuse one.

On the whole, therefore, the Florentine burgher did not regard the peasant with the perfect scorn of a French lord for his villein; and in any case the *villano* would not care a rap. 'His shoes are rough, but his brain is subtle.' Although violent on occasion he is by nature independent, cheerful and gay. His amusements are simple. At a country fête he brings out a donkey with cymbals tied to its back and a thistle under its tail, so that it is constantly fidgeting and making music for everyone to dance to.

Country-life in Tuscany had from early times afforded a subject for art. A fresco in the city-hall at Siena (fourteenth century) depicts a peasant dragging his pig to market; *contadine* dancing roundelays; farm-servants leading an ass; women with baskets on their heads; and ploughmen at work. This feeling for nature and the open air is well expressed by Lorenzo de' Medici in a passage describing the advent of Spring: 'When the Earth, clad in her new vesture, appears so fair to the eye, she will be saying to herself: "So now I am a little girl again".'

The tyrant took a personal interest in the peasants who were his neighbours. Nencia da Barberino was the girl whom he selected as typical and whose love-affairs he recorded in the rustic vein. 'She is a lily-flower, without leaves, so soft and white that she makes you think of the fat round a kidney.' She shines more brightly than a goblet; the dimple in her chin enhances her charms; she has seven rings in a little box, and makes prettier curtseys than any lady in Florence. No one is her equal for plaiting wicker-baskets and straw-hats, and everyone admires her when she goes to Mass in her Sunday gown. Vallera, the young contadino, has fallen in love when watching her gathering herbs one April for a salad. He goes to town to buy her a pennyworth of needles, some rouge in a box, and a ribbon of blue silk. But he has rivals who are promising her a pair of pretty little shoes.

When the lord of Florence took this tone with his peasants, the merchant would have shown ill grace by being haughty or distant.

To draw a complete picture of the environs of Florence, we should have to push as far as the subject-cities of Pisa, Volterra, Pistoia, Arezzo and Cortona, the many territories where the gates 'were closed at night and opened in the morning'. As a mark of submission and by way of tribute, the hundred wealthiest territories were required, on Midsummer Day, to offer a *palio*, a roll of cloth which served as a prize for the races that were run on that festival. The poorer lands, to the number of thirty, gave a candle as symbol.

One should add that, internally divided as she was and often torn between rival factions, Florence never contrived really to attach these vassal-cities. She treated them loftily, without regard or affection, and she was to pay the penalty when evil days came upon her.

CHAPTER VIII

HOME-LIFE IN FLORENCE (I)

*Marriage – Regulation of weddings – Life in the household –
How a husband instructs his wife – Birth and education of
children – Pedagogues and pedants – A model wife*

A FLORENTINE liked making regulations. From the day of his birth to the day of his death, no one in principle escaped the observation of a great number.

In medieval Florence young girls married at the age of twenty or above. In the fifteenth century they did not wait as long. Marriage was arranged by the *sensale*, a go-between, who informed the state-official of the names of the couple in question; but it could not actually take place unless the bride had a dowry which had been amassed and recorded in the 'Great Book'.[1] Towards the end of the fifteenth century, a modest middle-class dowry amounted to 2,500 or 3,000 florins.[2]

The gift of the ring, as a symbol of engagement, was celebrated at a lunch and a supper. Presents were exchanged; but the fiancée's must not have cost more than a hundred *lire*. On the wedding-day the young men stretched a ribbon or a garland of

[1] In the *Monte*, which was the State Bank, a man who wished to establish for his daughter a dowry of say 1,000 florins signed himself at the *Monte* as in debt for 104. The Commune paid no interest, but after fifteen years the dowry was ready. If he left it with the *Monte*, then he received interest.

[2] According to Varchi, the gold florin, which was still called a ducat, and later a crown, was worth seven *lire*. The *lira* was worth twenty *soldi* or sixty *quattrini*. But there were different kinds of florin; there were *fiorini larghi* or *di camera*, and *fiorini di sugello*. It is therefore difficult to estimate their value in present-day currency. According to Rodocanachi, the gold florin was equivalent to 12 francs in French pre-1914 currency. Multiply this by 250, and the florin would be worth 3,000 French francs at the rate current in 1957. The French gold crown under François Ier was equivalent to about 750 francs at the 1957 rate.

flowers across the street. The most handsome of them then complimented the bride, offered her a bouquet, and received a present; after which the bridegroom broke the obstacle. The party then proceeded to the church of San Giovanni. Here, near the Baptistery, above the Loggia of the Bigallo, the trumpets sounded, each trumpet carrying a square pennon with a red lily on a white ground. The bride then advanced to the altar, wearing a conse-crated veil as a symbol of chastity. Before the ceremony she was allowed to ride from her parents' home on horseback, escorted by at most ten women. But she had to return on foot, with only two women or two men, under pain of a fine of 100 *lire*. Marriage was not consummated the first night, out of respect for the sacra-ment.

At the marriage-dinner there were not to be more than twenty-five women, apart from members of the family, and not more than ten men and eight serving-men. After the two days devoted to the wedding, no trumpet or timbal-playing was permitted, and no dancing, or *carole*, outside the house. The cook was required to report to a public official what he intended to serve, the menu being strictly controlled. Only three dishes were allowed and twenty-five trenchers (or plates) with each. If veal was served, no other kind of meat might be consumed. Supper was limited to two courses: a stew, followed by a jelly or a tart. And the bride was not allowed to distribute or send any trinket, purse, waist-band or wallet, but only a few gratuities. The Signoria insisted on economy.

But what happened in fact? One can guess by turning to the journal of the coppersmith Masi. He wrote here, on his wedding-day: 'We had a fine banquet as befitted our quality in the ground-floor room, and there were more than thirty people at the first table. This was an honourable marriage-feast for people of our class.' Thirty people, merely at the first table!

The moralists stigmatized 'marriage customs' as deplorable. Among the Romans, they said, people scattered nuts to make a noise and prevent anything being heard from the bride's chamber. Today, under Christian laws, young maidens ride on horseback, in public, decked out, 'lasciviously painted', and preceded by trumpeters as though the people were being summoned to witness the unbridled audacity of a courtesan.

Wedding regulations often therefore remained a dead-letter, especially in the case of great families. Certain marriages cost several thousand ducats. The wedding of Lorenzo and Clarice Orsini has been already described; that of another Lorenzo de' Medici, a rather second-rate person, with a French lady in 1518, shows how far the old republican habits had fallen into disuse.

Masi, who was an eye-witness, describes the event as follows. The garden in the Via Larga was surrounded with new silk tapestries representing animals and imaginary figures, which would not have been more beautiful had they been painted. There were more than three hundred of these tapestries, and the smallest was worth over fifty gold ducats. Banquets were served to a succession of guests for three days running. More than two hundred calves were disposed of, as well as kids, hares, capons, geese, pheasants, peacocks and every other kind of poultry. And how describe the splendid attire of the people who devoured all this food? Masi was overcome with amazement.

But celibacy was gaining ground at the expense of marriage— a sign of the decadence of morals which was partly due to the example of the debauchees of Athens and Rome in ancient times. 'If everyone were like you,' a mother told her sons, 'the world would long ago have come to an end. The devil is not as black as he is painted.'

The devil, in the eyes of these youths, was a wife—a woman who usurps authority at home and expects to be boss. The Signoria tried to react against the trend, but many people persisted in thinking that to take a wife was to saddle oneself with an unendurable burden.

* * * *

Here, on the other hand, is a picture of a model household. After their marriage the burgher takes his young wife over the house from top to bottom, from the attic, where grain is stored, to the cellar, for wine and wood. He shows her 'where to put everything', and then, after shutting the door, shows her the great chest in the bedroom where valuables are kept, money, clothes and jewels. He does not show her his ledger and account-book. Next, kneeling beside her at the tabernacle of Our Lady, he prays to God to give her grace to make good use of all the things which in his bounty he now shares with her; he prays that they may live long together in joy and concord and have many *male* children. For himself, the merchant asks for riches, powerful friends and great honours; for her, a stainless reputation—that her desire should be to her husband (she blushes and lowers her eyes)—perfect respectability and the virtues of a good housekeeper.

After which, instead of playing the fool like so many people, he explains to his better half what he expects of her. 'Remember all this,' he says, 'because I shall not say another word of it.' He flatters himself.

The wife, who has been used to obeying her mother, is rather timid at the outset: melancholy, out of her element and listless—*oziosetta*. So when the husband returns after the day's work he greets her good-humouredly, to make her smile and understand that joy should reign in the home.

Gradually she grows used to things. The husband, as a good business-man, teaches her a horror for waste, a respect for economy, for 'he who finds no money in his wallet will find less in other people's'. Expenditure should be proportioned to income. A villa, if one owns one, provides all the food that is needed, and the income from trade, whether in wool or silk, adds to the credit balance.

If the housewife is a spirited woman, her consort teaches her not to raise her voice like those arrogant creatures who shout as though the whole family were deaf—an imbecile habit, worthy of country wenches who call to, and answer, each other from hilltop to hilltop. She should also prevent certain classes of people from collecting in front of the door—buffoons, itinerent singers, ne'er-do-wells and hooligans who, in their fantastic costumes, try to wheedle money out of spendthrifts.

Here is another chapter of the marriage-code: how to train the servant. She was often a slave[1]; in the market at Venice, she would have fetched from six to eighty-seven ducats, according to age and ability. She might be an Italian; but in any case she had to be kept well in hand. Listen to Fra Bernardino of Siena on this subject:

Is there sweeping to be done? Make her sweep. Pots to be scoured? Make her scour them. Fruit or vegetables to be peeled? Make her peel them. Laundry? Set her to washing. Make her look after the children, and everything else. If you don't accustom her to doing everything, she will become a good little lump of flesh, *buon pezzetto di carne*. Don't give her any leisure, I tell you. As long as you keep her on the go, she will not remain leaning out of the window.

These precepts seem to have been literally followed. And there was little generosity. Rare were the housewives who could boast of having given their servants 'enough cloth to bandage a finger'; and the wise would exclaim: 'After all that, how can you expect them to be faithful, affectionate and hard-working?'

The housewife should know how to cook, to prepare the most delicate viands and add the appropriate condiments. For this purpose, she will take lessons from the professional cooks who are engaged for big dinner-parties; she will watch them attentively so as not to be obliged to have recourse to them on every occasion, which would be difficult, for that matter, in the country where the cooks are not good and where one entertains more strangers. Not that she is personally to handle the food and dishes; but she must be able to instruct and direct the maids. Thus will she bring great honour to her husband, and win him many friends.

But let her not take it into her head to wear the trousers[2]! Some did so. A caricature dating from 1450 depicts the women struggling violently to seize this badge of authority. And let her not spy on her husband to discover his thoughts, like 'the moon who is a woman and peers and pries in everywhere at night, in defiance of blinds and shutters'. Let her be always correct and

---

[1] A Circassian or Tartar. Cosimo de' Medici, the '*pater patriae*', had a bastard named Carlo by a Circassian girl.

[2] The trunk-hose, strictly speaking.   (Translator)

D*

reserved, and let her avoid make-up! One day when Agnolo Pandolfini had invited some of his relatives, he saw that his wife had put on paint and face-cream and was playing the coquette. He took her aside and said, smilingly: 'Poor me! Wherever did you go and daub your face in that way? Did you put it in the frying-pan? Go and wash yourself, so that people won't laugh at you.' The wife listened and cried, and Agnolo gave her a cloth to wipe away the tears and the paint.

Somehow or other life settles down into its humdrum routine. The housewife gets up early, gives the necessary orders and sees that everything is in its place. Orderliness comes first. There must be no disputes or scenes with the servant, none of those grumblings and outcries that make a house sound like bedlam, no rows because the servant has not received her ration of dried figs. The wife will work on and off until the return of her husband, and she will give him a nice welcome, if not from her heart, at least in appearance. If a stranger arrives unexpectedly, she is to do the honours of the house without bustle or excitement, without a great shifting of chairs and stools, and without fussing round the room and making him wait two hours for a meal and then offering him as the main dish a couple of fritters, with an egg and a half in each, as a special treat! Given these conditions or rather the avoidance of these horrors, domestic peace will be possible.

Material conditions had quickly become more elegant and refined in Florence than elsewhere. Formerly, after a meal, the bones of game or fish were thrown under the table, the room was cleaned only on Saturday, and people lived among their animals. It was the fashion to keep house-dogs wearing silver collars, and geese; the former to keep an eye on the latter, and both to guard against burglary. Fallow-deer and chamois sometimes roamed in the gardens and courtyards. The Signoria, as we shall see, set an example with its menagerie; and Rabelais speaks of the ostriches and porcupines he saw in the Palazzo Strozzi.

Florentine houses were now equipped with large beds for several people, soft and springy, where you slept naked; they had valuable carpets and fine toilet-sets. Tapestries or other hangings covered the walls, and splendid vases stood on the sideboards. There were big chests (*cassoni*) too, for the trousseau, and these were decorated with genre-paintings or marquetry. Artistic woodwork, or *intarsia*, was now competing with sculpture.

The linen seems to have been abundant. One mother is recorded as having made for her son 'four large towels for washing, small ones to put round his shoulders when he did his hair; and some rather rough, round towels which were most suitable for removing dirt from the face'. Machiavelli, however, was less well treated when setting out on a diplomatic mission. His wife Marietta gave him only two shirts, two towels, two caps, two pairs of socks and four handkerchiefs.

The Florentine, who regarded the German as the very type of a dirty sloven,[1] changed his personal linen on Saturdays and went to the public baths—of which there were four in the city. Like Montaigne he considered 'bathing salutary', and did not believe that a man was any better for keeping 'his limbs encrusted and the pores of his skin stopped up with filth'. Economy should not favour dirtiness.

*   *   *   *

When a baby was expected, the mother went to church for confession. She was advised not to sneeze, as this would be harmful to the child. When the event had taken place, her friends came to visit her. We see them in Ghirlandajo's fresco in Santa Maria Novella, one offering the mother a cordial on a tray, another amusing the baby, while a splendidly attired lady of quality advances gravely into the room, followed by a buxom servant-girl carrying a basket of fruit on her head.

This can scarcely have been typical. When Marietta, Machiavelli's wife, had given birth to a little boy in 1503, she wrote as follows to her husband: 'The child is well for the moment. He is like you, with a skin white as snow, but his head is covered as

[1] The example of Maximilian Sforza of Milan was well known in Florence. This lord brought back from Germany, where he had been reared, such dirty habits that he never changed 'his body linen', and that the ladies of quality could never persuade him to do so.

with black velvet. He is hairy like you; but, as he resembles you, he appears handsome in my eyes. People think he looks a year old; he opened his eyes almost before he was born and made enough noise to fill the house.' This sounds more homely.

The standard principle was that a mother should nurse her own child. If a nurse were hired, she should in no circumstances belong to one of those savage peoples, like the Tartars or Saracens. She should be a young and healthy woman, of good character; and her husband should be kept away. The child should be left as much as possible in the open air. If he cried, he should be allowed to cry. He could sometimes be taken to church but never to the pleasure-grounds.

As the child grew older, he learned his first words. He said: *babbo* and *mamma*. Bread was *pappo*, wine *bombo*, *quattrini* (farthings) were *dindi*, meat *ciccia*, to sleep was *fare la nanna*. But for Heaven's sake don't spoil him too much! 'Ah!' cried an ill-tempered father, 'much will it profit you if you dandle the children all day in your arms, embrace them and lick them, sing them songs, tell them lying fables, frighten them with tales of ogres, deceive them, play bo-peep with them, and do all you can to make them handsome, fat, merry, laughing and well-satisfied with material pleasures.'

With all deference to this puritan, we must remember that such children are the ones which Donatello and Della Robbia depicted and which we now admire at Prato and in the Hospital of the In-nocents. Happily there were burghers more kindly and indulgent, such as the paterfamilias who once presented his quiver-full to Clarice Orsini: 'Madonna Clarice, here is my daughter. Come forward now, touch the lady's hand. . . . And this girl, and this one. This is my granddaughter, and so is this one and this one. All these are my grandchildren. See now, stand up straight, be nice. I want to make this boy a priest, this girl a nun. This young woman has just been married, this one makes Venetian fringes, this one makes ribbons. . . .'

It was traditionally held that a child born on Sunday was 'without salt', that is, a fool; because the salt-shop was closed that day, and you could not buy any to have the child baptized in San Giovanni's. One quarter of Florence harboured a number of deformed *barenzi*. Still, a fool was an exception in Florence.

As regards education, some people maintained that prior to the age of seven children were unable to acquire any knowledge; to which others replied that this was to show more concern for any trouble to the teacher than for the benefit of the pupil. It was better therefore not to waste time but to give the children at least a smattering of knowledge; they would thus, by the age of eleven, when they were handed over to a master, have acquired a few rudimentary notions.

The Florentine, always in the van of progress, had early desisted from the use of the rod. It was contrary to nature, he declared, and better fitted to promote servility than freedom; besides, it left behind it 'a resentment which weakens the natural affection of the heart. . . . Only donkeys should be beaten.' Rely more on reasoning than on command, or, as Fra Bernardino recommends, follow the example of Our Lord. 'Do you know how he pro-ceeded? Exactly like the mother with the small child who doesn't behave as he ought. She says: "Now, if I get up! Ah, if I get up!" And she threatens the child, and makes a semblance of preparing to punish him. God does likewise.'

The schoolmaster taught in a private family, who paid him, or in a regular school where he was paid by the State. He was usually a poor devil of a pedant, with his little bonnet and his threadbare gown which had seen at least five jubilees. His property consists of a small bag containing two shirts, four handkerchiefs and a few books. According to the satirists he is at once conceited and incurably stupid, with the stupidity that comes only of years of study. He is the ape of other men's books, incapable of grasping anything unless the authority of a book is behind it. To make study easy and pleasant is the least of his concerns: 'he has sweated so long to learn what he knows that others have to sweat in their turn'. Armed with his manuals, namely Donato's grammar, the Cornucopia and the Doctrinal, together with a few Latin or Italian works, he is an incarnation of Rabelais' pedant, whose knowledge is foolery, and who stultifies noble minds and corrupts the natural flowering of intelligence: filthy in his person, insipid in his teaching, closed to any feeling for charm or beauty, a perfect blockhead and the living negation of the aspirations of the time.

The 'house-pedant' spun out Latin periods in imitation of Cicero, and sold his words night and day in order to buy food, drink and clothing. He would try to win favour with the mistress of the house; hence many middle-class families preferred to send their children to school,[1] where however the master was scarcely of higher degree. 'This booby's discourses, half in Latin, half in the vernacular,' wrote a newsmonger, 'are like those mythological creatures who look human though they have the feet of a goat. If you happen to speak of love, he reels off a page of Plato; in the event of some misfortune, he quotes Seneca at you.' He was therefore generally despised, his trade was considered the lowest of all trades. He was to become a stock-type in satirical comedy, first in Italy and later in France.

How, in the meantime, was the young Florentine educated? In grammar, geometry and the paraphernalia of Latin. Machiavelli's son wrote to his father: 'I am today beginning to study the participles and Ser Luca (his master) has read to me nearly the whole of the first book of Ovid's *Metamorphoses*. As soon as you come back, I want to recite all this to you by heart.' Plutarch was the other author; although, as he was not always available in Florence, one had to write to Venice for a copy. The monks cursed this kind of pagan education as corrupting the hearts and morals of the young.

Austerity was a thing of the past, as even free-thinkers felt bound to recognize. 'Young men are more profligate than ever in their dress, and spend exorbitant sums on banquets and lascivious enjoyments. They are idle, they waste their substance on women and gambling. Their whole study is to go about in fine clothes and talk craftily. The man who is cleverest at biting his

---

[1] The number of children who were then learning to read has been calculated as 8,000 or 10,000; those learning arithmetic as 1,000 or 1,200; and those taking lessons in grammar and logic as 600.

fellows is esteemed the wisest and is the most admired.' The fault had often lain with the family: parents had decked out and titivated their son, and entrusted him to a master who let him read things shocking enough to raise the dead, and turned him into a thorough-going wanton.

The pedant's influence, fortunately, was limited. His pupil was expected to become 'a man able to maintain his family's honour and to defend his country'. In this respect, the educational programme was like that of ancient Greece, calculated to achieve an harmonious balance between the physical and intellectual sides. Thus the schoolboy and the youth were allowed many hours for recreation, hours devoted to gymnastic exercises of a 'manly' nature, such as football, running, jumping and wrestling, which developed grace and suppleness of body. The stadium was never empty.

*   *   *   *

The education of girls had also undergone notable changes. In former times, parents had been mainly concerned with teaching them how to spin and sew. This would occupy their leisure and in case of misfortune serve as a means of livelihood. Reading and writing might, at a pinch, be suitable for the daughter of burghers; for a daughter of the people, it was perfectly useless and even harmful. 'It is not too good for a woman to know how to read unless you want her to be a nun.'

At the age of seven, a girl was separated from her brothers and trained in housework: sweeping, polishing the silver and scouring the pots. Her conduct was strictly supervised. If she was allowed to dance, it must be with decorum. Her parents would tell her anecdotes like the following: the daughter of a knight, who had been promised in marriage to the Duke of Sterlich, danced so vivaciously that she fell and broke her leg. The Duke was no longer willing to marry her.

In the street, a girl should neither greet people nor answer any signs that are made to her. She is to shun society-games. To avoid the love-passion she wears a topaz, that precious stone that quells the flames of Eros or helps you to resist them. Finally, if she marries, she should on receiving the ring lower her eyes as a mark of emotion, while maintaining a quiet and modest demeanour.

All this was now quite out of fashion, and we shall later on be able to measure how far feminine education had progressed. Suffice it to note that by now girls were not only learning to read and write but they were also taught Latin. 'A little girl', says the poet Bembo, 'should learn Latin. It adds the finishing touch to her charms.' The hour of emancipation had struck. A Florentine maiden no longer wore a topaz, and she openly sang of the beauty of young men:

> Young man with the goodly locks, let them hang loose, do not tie them up. They look like threads of gold or silk. ... Young man, how noble is your step, how fair your countenance! Wherever you pass, the trees burst into blossom. Your eyes are dark as jade: what love they inspire! Young man with the curly locks, the golden locks that adorn your face, you look like an envoy from heaven, an angel of paradise. ...

Such a youth might have stepped out of a picture by Botticelli.

The old educational system, with its gloom and confinement, had gone with the snows of yester year. Before long, people would be saying the riskiest things in the presence of 'nice, respectable girls'; they would be telling stories that would make a gargoyle blush.

*   *   *   *

But before we forget the old times when morals had been strict, let us glance at the life of Alessandra de' Bardi, the model of her sex and the honour of Florence.

She was a lovely creature, so tall that she never wore pattens. Reserved and at the same time active, she would be first up in the morning, constantly busy about the house or sewing or making clothes. Never was she seen idling at the door or window. When going to Mass with her mother she wore a veil, whereas other girls of her class thought only of making themselves conspicuous.

Her parents wished to marry her to Lorenzo Strozzi, a son of the good Palla Strozzi whom we have already encountered. After the interview, which was 'modest and proper', the marriage was celebrated in the Piazza della Signoria. A platform extended from the Statue of the Lion to the Palazzo della Mercatanzia, and the reception was attended by the most distinguished members of Alessandra's generation, the young men clad in green, the girls wearing dresses very modestly *décolletés*.

After her marriage (1432) Alessandra became the ornament of every fête and reception. On such occasions she did not scorn to go round with a linen napkin over her shoulder offering trays of confectionery and cups of wine to the guests, making a pretty curtsey that was natural and not forced.

In the street she was always accompanied by an elderly maid. In spite of this, a young man was so much bewitched by her beauty that he ventured to declare himself, although Alessandra obstinately lowered her eyes. As he persisted, she tried to cure him of his folly. One day he went down on his knees and held out a knife, exclaiming: 'Since you refuse to see me, take this knife and kill me!' She made no reply, but remained firm and pure as a diamond; in face of such constancy, the youth at last desisted. Her husband simply laughed.

Two years after her marriage, Alessandra's father and father-in-law were banished; four years later her husband Lorenzo suffered the same fate; while she herself remained alone with her three children. Happiness was now a thing of the past. 'One comes to know God better in adversity', she murmured. As gold is tried and refined in the furnace of affliction, so misfortune seemed bent on afflicting her. She lost her mother, and then her husband, who, to make a living, had become tutor to a young lord of Gubbio and was murdered by him.

From her youth upward Alessandra had deprived herself of material comforts; she wore rough undergarments and slept on a mattress on the floor. Dressed now as a widow in a narrow skirt, with an unpleated hood and a headband above her eyes, she wore a cloak that almost concealed her face. Still beautiful, she resisted an avalanche of misfortunes, and brought up her children decently and respectably.

At the age of fifty-four, when she had been a widow for fourteen years, she caught fever, and said: 'I want to leave my body, and dwell with God.' And so she died.

A good life, and one to meditate, concludes Vespasiano Bisticci, the Plutarch of Florence.

CHAPTER IX

HOME-LIFE IN FLORENCE (II)

*Eating and drinking – The rules of good manners – Palmistry
and medicine – Funerals*

THE Florentine was a home-bird because he was economical. He considered it 'harmful, costly, annoying and inconvenient to change houses', and, as far as possible, he tried not to sink to the level of a lodger; but to have his own house in a respectable quarter so that his wife should make only honourable acquaintances. He did not like separating his family because to live under the same roof appeared to him to have solid advantages, if only because it economized lighting and heating.

Like most Italians, he was neither a drunkard nor a glutton; but, though the excesses of the Swiss and the Germans disgusted him, he was not averse to good cheer.

The first family meal was taken between 9 and 10 in the morning, the second before nightfall. In the days of 'modesty and sobriety' these meals had been of the simplest. Husband and wife ate from the same dish and drank from the same cup, the menu being mainly composed of bread, 'herbs', jam and fruit. Meat was eaten only on Sundays, and when a pig was slaughtered, one gave black-pudding to one's neighbour, who was angry if one forgot to. The fare became more delicate as the years went by. Boiled kid or peacock might now be served, followed by coloured jellies in the shape of little men or animals. This Florentine invention was made of almond-milk and other ingredients, coloured with saffron, or *zafferano* as it was called, and sometimes even scented. Pastry came in only with the sixteenth century.

For a burgher or merchant—it was the same thing in Florence—entertaining was an obligation. It meant business-customers as well as friends. Here, according to an expert adviser, were the requisites for a pleasant dinner-party: the guests should not be less

than three, or more than nine, because, if more are invited, they
will be too many to listen to each other or hold consecutive conversation—which may be profitable—and because asides spoil
the pleasure and create confusion. One should therefore invite
a reasonable number of people, sociable and on good terms with
each other; they should be entertained in a pleasant room, at a
convenient hour, and the service should be faultless. The guests
should be neither babblers nor of taciturn disposition, but moderate talkers. The topics of conversation should not be subtle,
uncertain or hard to understand, but gay, amusing and useful.
One must not forget to be practical.

The table is set facing the garden-door which lets in the fresh
air. The host has a ewer of water passed round so that the company may wash their hands. They then take their places, ladies
alternating with gentlemen. Slices of melon are served, then a
berlingozzo, which is a cake made of flour, eggs and sugar. This
is followed by boiled capon, fat and in perfect condition, prime
quality sausages and veal, a good stew, roast chicken,[1] or else
thrushes, pigeons or pheasants, and sometimes trout, 'to appease
the voluptuous and so fit the mind to cope with the things of this
world. Something must be allowed to the weakness of the flesh.'

This was a rich man's menu for festive occasions. There would
be music for merriment: the kettle-drum, played with two sticks,
or the jew's harp, an iron band bent double and fitted with a
steel tongue to serve as a spring. It was held between the teeth,
and the tongue vibrated as you pushed it with your finger.
While this was going on, the servant would be running back-
wards and forwards from the kitchen and grumbling about her
mistress: 'She works hard talking, and I walking, and I have only
two legs and down-at-heel shoes.'

These Florentine banquets were, by the way, matched by the
meals usually eaten in France, at least in the sixteenth century, if

[1] Did all the guests take all these courses? Probably not, but we do not
know. If however (another query) the Florentines were still on the two-
meal-a-day régime, this would make a great difference to their capacity.
(Translator)

we are to believe the economist Jean Bodin, whose strictures are violent: 'People are not satisfied, at an ordinary dinner, to have three dishes; boiled meat, roast meat and fruit. They must have meats prepared in five or six different ways, with so many sauces, mince-meats, pastries and every kind of hotch-potch and other fancy dish, that there is great intemperance.'

But Florence was ahead of France in the use of that instrument which the Latinists designated as a *fuscina* and we call a fork. It was considered vulgar to dip one's fingers in the gravy; one should pick up the food one wants either with a knife or a fork.[1]

The average Florentine, of course, dined less expensively than the rich merchant. He would begin with a salad, followed perhaps by a small pigeon, goat's milk cheese and fruit. He was very fond of *fegatelli*, a sort of liver sausage. But his basic diet was already *pasta*, which he prepared in various ways, while the preachers railed at his self-indulgence. 'You are great gourmands', cried one of them. 'It's not enough for you to eat fried *pasta*, but you must flavour it with garlic. When you eat *ravioli*, it's not enough for you to boil them in the pan and eat them with the broth, but you must then fry them in another pan, together with cheese.'

Wine, too, had its votaries, and everyone sang the praises of Vernaccia, Trebbiàno, etc. 'Drunk in moderation, it nourishes the body, improves the blood, hastens digestion, calms the intellect, makes the heart joyful, enlivens the spirits, expells wind, increases the warmth of the body, fattens convalescents, rouses the appetite, purifies the blood, removes obstructions, distributes nourishment in the right places, gives colour and health to the cheeks', and so on. It was the object of a cult. Luigi Pulci writes in the *Morgante Maggiore*: 'I believe no more in black than in white, but I believe in boiled or roasted capon, and I also believe in butter and beer. . . .[2] But above all I have faith in good wine and deem that he who believes in it is saved.'

[1] The fork, like so many of the amenities of civilization, was invented in Italy. It does not appear to have been much in vogue in England before the end of the seventeenth century. (Translator)

[2] 'Cervisia', to be exact. It was the kind of beer the Romans made.

Drunkards and gluttons were not however in favour. To have a good time but without swilling and gormandizing—that was the rule for most people, and they practised a delicate epicureanism. An English protonotary apostolic, who was staying in Florence and had been accustomed like his fellow-countrymen to spending four hours at table, was amazed by Florentine sobriety and ended by conforming to it.

There was no lack of inns and taverns in the city, and one of them, the Tavern of the Snail, near the Mercato Vecchio, was famous. Better-class citizens did not usually frequent them; but if a merchant's wife and children had left for the country, he would take his meals there—unless friends had invited him out—and return home only at bedtime.

*   *   *   *

The rules of courtesy and good manners are set out by a talented writer, Giovanni della Casa,[1] in the *Galateo*, a sort of manual which shows how Florentines behaved—or should behave.

When you are eating, do not masticate noisily[2] 'or crouch gluttonously over the food without raising your face, as if you were blowing a trumpet. Don't hiccup. That is not eating but devouring; and then too you soil your hands and even your elbows, and dirty the cloth.'

Avoid rubbing your teeth with your napkin, or, worse still, with your fingers. Do not scratch yourself, or spit, or at least only do it 'reservedly'. 'I have heard', remarks Della Casa, 'that there are nations so polite that they never spit; and we might well

[1] Della Casa was born in the Mugello; he published the *Galateo* in 1558. He is famous also for his sonnets, of which the form influenced Milton. (Translator)

[2] A Frenchman observed in this connexion: 'The Germans keep their mouths shut when masticating, and consider any other way unsightly. The French on the contrary half open their mouths and consider the German way unsightly. The Italians go about it very gently, the French rather more briskly, and they consider the Italian way too refined' (cf. A. Lefranc, *La Vie quotidienne au temps de la Renaissance*, p. 150).

refrain from spitting. . . . Inviting people to drink repeatedly is not one of our habits and we describe it by means of a foreign word: "*fare brindisi*", a reprehensible custom which one should not adopt. I thank Heaven that, among the scourges that have come from beyond the Alps (a reference to Germany and France), this one, which is the worst, has not gained a footing here; I mean, to consider it amusing and even estimable to get drunk.'

In no circumstances should you bend over the glass of wine or the plate, where someone else is going to drink or eat, in order to take a sniff. And do not offer your neighbour a pear or other fruit which you have already bitten.

On rising from table, do not stick your tooth-pick in the back of your mouth, which makes you look like a bird carrying a twig to its nest; and do not wear your tooth-pick in your collar—a strange accoutrement for a gentleman. After blowing your nose, do not look into your handerkerchief as if pearls or rubies had been deposited in it; and do not drum with your fingers on the table or wave your legs about. This shows little consideration for other people.

If you wish to speak with someone, do not go so close to him as to be breathing in his face. One does not always like to smell other people's breath. And do not nudge people with your elbow, and repeat: 'Isn't that true? And what do *you* think? And Messer So-and-So?'

Avoid expressing yourself affectedly, 'with the point of the fork'—*favellar in punto della forchetta*. Do not for ever be talking about your wife, or the children, or the nurse; and refrain from long descriptions of your dreams, as though they were wonderful or important.

To lavish advice on those who have not asked for it is equivalent to saying that you are wiser than they, and that they are incompetent. This can only be done between close friends. And the same applies to counsels of health. To say with the gravity of a physician: 'You ought to take *this* electuary, or *that* kind of pill', is like trying to clean another man's field when one's own is full of thorns and nettles.

In conversation, generally, do not be so anxious to hold the ball that you snatch it from your neighbour, 'as one often sees a hen in a farmyard snatching a straw out of the beak of another'. And if you want to make the company laugh, refrain from twisting your mouth, rolling your eyes, puffing out your cheeks or making other grimaces. 'The goddess Pallas amused herself for a time by playing on the bagpipes. She became an expert player. But one day, being thus occupied at the edge of a pool, she happened to see her image in the water and was so much ashamed that she threw away the instrument.' Imitate Pallas, and shun ridicule. . . . And stop making noises with your mouth to express surprise or contempt.

A few instructions now as to how one should appear in public. Do not be seen wearing your nightcap, or put on your garters in front of other people. Do not leave your office with your pen above your ear, or holding a handkerchief between your teeth. Do not put a leg on the table; avoid spitting on your fingers.

Your dress should be neither so pretty nor so elaborate as to make people remark that you are wearing Ganymede's hose and Cupid's doublet. If your legs are too fat or too lean, or slightly twisted, do not order from your tailor hose in gaudy colours or of a conspicuous cut, which would simply invite attention to your defects.

Observe the code of the *Galateo* and you will be an accomplished man of the world.

*   *   *   *

Well-informed though he was, the Florentine did not refrain from consulting palmists and having his hand read. It has in fact been established that the hand is the organ of every part of the body and that the natural disposition of the individual is revealed in its lines and contours. Why are there four lines in the hand? Because we have four principal organs: the heart, the liver and the brain, which counts for two. The palmist Bartolomeo Cocles says so. A short hand is the sign of a person subject to 'cold humours'; a long hand with short, stiff fingers denotes a phlegmatic individual, without much courage; a long hand with a broad palm warns us that the person will be mischievous, even a knave and a thief. As to a woman, if her hand is short but her fingers excessively long, she will be 'in peril of child-birth'.

Palmistry was of course no antidote for sickness. What then of the physician? He belonged to the fifth of the major 'arts', the art of drugs and groceries, which included the *speziale*, or apothecary, with whom the physician sometimes lodged. He had formerly been a man of modest appearance, in spite of his tall hat trimmed with fillets. He had worn a long fur gown, so shabby and thread-bare that 'a furrier could not have guessed what animal had provided the skin'. In these days, however, he dressed with studied elegance, wearing a long and capacious robe, trimmed with squirrel-fur and bands of scarlet, heavily begemmed rings, and gilded spurs, like a knight's. Following the example of Pier Leoni, Lorenzo's doctor, he had abandoned Arabic medicine in favour of Greek. Educated until recently in the medical school of Salerno, he practised astrology as much as medicine, and was now acquiring a reputation abroad, especially in France.

In 1479 sixty-six doctors are recorded as practising in Florence. They mainly prescribed simples, cabbage for example, which they regarded as a panacea. But in spite of his noble appearance, the physician was not taken very seriously, hardly more than the pedant. Years before this, Petrarch had described doctors as ignorant 'spectators of maladies and sick persons'. The facetious Poggio addressed them as follows:

You visit the patient, inspect his water and excrement with attentive eye and puckered brow as if his malady required the most important attention. Then you feel his pulse, where you recognise the forces of nature. Next you consult your colleagues and after much discussion agree as to the remedies, as you call them. If by chance the beverage you prescribe has been effective, you never cease from extolling the cure; if it has done harm, you blame the patient.

Machiavelli is said to have died from taking too many pills containing aloes and cardamom, which a doctor had prescribed for him.

In cases where the patient entered one of the city's numerous hospitals, he found a high degree of comfort: abundant food, choice wine, competent nurses, and great cleanliness in his room and bed.

*   *   *   *

When a Florentine died—or 'entered the great sea', as dying was called—the Signoria regulated the procedure. The body was to be simply dressed in white muslin lined with taffeta, with a plain cap on the head. In burying a woman, no ring was to be left on her fingers, unless it had little value. With a man, no armour was to be buried, no doublet, penon, flag or shield. The body rested on a common palliasse.

At the interment, two candles were permitted, or two torches containing at most thirty pounds of wax between them, or else four small torches. Candles or torches were to be extinguished immediately after the ceremony and returned to the dealer, the *speziale* in this instance, who was not allowed to sell candles weighing more than fifteen pounds, including the paper and candle-end. It was unreasonable to provide lighting for the dead, a useless display; and those who infringed the law were liable to a fine. This went into the *opera*, the fund for church-building and repairs.

The body was followed to the grave by mourners garbed in black; but this funeral attire was only loosely stitched 'so as not to spoil the material which would later serve to make clothes'. The wages of those who 'announced' deaths and of the under-taker's men—the *beccamorti*—were fixed at a maximum of eight soldi. The widow was not to receive from the heirs either a gown, or petticoat, or girdle, or head-dress, but simply a skirt and a cloak lined with taffeta. Two courses only might be served at the funeral dinner.

The interment took place at the charnel-house, or in the case of important persons, in the church. In Paris it was not until the middle of the sixteenth century that, on the occasion of an epidemic, the famous Dr Fernel and a colleague, having heard of the fetid smell that hung over the Cemetery of the Innocents, recorded the fact that 'in dangerous times the houses near the said cemetery have always been the first to catch the contagion and have remained infected longer than other houses in the city'. But this warning remained a dead letter.

In Florence, however, as early as the fifteenth century, Bishop Narcissus, who was of Catalan origin and who had observed how crowded the Florentine churches were with sepulchres, gave the following warning: 'The House of God, being clean and pure, should not be sullied with the presence of corpses. It is the monks who have introduced this custom. The primitive Church not only did not permit the burial in church of those who are now buried there, but even raised objections to the interment of holy men.' And Narcissus cited the reply which a Pope had made when asked by some prelate for permission to inter the bodies of two martyrs in his church: 'Place them at the entrance, but not elsewhere.'

The Florentines unfortunately remained deaf to the words of this foreigner who was so concerned for the purity of a holy place and, perhaps without realizing it, for public health.

PUBLIC LIFE

I N the ancient times praised by Dante, Florentines dressed in coarse cloth or even in skins. A cloak and hood, a plain cap and 'leather on their feet' made up the whole of their accoutrement. Even well-to-do women were content with a scarlet petticoat of coarse material, an old-fashioned waistband and a cloak of coarse green linen. They did not deck themselves out 'with little chains, necklaces, fine buskins and girdles prettier than those who wore them'.

The average artisan often remained faithful to these customs. Thus Masi the coppersmith ordered a 'monastic cloak' in a reddish-black fabric and a hood of the same material, for which he paid eight florins and of which he was very proud. His shirts were made by nuns. If he found a good bargain at the second-hand shop, he bought a pair of linen sheets, twenty handkerchiefs, six napkins and two towels. All this, together with a gold ring set with a red stone, cost him a little over thirty-four lire.

In the time of Lorenzo the Magnificent the standard dress consisted of the *lucco*, a long gown usually black, which fell to the ankle; a jacket underneath, and a hood or black bonnet with a ribbon hanging behind, 'the civilian cap'. But fashions were changing. Most of the citizens who had hitherto worn long hair falling on to their shoulders, now had it cut short and were beginning to wear a beard, though this was still exceptional. Those who did not follow the mode were called 'hairy' and considered antiquated.

A noble or a doctor now wore a cloak that might be pink or

purple, open in front, gathered in at the top, and held at the neck by a clasp. The hood, which is said to be of Flemish origin, now contained three parts: the cap proper, which was made of flock covered with cloth; the *foggia* which protected the left cheek; and the *becchetto*, a long strip of cloth, sewn double, and thrown over the right shoulder or rolled round the neck. This was the correct dress. A man who simply wore a sleeveless cape was regarded as a mercenary or a cut-throat, and Benvenuto Cellini, who dressed in that fashion, was held in contempt by the magistrates.

In spite of the regulations which these magistrates issued, the well-to-do citizen had a passion for novelty, for some kind of singularity that would please the ladies. It was called: 'ingentilire per donne'.

This youth you see wearing a pink cape edged with a broad band of velvet, white velvet hose variegated with silver lace-work, a white satin jacket, a velvet cap set off with a feather, velvet shoes, scented gloves, a gold medal, a dagger, a sword, a gold chain worth sixty crowns, and so many rings that his fingers are invisible—he is truly the lion of the day, the Beau Brummel of Florence.

But this pursuit of the rare and unexpected was nothing to that which possessed the ladies. Already Giovanni Villani, the old chronicler, had written with some bitterness that 'the reason and common sense of men are overthrown by the excessive appetites of women'.

There were sumptuary laws, it is true, as in all well-regulated republics. Thus in 1330 women had been forbidden to wear painted dresses—painted no doubt by professional artists. Only dresses with embroidery, 'paintings in needlework', were tolerated. But what needlework! We read of a dress of which both sleeves were embroidered, one with an arm emerging from a cloud and scattering flowers, the other covered with a design of flowers with little branches of pearls; and the buttons were so delicately worked that they looked as though made of thread. And what was one to say of a cloak on which were 'painted' parrots and other birds, white and red roses, dragons and pagodas, the whole intermingled with letters composing a device? And in crimson, green, red and scarlet! Prices varied, of course, according to the quality: 100 florins for a silk dress *de luxe*; 75 for a dress in ordinary fabric. Women wore their fortune on their backs.

Sometimes it amused them to imitate men's fashions. They would wear the *cioppa*, or short cloak, and high-heeled sandals. Others who affected simplicity would sport a petticoat of *ciambellotto*, a fabric made from goat's hair.[1]

The preachers railed against them: 'O women! You provoke God by your extravagance, by the excessive length of your trains, your low-cut dresses, the paint you daub on your faces, and your indecent garb in church.'

The disgruntled burgher of old-fashioned outlook was especially shocked by the somersault changes of fashion. One of them wrote as follows:

The fashion-modes of courtesans, once regarded as indecent, have now been adopted by the noblest ladies, worn at festivities and considered graceful and engaging. At one moment the Florentine dames wear dresses so low-cut that they display their bodies well below the arm-pits; at another, they suddenly make a jump and conceal themselves in little collars that come up to their ears and gowns as tight as strait-jackets—so tight that they cannot look at their feet. After which, having tried the too little and the too much, they resign themselves to the intermediate; and this will last until the next new moon.

Everyone was running after the newest fashion. Cried a moralist:

A fine thing it is to see girls who normally look respectable decking themselves out in finery, sporting helmet-shaped headgear like society-women, wearing necklaces with strings of little animal-trinkets, and sleeves that are more like sacks! What a stupid, damnable and useless fashion! They cannot raise a glass from the table without soiling their sleeves or when they set it down, the table-cloth. When helping themselves to gravy, they drop more of it on their gloves than could be held in a hood.

Ladies thus attired might easily be confused with public women. *Chi imbianca la casa la vuole appigionare* (He who

---

[1] Hence the modern French word *camelote* (our 'shoddy'—Translator).

whitewashes his house wants to let it) was a proverb applied to coquettes who used rouge and make-up to excess. When one such person was arriving for Mass she noticed a *villano* standing under the church-porch and apparently apeing the gentleman. She asked him mockingly whether the Mass for rustics was over. 'It is, Madame,' he replied, 'and they are just beginning the Mass for harlots. Be quick and join them.'

So great was the scandal that the authorities introduced a new sumptuary law, but the women dressed as conspicuously as ever. When the lawyer who had been instructed to draw up a list of offenders was taxed by his superior with being too indulgent, he replied:

Monsignore, I have studied law all my life; I thought I knew something about it, but I now perceive I know nothing. When on the look-out for adornments which, according to the orders you gave me, your women are forbidden to wear, I could not in any law find arguments equal to those they brought against me. I will give you a few examples.

I meet a woman wearing a lace headband above her head-dress. I stop her: 'Give me your name. You have a lace headband.'

The good woman removes the pin that holds the thing in place, takes it in her hand and tells me it is a garland.

Further on, I see a person wearing long rows of buttons on her dress. I say: 'You cannot wear those buttons.' She replies: 'Oh yes, Messer, I *can* wear them. They are not buttons, but cupels, and if you don't believe me, just look, they have neither eye, nor holes.'

In the same way, if I see a lady wearing ermines, she tells me: 'This is suckling's fur.'

'What is this suckling?' I ask.

'It's a kind of animal.'

The man of law declared himself beaten.[1]

It was generally held that Florentine women knew how to look nice. See the young lady who is wearing a skirt of red satin with gold embroidery and silver buttons, and a blouse of gold tissue.

---

[1] Savonarola, who managed to impose real reforms on Florence, was held up when he asked for laws to regulate the use of silk and jewellery, and to prohibit excessively low-cut dresses, curls, ringlets and so on. Although he brought up the subject again and again in his sermons, the Florentines refused to give way; they would accept no reform in feminine attire.

She carries a lace handkerchief, her hair is arranged with a flat bun behind and ringlets round her face, and she has a cluster of pearls hanging on her neck: the sort of girl of whom people say: 'She's made of such fine flax that she will easily get a spindle and distaff to spin it.'

An excellent handbook was published in the sixteenth century by the Tuscan Alessandro Piccolomini, with a view to saving the dames of Florence from being baffled by problems of good taste. Here, through the mouth of an experienced person, the Raffaella, one received such advice as the following:

> I like a woman often to change her style of dress, and never to neglect a good fashion. If she invents a new one, she should not hesitate to bring it forward. . . . The gown and bodice should be ample, not skimped, and yet not so full as to be inconvenient or to make it necessary to raise the skirts behind so that they do not trail in the dust. Do not behave like those women we see hurrying along the street in a sort of fury, and with such a clatter of pattens that they seem to have the devil at their heels.

Dress as a whole should sometimes be elaborate, slashed, braided, or daintily embroidered; sometimes the *ensemble* should be plain. Variety is the sign of elegance. And colours that clash should be avoided, as, for example, green and yellow, or red and pale blue. A lady should take care that the fashion she adopts brings out the advantages of her person and conceals its defects. Nor should she forget the importance of *portatura*—carriage and deportment.

*   *   *   *

In winter the middle-class citizen wore a smock and a fur cap; in summer a serge gaberdine and a light-weight cap. At night he wore a toque and a cape, which last however was considered bad form in the daytime, being suggestive of the soldier. The knight's costume consisted of a hooded cloak, more or less thick according to the season, a felt hat, and hose slashed at the knee with sewn-in strips of parti-coloured velvet. These, together, with his shirt, he changed at the week-end.

It was not customary to uncover when saluting someone, unless it were a bishop or cardinal. In presence of a knight, a doctor or a canon one lowered one's head as a sign of respect, and slightly raised one's forelock with two fingers. The second person singular was used in addressing people, and they were called plainly by their name or surname. Doctors and canons had the right to be called 'Messer', a physician 'Maestro', a monk 'Don' and a friar 'Padre'. But in general equality obtained. It was not for nothing that the Florentines had destroyed the social hierarchy.

As soon as he had laid down his work, which was often late—as he was a great worker—the artisan, according to Varchi, lived better than the merchant. He went from tavern to tavern, and then into the street or on to the public square, and enjoyed himself, observing the crowd or arguing endlessly. He might be seen at the Banchi, unrestrained in his speech, prompt in retort, and not in the least disillusioned by political and other kinds of gossip which were the daily bread of his existence. The atmosphere was joyous, noisy and sometimes feverish; and people spoke with their hands:

'With the hands one summons or dismisses, one rejoices or sorrows, calls for noise or silence, for prayers or threats, for peace or rioting; one affirms and denies, demonstrates and counts. The hands reason, argue and finally agree; they adapt themselves to each one of our intentions.' So writes Matteo Palmieri, a merchant who knew all about it.

Sometimes on summer nights the strains of a concert, or the human voice, might be heard. In the days of Lorenzo the Magnificent it was a virtuoso named Luigi Pulci (different from the poet Gigi) who improvised; and so great was his talent that the young Michelangelo rushed to hear him as soon as he discovered his whereabouts.

Every Florentine loved music. It beguiled the fatigue of the workman toiling under the hot sun; it cheered the peasant girl who had risen before dawn to spin and weave; nature had taught music to the nurse to pacify the wailing infant. The study of music therefore was recommended. Its rapid measures made the body alert and 'trained it to adopt graceful attitudes'. It exercised and nurtured the mind, corrected the voice and rendered pronunciation soft, accented, grave or sonorous.

E

In the course of time the sway of music increased, instruments were improved and diversified; organ, harpsichord, violin, lute, lyre, 'cello, harp, horn, trombone—all shaped in forms elegant or bizarre. In 1480 a school of harmony grew up in the entourage of Lorenzo de' Medici and under the direction of Antonia Squarcialupi, a famous organist. It was a sort of academy, and included painters and sculptors who were also musicians (note by the way the part played by musicians in Italian painting).[1] Here recitals would be given by a quartet of stringed instruments, *quattro viole da arco*. For song, one voice was preferred to a choir, because one voice could be better heard, enjoyed and judged.

At the beginning of the sixteenth century a revolution was initiated by Stefanello, who was organist at St Mark's in Venice. Music was now allied to drama, which it supported and developed. There was now not one orchestra but several, with different instruments, each orchestra being attached to an individual actor. Thus in Poliziano's *Orfeo*, the contrabass viols accompanied Orpheus, the treble viols Eurydice, the trombones Pluto, the flutes and bag-pipes the shepherds. Curiously enough, Charon, the ferryman of Hades, was accompanied by guitars. In the preludes and *ritornelli* all the instruments took part; the accompaniment was then a symphony, the musicians executing the same partitions as the actors were to sing, or had sung, on the stage.

To return to the open street, here complete liberty seemed to obtain, although the police-spies kept an eye on certain classes of men, such as former exiles who had been recalled in cases where their ability or their work was advantageous to the city. The carrying of arms and observation of the curfew were also supervised. Yet, on the whole, the Florentine had no feeling of being curbed or bridled, and he also enjoyed great freedom of mind in the midst of civic disturbances.

Street-scenes delighted him, and some of them are worth recording. Thus in April 1489, when the foundations were being

---

[1] As, e.g., in Raphael's *Santa Cecilia* in the *Accademia delle Bella Arti* at Bologna: a small picture, rather brightly coloured, which inspired Shelly to transports of admiration.   (Translator)

laid for the Palazzo Strozzi, a small tradesman named Tribaldo de' Rossi arrived at the spot and threw into the trenches an old soldo, bearing a 'commemorative' lily. He then called his little boy Guarnieri and his daughter Francesca. 'Tita, our servant,' he relates, 'had come to the shop for meat, as it was Thursday. She then went to fetch the children, and my wife Nannina sent them both dressed to me. I took them to see the foundations, and raised Guarnieri in my arms, so that he could look down into them. As he had a little bunch of Damascus roses, I made him throw them down and said: "You will remember this, won't you?" He replied "Yes." They were with Tita, and Guarnieri was exactly four years and two days old. Nannina had recently made him a new jacket of shot-silk, green and yellow. . . .'

The foundation of a palace for a great family was a public event in Florence. But Tribaldo and his fellow-tradesmen were never at a loss for diversion. They could visit the botanical garden at Careggi, the Medici villa, where many different kinds of trees were growing; and in Florence itself, near the Palazzo, the *serraglio* or menagerie. Here there was a den of lions, who were held in special esteem as the lion was the emblem of Florentine independence. He figured on the city arms. To touch him was a crime. His sicknesses or his death were a presage of catastrophe; when on the other hand a lioness bore many cubs, this was a sign of prosperity. The lion-keeper, a bearded and hairy fellow, was held in fearful veneration.

In addition to lions, leopards, bears, wild boars and bulls played a part in public festivities, as for example at the reception of Pope Pius II, a Siennese, in 1453. That day, however, the lions were a disappointment, as they lay down and refused to attack the other animals. A ball was given in the Mercato Vecchio by way of consoling the public.

Stags and buffaloes were sometimes brought in, and the fête then took the form of a hunt. The apothecary Landucci describes one which took place in 1514 in the Piazza della Signoria. In the middle of the square a grove of verdure had been arranged, with a fountain, where the animals could rest and quench their thirst.

Never had there been so many visitors and strangers. There were even cardinals in disguise, garbed in black, wearing swords and concealing their faces.

The joiners and contractors had paid up to forty florins for building platforms along the house fronts. In the open were shelters known as 'tortoises', under cover of which men goaded the animals with lances. Once again the lions remaind torpid. One of them, after killing a dog, lost all interest in the proceedings. There were casualties, however, three men being killed and a fourth knocked senseless by a buffalo; but what Landucci especially deplored was that, in the presence of 40,000 women and children, a mare was loosed with a stallion.

Sometimes, for the sake of variety, there would be a sham assault on a wooden castle. In such cases the actors lost control and even killed each other. Fortunately, as we know, there were more innocent amusements like the *calcio*, a sort of football, in which one played less with the feet than the fists. This became a regular sport, with formal rules.

But the most popular diversion, the sport *par excellence*, was the *palio*. Immediately after dinner all the women, decked out in their finery and covered with flowers and jewels, took their children to some point in the street along which the horses would pass. Three strokes of the bell in the great tower of the Signoria were the starting-signal; whereupon the horses would leap forward, bearing the insignia of their owners, who were sometimes great lords from distant cities. The race-track traversed the city in its full length, from the Porta al Prato to the Porta Santa Croce. The magistrates who judged the race sat at the finishing-post. After which the *palio*, which was the prize, was set on a four-wheeled car, adorned with a lion at each corner. This *palio* consisted of a piece of crimson fabric, trimmed with fur and having a fringe of gold and silk, and it was worth three hundred florins.

The custom arose later of making the horses race without jockeys. Sometimes they would break into the line of spectators, when the city would pay for the damage. But the *palio* was too popular to be abandoned. There was even, on the festival of St

James, a water-palio, with boats on the Arno; and bitter was the disappointment if there was not enough water in the stream.

*   *   *   *

The theatre had for long remained exclusively religious. A *sacra rappresentazione* took place in a church, or cloisters, or a refectory, or in the open, and the actors were young boys who belonged to a religious association and who had been trained by the *festaiuoli*. These *impresarii* expended their ingenuity in devising scenery and stage-machinery. There would, for example, be a sky filled with moving figures, lights which came on and went out as in a lightning-flash, a celestial sphere with two companies of angels flying round it, and from which the archangel Gabriel descended in a machine shaped like an almond—a pretty invention of Brunelleschi's.

The torture and execution of martyrs were also represented: St Apollonia, when the executioner broke all her teeth, St Margaret, tied to the stake and crying out: 'Now I rise to a higher station, like gold which is refined in the furnace.' And people admired the fervour of St Barbara, who, when confined in a tower with only two windows, pierced a third one, so zealous a believer was she in the Holy Trinity.

The public did not feel out of its element when an angel advanced to explain the action by way of prologue. The actors were like the spectators, belonged to the same age, shot with bow-and-arrow, drank Trebbiano, paid in florins and were familiar with the inns of the *Buco* and the *Panico*.

All this was very innocent. In the 'sacred representation' of Nebuchadnezzar, one saw the sculptor Donatello summoned by the king of Nineveh, who had sent his seneschal to the studio.

'Master, I inform you that you are to appear before our king.'

'What does that mean? I haven't a moment's rest. I have to deliver a pulpit for Prato.'

'You must come at once.'

'I cannot refuse, but I have to carve the *Dovizia* (Abundance) which will be set on a column in the market-place, and for the next quarter of an hour, I cannot undertake more work.'

Such dialogue was well-calculated to please the artisan.

As time went by, the stage became definitely secular, pagan and realistic. Machiavelli's *Mandragora*, which was presented in 1526 by the 'Company of the Trowel', enables one to see how absolutely the tone had changed. The plot is far from edifying: a husband stupidly lending a hand to his marital misfortune, a casuistical monk, and, in the wife only, a rather half-hearted virtue. But this new kind of play was completely successful. The Florentines adored anything witty, astute or farcical, any ingenious ways of getting out of a difficulty. And Machiavelli achieved a similar success when, in the garden of his friend Fornaciaio, he produced the *Cliçia*, a play imitated from Plautus. The garden had been levelled so as to allow of a stage, artists were engaged to paint the scenery, and the play was followed by a banquet of which all classes partook, patricians, burghers and common people. The fame of this performance spread all over Tuscany, and even as far as Lombardy.

As the theatre became more exquisite, greater attention was paid to the wardrobe. It was popular now to attire the actresses as nymphs, in a blouse of crimson damask and a skirt of fine Cyprus fabric encrusted with gold, and raised half-way up the leg. They wore a garland of flowers and leaves round their heads, and carried a bow, with a quiver suspended behind the shoulder. These pastorals were accompanied by songs, now sentimental, now even free and hearty:

'With water from the fountain, my brunette bathes her face and tender breast.'

'Come, fair neighbours, attired in your skirts of white linen, come from plain and valley, from hill and mountain top, dance with joy and gaily bound,[1] and strew, your roses all around.'

Or again, in a different vein: 'O my goddess, appear at thy casement, show me thy angel face, bring thy Taddeo a bowl of soup and a slice of salt pork.'

[1] With acknowledgements to *Princess Ida*.   (Translator)

Poliziano, Pulci and Lorenzo himself composed some of these songs. And what conferred a peculiar lustre on the entertainment was that every class shared in it, everyone understood the bearing and symbolism of the show, whether historical, mythical or political.

Of the ecclesiastical festivals the most popular was that of May Day, when the village-girls, wearing their spring frocks and carrying leafy branches, danced in the Piazza Santa Trinità. Next came the Feast of St John, a patron of the city. On the previous day all the 'arts' had decorated their shops with silk and cloth of gold (enough to bedeck ten kingdoms), pictures and excellent engravings. Towards noon, the clergy formed a procession, bearing the sacred relics; they were escorted by laymen dressed as saints and angels, to the accompaniment of wonderful singing and music. In the cool of the evening the citizens marched, two by two, under the sixteen banners of their respective quarters, to offer candles in the baptistery of St John's.

On the day itself, the Piazza della Signoria presented a magnificent appearance. One hundred gilded towers, borne on wagons, symbolized the tribute paid by the subject-cities; these towers were covered with figures in relief representing horsemen, soldiers, girls dancing roundelays, animals, trees, fruit, in short, 'everything that could charm the eyes and the heart'. An interior mechanism caused the towers to revolve so that every side of them would be visible. From a hundred masts erected on the balcony of the palace floated the many-coloured standards of the tributary cities.

The morning was devoted to offerings, of which the first was made by the Captain of the *Parte Guelfa*. He was followed by the citizens and peasants, the workmen of the *Calimala*, and the money-changers, each group appearing in succession in the church of San Giovanni, while the square in front was covered with blue tents adorned with yellow lilies. Here and there one might see a foreign merchant from Flanders or Brabant, who had come to witness the *palio*—the race which was run after the midday meal and the siesta.

As you make your way along the streets [wrote an eye-witness] the houses are all hung with tapestries, and the chairs and benches covered with taffeta. Everywhere you see girls and young women dressed in silk and bedizened with jewels, precious stones and pearls. . . . The whole city, that day, is given over to revelry and feasting, with so many fifes and music, songs, dances, and other festivities and merry-making, that this earth seems like a paradise.

Another and exceedingly popular spectacle was the 'Triumph'. The chariot, which plays a great part in the *Divine Comedy* (Beatrice rides in one) and which symbolized the triumph, was perhaps at the origin of the custom. These displays, in any event, became more numerous in the course of time and acquired a more secular character. Rival societies displayed the utmost ingenuity in presenting allegorical triumphs. One would figure the three ages of man; another, the ages of the world symbolized by episodes from Roman history. During the Carnival, which went on for days and days, there would be a series of processions, with a swarm of masked participants, on foot or on horseback, escorting the chariots. The latter bore the figures of Jealousy with four faces armed with spectacles, the four Temperaments and their corresponding planets, the three Fates, and Prudence on a throne with Hope and Fear in chains at her feet.

Mythology was held in honour. Eros appeared at the Carnival as a child in swaddling clothes, blindfolded and with multi-coloured wings; while Bacchus, Ariadne and Paris were accompanied by hunters, nymphs, beggars, hermits, astrologers and devils, all chanting in chorus songs that were gay or moving, and sometimes obscene. And then would come the refrain proper to the Carnival:

'How fair is youth! and, alas, how fleeting! Let him who will, rejoice! For what will the morrow bring us?'

In the matter of triumphs as indeed of other popular festivals, the Florentines were innovators, thanks largely to a strange artist who deserves to be better known.

Piero di Cosimo, born in 1462, was the son of a goldsmith and had studied under the painter and alchemist Cosimo Roselli. A

solitary who was always building castles in the air, he led the life
of an animal rather than a man, so Vasari tells us. He allowed no
one to sweep out his room or hoe his vineyard. All should be left
to Nature. He loved rare plants and strange animals, and talked
nonsense about them. 'Sometimes he would stop to contemplate
a wall covered with the spittle of sick persons; on this he imagined
he saw dream-cities and battles of horses.' He saw similar things
in the clouds.

Comfort was unknown to him. He lived on eggs which he
boiled in the same receptacle as he made his gum; hated children's
crying or men's coughing, loathed the sound of bells; but loved
to see the rain streaming off the roof-tops. If however there was
thunder, he would hide himself under a cloak and crouch in a
corner of his studio.

Growing more eccentric as he grew older, he ceased to take
pupils, and though crippled with paralysis strove 'to vanquish
his hands and compel them to hold the brush'. The neighbours
were moved to pity. Piero however did not think he was going to
die, and, although a good Christian, kept putting off 'making his
peace with God'. He was furious with the doctors, their enemas
and syrups and other kinds of martyrdom such as not letting you
sleep when you want to, or having to make your will or to see
your kinsfolk weeping in a darkened room. The lot of a criminal
condemned to die seemed enviable to him:

'A fair thing it is to go to the place of execution in the open air,
while the multitude consoles you with sweetmeats and kindly
words. You have a priest, the people pray for you, and you go to
heaven with the angels. Lucky is the man who departs thus
suddenly!'

Piero departed suddenly, but not by the hand of the law. He
was found dead at the foot of his ladder.

Now this gifted savage had won popularity by organizing
triumphs. 'A fair thing it is, by night, to see twenty-five or thirty
pairs of horses, richly caparisoned, the riders attired to represent
the subject of the triumph, and each escorted by six or eight
armed lackeys wearing the same livery and carrying torches; while

E*

the chariots are full of ornaments and gaudy rags and quaint fantasies; something that sharpens men's wits and gives the people much pleasure and satisfaction.'

One day Piero di Cosimo conceived the idea of a Triumph of Death. The car and wagon he built secretly in a hall of the convent of Santa Maria Novella; a huge black vehicle with bones and white crosses painted on it, and drawn by buffaloes. Death stood in the wagon, very tall and armed with his scythe, while closed coffins were ranged all round him. When the wagon came to a halt, the coffins opened and from them emerged shapes garbed in black cloth, with skeletons painted on them, so that the white stood out from the black. The whole thing, with the torches and skulls, was terrible to look upon. Finally, to the strains of muffled instruments and lugubrious trumpets, the skeletons would arise and chant: 'Dead we are, as you see. So, one day, we shall see you', to an accompaniment of funereal music.

In front and behind rode dead men on horseback, and for this purpose the leanest and sorriest hacks had been selected. Each rider represented a skeleton, as did the four attendants who escorted him. These were followed by ten black standards painted with crosses and skulls, and during the whole march-past the *Miserere* was sung in chorus and with trembling voices.

The people were terrified and never forgot the Triumph of Death. It makes one think of an Italian Albrecht Dürer.

CHAPTER XI

BURGHERS, ARTISANS AND TAXPAYERS

Outlook of the average Florentine – Civic ambitions – Some representative men – Journals and those who kept them – Lives of artisans – Travel – The mercantile spirit – The budget and fiscal instability

A FRENCH bourgeois in the time of the Renaissance was a citizen with a home of his own and social ambitions. Whatever his profession, whether he were magistrate, man of law, banker, merchant, physician or master-craftsman, he invariably wanted to become a noble, he sought to obtain one of those offices which would distinguish him from his fellows.

Things were quite different in Florence, as we may judge from the example of Francesco Sacchetti, the author of a collection of *Novelle*. He came of an old family of *Popolani* and was a 'white Guelph', that is, a moderate. He revered the Pope as an enemy of the Emperor, but did not want him to have much hand in Florentine politics. It was not for clerics to intervene in civic affairs.

His own life was full of ups and downs. He conducted perilous missions in Slavonia, then became Prior of the Quarter of San Giovanni, and was ambassador to Genoa. He married three times, and each of his wives died. He lost part of his fortune and towards the year 1400 we lose trace of him. He had been a conservative; once his missions were accomplished, he looked no further than to the campanile of the Duomo, the palace of the Signoria, the Mercato Vecchio, the old fortified towers—symbols of liberty— and the dark little shop, where the merchant pocketed florins from every corner of the known world. His very Christianity, as Emile Gebhart observes, was municipal. Now this important citizen not only regarded the men of law as plagues to the commonwealth and promoters of civil strife, he jeered at the nobles, mocked the principles of chivalry and derided the merchants who wished to ape lords and parade in tournaments. This he regarded as the last word in the ridiculous, and herein he anticipates the *Morgante Maggiore.*

The Florentine was a man of positive, if not prosaic, outlook, who was averse to any excess whether in vice or virtue. The art of life, in his eyes, was to take account of men's good or evil attributes and to profit from them to the utmost. 'The art of managing men, within certain moral limits, is superior to useless or ill-conceived heroism.'[1]

Thus, when the form of government changes, the man who persists in thinking like his ancestors and criticizes the new institutions, is not wise. One should adapt oneself to the times. There is much to be said for opportunism; and, in short, the main thing is to make sure one has a credit balance. Agnolo Pandolfini gives exact instruction in this matter:

There is nothing that I esteem less than filling a public office. It is a source of peril, dishonesty, injustice and instability. Does it really suit you to give up your shop and your business in order to serve other people's ambitions? O stupidity of men who deem it glorious to march with the staff of office in their hand, while trumpets blow before them! and who thus abandon their tranquillity and their freedom. He who would ride the steed of the Commonwealth will be thrown by it!

He says elsewhere:

Distrust the plebs, the ignorant plebs, a glib-tongued and unreasonable breed, like a broken instrument that never rings true. Distrust the lords, who are always borrowing and never paying back. Remain in your shop. The merchant's hands should be ink-stained. He should write down everything: purchases, sales, contracts, goods received, goods dispatched. . . . Always have the pen in your hand. And keep an eye on your clerks. That is how to build up a good business.

These rules, which sound a little too theoretical, were not often observed. Take the case of Donato del Corno, a wealthy parvenu who tried to buy his way to civic honours. In the hope of being *imborsato,* or eligible to public office, he lent money free of interest

---

[1] Cf. L. Passy, *Francesco Vettori,* II, p. 38.

to influential men and got his friends to write to the *accopiatori*, or 'assemblers'. His shop had become a meeting-place for gossipers, gamesters, intriguers and politicians—worse still, a house of ill-fame, full of drunkards and prostitutes. And what good did this do him?

Fortunately, many merchants were able to hit the happy mean between their political aspirations and a strict attention to business. Matteo Palmieri was a case in point. A man of humble birth, he sold drugs and groceries in the Canto delle Rondini, a fact which did not prevent his serving on occasion as ambassador, as Gonfaloniere of his company, and as Prior. Being something of a mathematician, and dabbling also in literature, philosophy and theology, he was one of those who tried to leave a name behind him, following Dante's lines on *Como l'uomo s'eterna* (How man may perpetuate himself). This led him to authorship. He wrote a philosophical poem entitled *La Città di Vita*, in which he argued that our souls are the angels who had remained neutral at the time of Satan's rebellion and whom the Creator has sent into our bodies 'so that we should be obliged to take sides between good and evil'. Although the book remained in manuscript, it was condemned by the Inquisition. But Palmieri's principal work was the *Vita civile*, a kind of manual of good breeding, which shows how a man should behave in his family, in society, and in the State. It is written in dialogue form and in the vernacular, 'in that famous and glorious Italian tongue, more worthy of praise than Latin or Greek'. It remains as a valuable document for the history of manners.

Matteo Palmieri was a tall and handsome man, prematurely white-haired, *tutto canuto*, which made his appearance the more impressive; and he raised and ennobled his family by his singular virtues, or so we are assured by Vespasiano Bisticci whom we have already encountered in the company of Cosimo, the *pater patriae*.

Bisticci, who was the first bookseller in the wider sense of that term, had been born in 1421, and his career coincided with the rise of the Medici. Literary men foregathered in his shop. He knew the price of rare manuscripts and where to find or borrow them.

An oracle in his own line, he supplied books to burghers, lords and popes, and his business extended to every part of Italy. He declared he had no gift for fine writing, but undertook all the same to be the Plutarch of his age; and his new *Lives of Famous Men* is a work of unique interest, for he understood better than anyone else the curiosity and general outlook of his fellow-countrymen. He knew how to observe and express himself simply, and he conveys a vivid notion of his environment. Vespasiano was an ingenuous soul, a man pure in heart and mind, and one of the most attractive figures of the age. He died in 1498 and was buried in Santa Croce.

There were philosophers in his circle, like that Zembino da Pistoia who got tired of teaching and decided to live on his private income. After selling the corn he had harvested and putting his wine in casks for a year, he settled in Florence. The money he had made for his corn he kept in a sack, which hung by his pillow. He then fixed his diet and way of life. He would have two loaves a day and 'some little thing' with them. He never departed from this régime, and busied himself by writing a history of the world, beginning from the Creation, with the dates! 'A life without fraud or deceit.'

Bisticci's gallery, if one may so call it, of course contains many other figures. Salviati, once a great and wealthy merchant, had visited every trade-fair in Europe; but, convinced that the world was a hotbed of deceit and imposture, he restored, on his return home, 'everything he seemed to have on his conscience'. The rest of his money, which he had made honestly, he gave to God, and then took refuge 'in the well-shielded nest of religion'.

Bisticci introduces us also to the son of a poor peasant of Chianti who had been brought up by a Florentine burgher: a smiling little man clad in a purple jacket and a long cloak reaching to his ankles. Every morning, at Ave Maria, Ser Filippo attended Mass, and then went to the Palazzo to attend to civic affairs. In the course of the day he would visit his friends the monks, call at the bookshop to see if there were anything to buy and to chat with the literary men; after which he would return to the Palazzo to give interviews.

The remainder of his time was devoted to study, Although banished after a time, like so many others, he at last obtained permission to live near Florence, and settled down to work in the monastery at Settimo. From his speech, his manners and his attire, you might have thought him a philosopher of the ancient world.

One might recall other noble or inoffensive specimens from the Bisticci collection, such as Lappo Mazzi, an unquestionable Christian, a serious, charitable and rather simple-minded person who used to read to his small boys the *Fioretti*, the incomparable legend of St Francis. But little by little this atmosphere of decency and ingenuousness evaporates, and models for Plutarch become rare. Consider the illegitimate child who had been brought up in an orphanage but who one day attracted the favourable attention of a Bishop. The prelate sent him to Florence, where he was placed with an excellent woman who treated him as her own son. After reaching man's estate, he lived in a happy-go-lucky way on an allowance or annuity, and he thus accounted for himself to his companions:

> That is all I know about my birth. As I have never been capable of anything except running through my allowance, I take what I need from the public. I have made friends by my intrigues, and I could tell you of a great man who has often asked me to dinner without being able to get me. That's how I pass my life, and now let's have a drink!

*   *   *   *

Of all the Florentines who knew how to observe and how to record what they observed, the most useful for our purpose are those who kept a *diario*, and who thus convey a notion of what daily life was like. We will choose two such men.

Luca Landucci, whose impressions of various events we have already recorded, was born in 1436. His parents were well-to-do people, who lived in the parish of San Piero Maggiore. When Luca was fourteen, they entrusted him to a schoolmaster named Calandro with whom, he tells us, 'I learned my lessons to the praise of God.' Two years later, he was apprenticed to the apothecary Francesco, at the sign of *La Scala*, in the Mercato Vecchio.

But he hankered after independence, and at the age of twenty-six went into partnership with a certain Spinello di Lorenzo to open a shop in a house that had belonged to a second-hand clothes-dealer. It was not a good idea. 'The hope of greater profit', he tells us, 'led me to sacrifice a secure position.' The old shop had to be renovated and furnished, and Landucci spent a small fortune on it. A cupboard cost fifty florins, and, to make matters worse, Spinello was penniless. Less than a year after signing their contract they separated, Spinello undertaking to pay what he owed by a fixed date. Luca fortunately had money. At the age of thirty, he bought a shop in the Canto dei Torna-quinci, in a good situation at the angle of the Via Tornabuoni and the streets of the New Vineyard and the Sword. The undertakers, by the way, lived in that quarter.

Before occupying his new house, Luca had married. On May 24, 1466, eve of the Festival of the Holy Ghost, he took to wife Salvestra di Domenico di Pagni, a girl of seventeen. She brought him a dowry of 400 florins and the following trousseau: a light-blue dress with tight sleeves, embroidered with pearls; a purple skirt and gown with brocaded sleeves, twenty-four handker-chiefs and six towels, twenty-four child's handkerchiefs, eight chemises, twelve hats and three berets in various colours. Luca, for his part, expended a fair sum on trinkets, ribbons, jewels and brooches.

This time the partnership was successful. Luca described his wife as a 'dear companion and virtuous without a peer'. They were to live together for forty-eight years 'without her ever making him mad', and to have twelve children.

Taking as his model in business Cosimo de' Medici,[1] Luca prospered. He was the first to import sugar from Madeira, an island which had been colonized by the King of Portugal. In 1490 he opened a new shop, at the sign of the *Stelle*, opposite the Palazzo Strozzi. He was a man of equable temperament, religious, merciful in his dealings, and a lover of liberty. Though living in

[1] When Florentines were arguing about business matters, they would say: 'You think you are Cosimo de' Medici.'

Florence he was well-informed as regards foreign affairs. In 1477 he had noted the death of Charles the Bold, at the hands of the Swiss. Charles he held to have been as cruel as the Sultan of Turkey: 'Both took delight in the shedding of blood.' In 1492 he hailed the conquest of Granada by the Spaniards, the defeat of the Crescent, and herein he saw 'great gain for faith in Christ and the beginning of the submission of the infidels'.

But he was anxious for the safety of his own country. Florentine soldiers, he observed, were more interested in larceny than in fighting. 'One of these days the *Oltramontani* (the French and Spaniards) will have to teach us how to make war.'

Like every citizen he had his troubles. When there was an outbreak of the plague, he and his family fled to his villa of Dicomano; but in January 1490 this very villa was damaged by a fearful snowstorm followed by an ice-storm[1] which devastated the oaks and chestnuts 'so that those who witnessed it thought it was the end of the world.' Later, the house attached to his shop in Florence was destroyed by fire. He lost 'all his rooms, his reserves of cloth, his wardrobe, all his library with books worth more than twenty-five ducats', and there he found himself in a shirt, together with his children, one of whom had had to leap naked out of bed, when awakened by the fire. 'As for me,' he concludes, 'I accept adversity as I accept prosperity, and render thanks to God for one as for the other.'

Landucci's piety was associated with a taste for building. Having capital at his disposal, he applied to Simone del Pollajuolo, the architect, to carry out a plan he had long meditated, namely, to raise a temple with a fair cupola to the glory of San Giovanni, 'so that, in face of San Lorenzo, we may have an advocate in Heaven in the person of St John the Baptist, who was the favourite of Christ'.[2] But this plan he was never able to realize.

In 1514 he had the sorrow of losing his dear companion

[1] A phenomenon much commoner in North America than in Europe. (Translator)

[2] One wonders whether the good apothecary was confusing the Baptist with the Evangelist. (Translator)

Salvestra. Two years later he followed her to the grave and was buried in Santa Maria Novella.

*   *   *   *

After the apothecary, the coppersmith.[1] Bartolomeo Masi's father, who had married a baker's daughter, was in a very comfortable position. Apart from the house and shop which he rented in the Via dei Ferravecchi (now the Via Strozzi), he owned a parcel of land which he had bought from Filippo Lippi, the artist, in the Via Ventura (now the Via Laura), and another piece of land on which he built a new house. His coat-of-arms showed two lions facing each other, but separated by a mountain on the top of which appeared an arm holding a sword that pointed downwards. This was the sign of his trade.

His son Bartolomeo was born in 1480 and had as godparents a wool-comber and a coppersmith named Sandro di Giotto. Entering the Company of the Children of St John at an early age, he received a pious education. This company brought together a number of boys, of ages between thirteen and twenty-four, who desired to be well trained in the three ways of life, the contemplative, the active and the moral, under the patronage of St John. A secular guardian, who had to be a bachelor of at least thirty years of age, and who was assisted by other 'officers' and confessors, controlled the company and maintained it in purity, calm and peace. Lauds and prayers were sung in Italian, and sometimes one enjoyed a little collation of jam and wafers, cakes and wine of Trebbiano.

Bartolomeo, who had acquired a liking for these confraternities, later became a member of the company of the discipline of St Benedict, which met in the convent of Santa Maria Novella, and then of the Company of St Cecilia which met on the hill of Fiesole, under the Franciscan monastery.

At the age of seven he had been registered by his father in the 'art' of the locksmiths, his father paying the entrance-fee. After learning the rudiments of the trade, including arithmetic, at the

---

[1] Probably also a hardware-dealer.   (Translator)

school of Giovanni del Sodo, he began to work in the shop, the only one that he was ever to know. At the age of eleven he began to keep the ledger, which contained a record of goods bought and sold, with the prices. This early training was to serve him well. He became one of the notables of his guild, was councillor on four occasions, and never failed, when it was his turn, to entertain to dinner his colleagues and the notary of the 'art'. Had he failed to do so, he would have been liable to a fine of ten lire.

At the age of thirty-five Masi was free to go into partnership with his father and brother, in the hardware trade. 'May it please God', he wrote, 'that we make good and honest profits, for the salvation of our souls and bodies.' About this time his uncle, who was a notary, came to live at the shop, 'sharing bread and wine'. Again, a contract was signed. The uncle was to furnish annually sixteen bushels of grain, eight barrels of red wine, one of verjuice, and 'thirty lire on account'; in return for which he would be lodged 'with table, fire and candle'.

Masi did not remain mewed up all the time with iron pots and copper cauldrons. He liked to see the world and would occasionally take a holiday. Thus in 1502 he went away with a goldsmith, a mercer, a cobbler and a woollen-worker to visit a second-hand clothes-merchant whom they knew in the Val di Pesa. They arrived after midnight and junketed for a couple of days. On the return Bartolomeo conceived the plan of visiting Siena, of which he saw 'the whole'; then, after stops at San Gimignano and Volterra, the party returned to Florence It was the first time that they had ever left it.

In September of the same year Bartolomeo and his friends went to Arezzo, which had recently rebelled and been severely handled. The streets were full of filth, and the bed in which they slept 'stank worse than a stable'. There was little to eat, and that costly. They consoled themselves at Laverna,[1] where the Franciscan brothers received them with every courtesy, 'showed them all the holy

---

[1] Readers of Wordsworth will recall how much he was impressed with this monastery, which he visited in May 1837, and the poem it inspired, 'The Cuckoo at Laverna'.   (Translator)

places, including the spot where St Francis received the stigmata, and all his miracles'. Here they were given a decent little room with a good fire (for it was cold) and a good bed specially prepared for them.

When Bartolomeo had an attack of what he called 'French pustules', he took a vow that if cured, he would go to Loretto, on the Adriatic coast. On recovering, therefore, he accomplished his pilgrimage on foot. Here was his itinerary. He slept one night at an inn near the Lake of Perugia, and visited Perugia next day. On the morrow he left at dawn for Assisi, where he 'saw the land', visited Santa Maria degli Angeli and completed his knowledge of the Franciscan community. Then, by way of Foligno and Recanati he reached Loretto, paid his devotions and had dinner. On crossing the harbour at Ancona he met a boatman who was returning to Venice with four ladies who had come on pilgrimage from that city. As it was very tempting to see Venice, the competitor and adversary of Florence, he embarked. In the evening they touched at Sinigaglia, and being held up by a storm, bought food for their supper. Finally, by way of Pesaro, Rimini, Ravenna (Masi says nothing about Dante) and Chioggia, they reached Venice. The Florentine put up for five days at the inn of the Two Swords, near the Rialto; after which he returned home by Ferrara and Bologna. Apart from the lap between Ancona and Venice, he had made the journey on foot in three weeks.

And so now, serene and yet joyous, and rendering thanks to God and to the very glorious Virgin Mary of Loretto for giving him good company both going and coming, he regained the shop in the Via dei Ferravecchi and saluted his father, his brother and his uncle. For a Florentine artisan, by nature a stay-at-home, Bartolomeo Masi has the air of a globe-trotter. He was not long-lived, however, and was buried at the age of fifty in the family vault in Santa Annunziata.

*   *   *   *

One of the reasons for Italy's pre-eminence during the Renaissance lay in the country's wealth. Florence was continually increasing her trade and banking operations, and although the city's income was inferior to that of states like Venice and Naples, Florence none the less remained the 'source of gold', the city where there were the greatest private fortunes. In less than forty years in the fifteenth century the Medici expended over 600,000 gold florins, in charities, buildings and taxes.

Statistics, for which the Florentines had a particular bent, enable us pretty accurately to judge of the city's prosperity. In 1422 there were seventy-two counters of money-changers in the Mercato Nuovo, and two million gold florins were in circulation. The new industry of thread of gold and of silk stuffs was booming, and in this same year the first Florentine galley weighed anchor for Alexandria. The luxury-trade was constantly increasing. Fabrics spangled with gold and silver were produced, and various kinds of damasks, wood-carvings, arabesques on marble and sandstone, marquetry, portraits in wax, goldsmith's work and jewellery. Florence was now the home of elegance and refinement.[1] The trade policy was protectionist, as much to defend industry against foreign imports as to preserve the secrets of manufacture. Almost every import was subject to duty.

Wealth brought speculation in its train. The *stocchi*, by buying wholesale, caused a rise in commodity prices. While prices were high they sold the goods; then, when the market collapsed, they bought them back, and thus killed their victims as if with a *stocco* (rapier), whence their name. Still more terrible were the usurers, Jews for the most part or Jewish converts who charged from 20 per cent to 30 per cent interest. One of them ran four money-lending offices in the city; but a Pisan Jew destroyed and supplanted him.

It was to limit or hinder this trade that, with the approval of the Holy See, the Franciscans founded offices where any citizen could borrow against the deposit of security, but free of interest. The capital was provided by voluntary contributions, collections and endowments. This was the origin of the *Monti di Pietà*—

[1] As early as the fourteenth century, the forty-four goldsmith's shops on the Ponte Vecchio were worth 800 gold florins in annual rent to the State.

'mountains of money'[1]—of which the mass of poor folk were supposed to be the owners. The Franciscans were, in point of fact, extremely well-versed in questions of finance. In the fifteenth century one of them, a Tuscan named Luca Paccioli, wrote a methodical treatise on the money-market, a treatise based not on canonical texts or the interpretations of casuists, but on an exact analysis of the various kinds of exchange: the *cambio minuto*, or ordinary kind, the 'royal', the 'dry'[2] and the fictional; and his compatriots derived much benefit from this. It is evident that everyone, whether layman or cleric, had a practical and realistic outlook.

*   *   *   *

This outlook will lead us to take a glance at the State Budget, and to ask how it was made up.

On the side of receipts, there were the sales taxes, municipal tolls, collected at the city-gates, on salt, meat, wine, etc., and also the tithes or 'tenths', ordinary, extraordinary and arbitrary. In the sixteenth century the total amounted to roughly 300,000 gold florins, and it had not been very different in the fifteenth. But in finance as in politics the Florentines never had leisure to suffer from monotony, because taxation, like the form of government, was perpetually changing. At the outset only real estate had been taxed, but this encouraged reasonable people to put their money into moveable property or even to conceal their wealth. In 1427, on the motion of Giovanni Bicci de' Medici, the *catasto*[3] was introduced. This affected all kinds of property, moveable or immoveable, including credits, goods in hand and rural livestock. In each quarter of the city, ten persons assessed the capital of the taxpayer, who paid so much per cent; and the money was rigourously collected.

In pursuance of his policy of flattering the lower classes, to

---

[1] And of course 'of pity'. (Translator)

[2] '*Cambio secco*' means exchange without endorsements.

[3] Today, *catasto* means a tax on real estate, or the office where it is assessed. In the fifteenth century it appears to have designated income tax in general. (Translator)

whom he opened the highest offices in the State and whom 'he clad in the scarlet cloaks of the old nobility', Cosimo de' Medici in 1442 replaced the *catasto* by the *arbitrio*, a sort of forced loan which was assessed not on stable property but on trade and credits. This mainly hit the well-to-do, and was applauded by the lower middle-classes and the artisans. 'The nature of the people', observed Guicciardini, 'is to overburden those who are in a superior position'; and the Medici, who studied to remain popular, used the *arbitrio* 'as a dagger and a stick'. The taxpayer's declaration of income was public and subject to examination; any sums he concealed were confiscated to the benefit of the State and the informers. Confiscation was subsequently replaced by a fine; the poor scholar, Gianozzo Manetti, had a bitter experience of what this meant. The Medici, who disliked him, condemned him to a fine of 135,000 gold florins, which reduced him to beggary. Thus taxation was an instrument of policy.

In 1443 a new tax, known as the *graziosa*, was introduced. Under this system an assessor fixed what every individual was to pay. The rate varied from 4 per cent to $33\frac{1}{3}$ per cent, and anyone who did not pay cooled his heels in the State prison. Others, to escape the tax, went to live in the country; but they were stigmatized as *morosi*, men in arrears, and some of them were banished. 'One does nothing but pay', sighed poor Alessandra de' Bardi, 'although the city is quiet and we are at peace. It's miraculous how much money they take from us.'

But by thus overburdening the wealthy, who contribute to maintain a balance in the State or to restore the situation in times of financial difficulty, the city as a whole was impoverished. In the end the Florentines discovered a more equitable and less arbitrary tax. This was the *decima*. All the citizens (except the workmen as regards their wages) were to pay a tenth of their income from land, or industrial profits, or of their salary or pay, or from bonds registered at the *Monte*. This was the advent of income tax and its obligatory accompaniment of fiscal inquisition.

The interlude of Savonarola's régime brought about a complete change. Now, only real estate was taxed at 10 per cent. Commerce and banking escaped; and yet Savonarola imagined he was making the rich pay, from their superfluity, in order to benefit the poor. 'Work', he said, 'falls only on the poor; it is from the poor that the lords[1] draw their salaries and income and tolls, while they neglect their duties. They think only of pleasures and festivities. And it is the same with the Bishops, and prelates and beneficed clergy. No fatigue for them. They are rich in land while their subjects are dying of hunger.' St Ambrose had said that the superfluous is robbery. Proudhon was to enlarge the formula.

After the fall of Savonarola the experts considered what forms of property could best be taxed. A tax on income from landed property would not meet the needs of the State. Profits from trade and banking were difficult to estimate and dangerous to publish, because business was mainly founded on credit. Food and commodity-goods could not be over-taxed without the risk of a popular revolution.

Florence was in fact ready for a graduated income tax. The city now returned to the *decima*, but it was *scalata*, or graduated in such a way as to hit the upper classes. A man with 50 ducats of annual income paid only 5; a man who had 300 paid 80 or 100, so that the former was taxed only at 10 per cent whereas the latter was taxed at 25 per cent or even $33\frac{1}{3}$ per cent. But now came the rub. The *decima scalata* could be raised twice or three times in one year. So, an income of 50 ducats paid a quarter or a third, while at 300 ducats one paid one's whole income; and, as the rate steepened, one might reach the point of paying one and a half times or even twice one's income. The lower class thought this wonderful, but the rich, who had been lightly touched hitherto, felt themselves 'cut to the quick'.

The 'popular' government which ruled Florence between 1527 and 1530 extracted nearly a million and a half gold florins from the population; at this rate the source of taxation dried up and dis-

---

[1] Meaning no doubt the wealthy classes in general. It would be interesting to know what remnants of the feudal nobility had survived; most of them had probably been driven into commerce or had intermarried with rich *parvenus*. (Translator)

appeared . . . and the Republic with it. The fact is noted by the wise Guicciardini in a passage which explains the close connection between crises in public finance, uncertainty as to a quiet and stable régime, and the faults or incompetence of government:

There was disorder in the great assemblies, debates were long and held too late, State-secrets were divulged. We were not enlightened as to the general trend of Italian politics. . . . Then we were unexpectedly surprised by misfortune. As the public funds were now handled by various people, divided among a number of negligent officials, the money was squandered even before it was collected. It was thrown away uselessly and too late. Hence the enormous taxes which crushed the citizens. The Signoria, being always short of money, was continually extracting forced loans from the wealthiest members of the community. Honest men turned their back on politics. The city, bled white and dishonoured, was going to its doom at a hundred miles an hour (*andarne all'n giù cento miglia per ora*). The rich, incensed by arbitrary taxation, desired a form of government such that, whoever might be in control, they themselves would not be ruined. Even the lower class was weary of taxation and ready to accept reform, provided it was not aristocratic.

Good finance, good government, and vice versa. The principle is not a new one. To this dark and melancholy chapter, which affords a lesson for tax-payers in all ages, one may add a few minor documents in illustration.

Here, for example, is the tax statement made by Donatello to the officials of the *catasto* in 1427: 'He has no fortune apart from a few pieces of furniture for himself and his family. He lives on the proceeds of his shop, in company with Michelozzo, a sculptor and coin-designer.' And the beginning of this declaration by the notary Pietro di ser Guidi da Vinci (Florence 1470) who mentions among 'the mouths' he has to feed, that is, his dependents, his wife (aged 74), two sons, two daughters, and at the end *Lionardo figlulo de ser Pietro non legiptimo d'età*: the illegitimate Leonardo da Vinci.

As an illustration of the history of contraband through the ages, the following anecdote has its charm. A well-to-do citizen named Messer Antonio wished to avoid paying the toll on eggs. So, before coming into town, he stowed away thirty in his breeches' seat. The toll-collector, being suspicious, made him sit down. 'What have you got there that I hear cracking?'

The yellow yoke was flowing down Antonio's legs, and he had to bribe the collector to keep his mouth shut. One can imagine his reception on reaching home. 'What!' cried his wife. 'Did you want to hatch eggs as though you were a hen? A curse on your meanness, and the shame you've brought on us! Everyone will be pointing his finger at you, and all for two farthings!'

CHAPTER XII

THE BARBARIAN AND THE PROPHET

The French in Florence – An outburst of mysticism – The
city becomes a monastery – Savonarola and the burning of
the 'vanities' – Resurrection of political parties – Martyrdom
of the prophet – End of the theocracy

THE successor of Lorenzo the Magnificent was not the man
his father had been. Robust, and at the same time frivolous,
impulsive and unintelligent, he had inherited from Clarice
Orsini, his mother, the haughtiness of the Roman barons. He
meant to be blindly obeyed; and as he found two of his cousins
antipathetic, he placed them under police supervision and thus
created a centre of opposition within his own family.

And yet Florence had never been in such need of a governor
who could unite everyone under his leadership.

Called in by Ludovico il Moro, tyrant of Milan, the French
King Charles VIII was planning the conquest of Naples. He had
ancestral claims on that kingdom; and he now descended into Italy,
although it had been described to him as 'the lion's den': you see
the tracks of those who go in, people said, but no tracks coming
out. However, the invasion of the 'Barbarians' was beginning, and
with it the era of calamities. On January 17, 1494, a Florentine
ambassador wrote to Piero de' Medici: 'If we are beaten by the
French, it will be the end of Italy, *tutto a bordello*. If we prevent
them from marching through, there will be enduring hatred and
great expense. The first florins to be expended will come out of
your pocket.'

The alternatives were not attractive, and Piero scarcely knew
what to do. He at last decided to go and meet the King of France
at Sarzana; and as he had neither the skill not the force of character
of his father, he ended by signing a shameful treaty, handing over
several fortresses which were the keys to Florentine territory.

Florence immediately rose in opposition; a 'parliament' was called, and the people brought out the rusty swords and daggers which had lain unused since the conspiracy of the Pazzi. On the morning of November 9, 1494, Piero found the Palazzo della Signoria closed. He was ordered to go in alone. When the significance of all this dawned on him, he fled by way of the Porta San Gallo and made for Bologna. The city was now in an uproar. Young Cardinal Giovanni, the future Leo X, was seen on a balcony, trembling with fear and commending himself on his knees to God. He then disguised himself as a Franciscan and fled with his brother Giuliano.

The Medici were proclaimed rebels, their palace was pillaged, and of the booty, worth at least 100,000 crowns, the Signoria had its share. The exiles returned, and notably Piero's cousins, who, to make it plain that they had nothing in common with the family of the tyrant, replaced the balls on their coat-of-arms with the red cross of the Guelph party, on a silver field. Like good demagogues they styled themselves *Popolani*.

The Signoria had given orders that everyone should be ready to receive the French billeting officers, and these, on their arrival, marked with chalk the houses and rooms that most appealed to them, this one for Lord X, that one for Baron Y. Then, as Landucci writes in his journal, the men-at-arms knocked on the doors, crying: 'Open there!', without troubling as to whether it was a poor man's house or a rich man's. They intimated that they would pay, but few did so, and if they paid, 'It was with the ox's horns, while they ate the flesh'.

As a measure of precaution the young girls had been sent to convents or to relatives in the country; but the fact was that these strangers behaved very properly, and not one used indecent language to a woman. Landucci thought they were afraid. When they asked what was the population of Florence, they were told that at the sound of the bell 100,000 people would assemble, from the city and the environs; and this dissuaded them from any inclination to pillage.

On November 16th, two columns adorned with the arms of the

King of France were set up outside the doors of the Medici palace (which had just been sacked). 'It was truly a triumphal sight.' And on the 17th, according to a French chronicler, in Florence 'surnamed the beautiful or the pleasant . . . there took place the fairest entry of armed horsemen and footmen that ever was seen in the Italies'.

Entering by the Porta San Friano, Charles VIII appeared on horseback under a canopy of cloth of gold. Wearing a great white hat, a doublet of gold brocade and a blue mantle, he carried his lance on his thigh, like a conqueror. Behind him rode barons superbly armed, dressed like princes and mounted on great maned horses whose ears had been cropped to give them a more ter-rible aspect. Saluted with acclamations of *Viva Francia*! the King advanced to the sound of music, along streets strewn with sweet-smelling herbs and under houses hung with tapestries and banners. After crossing the Arno by the Ponte Vecchio, he proceeded by way of the Piazza della Signoria to Santa Maria del Fiore, where he kissed the altar which was illuminated with thousands of candles. At nightfall he dismounted in front of the Medici palace.

'When people saw him on foot his renown seemed to diminish, for in truth he was a very small man, ill-favoured of countenance; he had big shoulders, an aquiline nose and feet like those of a goose, with all his toes tied together.'[1]

But, as he was not really antipathetic, he received a sincere and hearty welcome. 'Everyone's body was full of lilies.' Were not the French old friends and good customers? Could one receive them inhospitably without compromising the position of all the Florentine merchants who were living in France? And then, never had such an army been seen! The long halberds of the Swiss infantry caused a sensation; and a still greater one was produced by the fifty-four pieces of artillery drawn by horses, when Italian canon were merely mounted on wagons and drawn by oxen. All this gave one furiously to think.

While the King was in Florence, everyone with a house over-

[1] Charles was wearing square-toed slippers of black velvet. Another Italian said that he had the feet of an ox.

looking the street was required to keep a light burning in one window; it gave a festive air to the place. Yet no one felt easy. The French had just liberated Pisa, which Florence used as her seaport, and people were now wondering exactly what this web-footed king meant to do. Was he going to enslave the city, and bring back Piero de' Medici?

The atmosphere grew threatening. The citizens, preparing to defend themselves, laid in a store of bread, weapons and stones; and contemplated, in case of need, a repetition of the Sicilian Vespers.[1] The rich gathered round them the peasants of the *contado*.[2] The French for their part felt little stomach for fighting in these narrow alleys, among palaces which looked like citadels and from which they could easily be subjected to a hail of stones and rocks. By way of precaution, they occupied the Porta San Friano and the Carraja bridge.

Charles, meanwhile, adopted a haughty tone. He told the commissaries of the Signoria that he intended to occupy the city he had conquered; to which they replied that the Republic had received him as a friendly guest, not as a victorious enemy. Negotiations regarding the terms of capitulation now became acrimonious, ending in a scene famous in history.

'Well, we shall sound our trumpets', the King is recorded as saying. 'And we shall ring our bells', retorted the commissary Capponi, who proceeded to tear up the capitulation, and then withdrew with his colleagues. The French again became prudent. Charles recalled Capponi and treated the matter as a joke. 'Ah! Chappon, Chappon!', he cried. 'You are a naughty capon.'[3]

Calm was restored, and an agreement was reached and sworn to in the Cathedral. The freedom of the city was recognized in return for a payment of 120,000 gold florins. The King ordered that the Florentines should be paid what was owing to them, and

[1] The wholesale massacre, in 1282, of the French in Sicily.

[2] The farming-districts round the city.   (Translator)

[3] In later years, Machiavelli celebrated the crowing of this capon, sur-rounded by so many cocks—*Galli* (which means Gauls, as well as cocks. Translator).

the Signoria, unwilling to do less, instructed the population not to exaggerate the bill. Anyone who should give offence to a Frenchman was to have his hand cut off.

On November 28th Charles left Florence and marched towards Rome; but a taxpayer had already seen the moral to be drawn from this experience. 'We Florentines', he said, 'follow the wise custom of giving money to those who come to pillage our country, and so, of paying for the damage they have done. It will be the same in the future. Let anyone who wants our money come and ill-treat us.'

Looking back on these times Guicciardini was to regard Charles VIII's passage through Florence as the beginning of an avalanche of misfortunes. States would be transformed, kingdoms fall, cities and whole countries be ruined. There would be fearful butcheries, new ways and morals would arise, and war would become more bloody. The picture is scarcely exaggerated. One might add that economic prosperity was declining. But at the end of 1494 the Florentines were overjoyed at being freed from French occupation, and they ascribed it to the monk Savonarola who was presumed to have persuaded Charles VIII that by going away he was obeying the will of God.

*　　*　　*　　*

Whence came this monk who was to transform Florence and carry the city with him on a wave of mystical enthusiasm? He had been born at Ferrara in 1452. His parents had hoped to make a physician of him, but his vocation was for something quite different. One day, while he was playing a sad melody on his lute, his mother suddenly turned to him as if possessed by a spirit of divination. 'My son,' she cried in despair, 'this is the sign that we are soon to be parted.' He arose and continued, though with trembling hand and lowered eyes, to touch the lute-strings.

A visionary who believed himself to be inspired by God, Savonarola felt no respect for temporal princes. When appointed superior of the convent of San Marco, he had not even troubled to call on his patron, Lorenzo the Magnificent. Yet this puny and ailing little monk, this hollow-chested creature, had the nose of an eagle, and his great dark eyes glittered under thick red eyelashes. When he spoke, his prophecies inspired terror, and his thin transparent hand was a herald of the Apocalypse. 'The judgment of God', he cried, 'is nigh at hand. A sword hangs over your heads. Italy has been condemned for her iniquities, condemned for the sins of the Church and of the tyrants, condemned for your sins, O people! for the sins of your fathers and mothers, and of you, young men, blaspheming children that you are!' A new and menacing voice, which echoed strangely in the hearts of the Florentines, who were Christians rather by habit and not particularly subject to spiritual torments.

But Savonarola did not lose himself in vague declamation. Although stating that he had never wished to concern himself with politics, he resolutely grappled with the political problem, and once the Medici had been driven out and a treaty signed with the French, he set himself to consider the best form of government.

It was not easy. As a disciple of Aquinas he had a theoretical preference for monarchy, but he thought such a régime unsuited to Florence. To see more clearly, he consulted the citizens. The debates dragged out interminably, as usual, and there was little sign of agreement. 'One wants boiled meat, another roast.' In the end Savonarola decided for a republican and democratic constitution. He even exploited the jealousy of the lower classes as regards the well-to-do, and he warned the latter. 'I will come out of my convent,' he told them, 'and armed with the fury of the people, I will enter your palaces and I will say: "Here we remain".' It was the tone of the *Ciompi*, a recognition of the right of insurrection.

By the new constitution of December 1494, Florence was to be governed by a Great Council composed of citizens whose parents or kinsfolk had occupied certain offices. Invested with legislative power, this council was also empowered to appoint all State officials. Thus 3,200 citizens were placed at the head of 90,000 or 100,000 people; but this democracy, which wore something of the aspect of a Venetian Oligarchy, was of a particular kind. In principle it had no master, apart from the man who was 'the voice

(*above*) Cosimo de' Medici (the ~~lder~~) is presented with a model of ~~~~e church of S. Lorenzo by ~~~~runelleschi (*left*) and Ghiberti (~~~~*right*). Fresco by Vasari in the Palazzo Vecchio

(*right*) Façade of the Duomo, Florence

9. Vasari's portrait of Lorenzo de' Medici (Uffizi, Florence)

of God announcing His will to the faithful'—Savonarola the Judge, as in ancient Israel. And by a natural trend the new government, in which the Signoria was obsessed with the visionary, took on the appearance of a theocracy.

'Florence,' cried the Judge, 'God wishes to content you. He wishes to give you a leader, a king who will govern you. This king is the Christ.'

Gone were the times when Cosimo de' Medici used to say that men are not governed with paternosters.

'Will you have Jesus for your King?' Savonarola asked the people.

'Yes, long live Jesus Christ, our King!'

Foreigners and older citizens rubbed their eyes—they no longer recognized the City of the Lily, once so lively and noisy with festivals and joyous songs, a city where men scarcely worried themselves with thoughts of the inevitable end. You would have thought now that you were in a monastery.

Thirteen or fourteen thousand people would sometimes throng the Cathedral when Savonarola was preaching. They reserved their seats from early dawn. One devotee took down the prophetic words in short-hand, 'without missing an iota, and that by divine permission, for he is a good man'. The children were accommodated on tiers of benches, modestly dressed, with their hair cut short and each carrying a red cross in his hand. And they sang the Lauds so sweetly that everyone wept, saying: 'This is the work of the Lord. There is such holiness in this church that it seems full of angels.'

Then there were processions. Five thousand girls and boys clad in white, wearing crowns of olive-leaves and carrying branches, followed the tabernacle on which was painted Our Lord riding into Jerusalem on an ass. At the sound of fifes and trumpets all the children would sing in chorus: 'Long live Christ our King!'

Rough amusements, 'bestial and stupid' games, were abandoned. Noisy street-cries were replaced by hymn-singing. The population fasted and, in accordance with the *frate's* command, brought their savings to the Monte di Pietà. The women laid down their finery

F

and read the service of the Mass as they walked though the streets. Workmen beguiled their leisure by studying the Bible. People met to pray and converse of holy matters. And they grew more and more emotional, whence the name of *piagnoni* (weepers) which was given to Savonarola's partisans.

The prophet in fact subjected these 'Athenians of Italy' to a severe discipline. The taverns closed at six. On Saint's Days the shops were shut and no trade or business might be transacted. There was to be no more luxury-trade in clothing, no more licentious pictures or indecent books by pagan writers, 'works of the devil'. Blasphemers would have their tongues pierced; debauchees and those guilty of sodomy would be in danger of the stake. As to the courtesans, the *frate* desired that, to put shame upon them, they should be conducted to the Signoria amid a blare of trumpets; and when it was pointed out to him that they were so numerous that the whole city would be thrown into disorder, he replied: 'Begin with one, then you can go on to the others.'

Savonarola in his zeal engaged servants to spy on their employers. The very children who, when singing Lauds, sounded like choirs of angels, became his policemen. They went about the streets snatching from young girls any ornaments they thought unseemly, demanding from passers-by alms and gifts for the Monte di Pietà, hunting down dice-players and card-players. When the cry arose: 'Here are the *frate's* children', every gamester took to his heels.

These beardless policemen, none of whom were over fourteen and who carried a crucifix instead of a truncheon, entered private houses confiscating harps and flutes, boxes of perfume and books of secular poetry. These all went to swell the 'pyre of vanities', the *talamo* which the Judge Savonarola was having built in the Piazza della Signoria for the Carnival of 1497.

It was a grotesque and lamentable sight. All these trinkets, these often charming knick-knacks, articles of beauty or pleasure, were piled up along with valuable books. Above them were set paintings of celebrated women such as Lucretia and Cleopatra or of courtesans like Bencina la Bella and Lena Morella; for such was the persuasive power of the monk that he had won over the artists and that Botticelli, Lorenzo di Credi, Perugino and even Michelangelo were his devoted followers and that some, like Fra Bartolomeo, themselves brought their studies from the nude and threw them on the pile.

Then the flames went up. The priests, accompanied by the people, sang the *Te Deum*. Bells rang, trumpets sounded. All this was what Savonarola and his *piagnoni* called sacred folly for the love of Christ. But when the pyre of vanities had been consumed, the sacred folly took another form. In the square in front of the convent of San Marco, of which Savonarola was superior, a great cross was set up and three circles were formed round it. In the innermost were ranged the Dominicans, interspersed with groups of children dressed as angels; next came a circle of young laymen and clerics; finally an outer circle of old men, priests and burghers—all crowned with flowers and dancing. Once again it was a revival of Biblical times: King David dancing before the Ark of the Covenant. But the Jewish money-lenders were banished.

The Judge admired without taking part in these pious Bacchanalia. But he continued to subject the faithful to a rule of iron. He whipped them and terrified them. 'You pass your lives in bed', he thundered, 'or in taking walks, in gossip, in orgies and debaucheries. Your lives are the lives of swine!' And in one passionate outburst on the theme of Death:

'The living will no longer suffice to bury the dead. There will be so many dead in the houses that men will go about the streets crying: "Bring out your dead!" and they will place them in wagons and on horses, and they will pile them up and burn them. And then they will proceed down the highways and cry: "Who has dead to bury? Remains there not one who is not dead? Who has no more dead?"'

Such images of the Last Judgment, other visions too in which Hell itself seemed to be gaping, pierced the Florentines to the marrow. They were an imaginative folk, and easily frightened. Even so, the Judge remained popular. Men were grateful to him for having overthrown tyranny, reformed the constitution, suppressed usury and improved the public credit. In October 1495, to celebrate the revival of liberty, Donatello's Judith was removed from the Medici palace and set up on the terrace of the Palazzo della Signoria with the following inscription: *Exemplum salutis publicae cives posuere.*[1] Judith, the murderer of Holophernes, a symbol of deliverance.

Savonarola had won gratitude also for having dissuaded Charles VIII, on his return to France after the failure of his expedition, from passing through Florence. It was true that Pisa and the various forts had not been given back; on the other hand, the merchants were in no hurry to pay what they owed the King. And if one needed further proof that the theocracy was accepted, it could be found in Piero de' Medici's failure when he tried to recapture 'his city' (June 1497). This failure cost the lives of five of the conspirators, including the old Bernardo del Nero, who, as he bared his neck for the executioner, said that at his age—he was seventy-five—'there was not much that they could deprive him of'.

The secret partisans of the Medici prudently refrained from making themselves conspicuous, and were jokingly referred to as the *bigi*, the grey ones. Many of them ended by inscribing themselves as followers of Savonarola, who indeed had proclaimed a general amnesty. But a certain minority hated the Judge and remained untouched by his teachings: these were the free-thinkers, the libertines, the *arrabbiati* (the rabid), and they made play with anything calculated to injure 'that pig of a dirty monk who is going to be boiled in his convent of San Marco'.

The open conflict between Savonarola and the Borgia Pope Alexander VI proved a trump-card for this opposition. The *frate*, who pointed again and again to the revelations he was receiving, stigmatized the vices of the Church, and attacked the 'Roman Babylon' so vehemently that the Pope, despite the lenient view he had taken of this visionary, ended by losing his temper. He forbade Savonarola to preach. 'But I cannot live when I am not

[1] The citizens set up this (statue as a) symbol of public safety.

preaching', cried the monk; and after some half-hearted efforts to obey, he again mounted the pulpit and renewed his attacks so vigorously that he was excommunicated.

The *piagnoni* were dreadfully upset. Being forbidden now to attend the monk's sermons, they debated the problem with anguish in their hearts. Just or unjust, however, excommunication was to be feared, and few of them now went to hear their leader preaching. As for Savonarola, he abstained for a time from any ecclesiastical function, then suddenly, at Christmas 1497, he celebrated three Masses, administered the Communion to his fellow-monks, and delivered a personal attack on the Pope.

'As for me,' he cried, 'it is enough that I have not been excommunicated by Christ!'

Such audacity disconcerted his followers. Fewer people now attended church and more and more haunted such taverns as the *Frascato*, a pothouse and gambling-den near the *Mercato Vecchio*. The child-policemen were no longer to be seen.

The *arrabbiati* and their friends the *compagnacci*, or fast-livers, felt that the wind was now in their favour; and when the Pope threatened Florence with an interdict, the members of the Signoria, who had hitherto favoured the *frate*, changed their tune. One knew what an interdict would mean: no more masses or sacraments; and moreover the probable arrest of Florentines living in Rome, and the probable confiscation of their goods. This was to touch the Republic in the tenderest spot; mystical as the city appeared to have grown, it was above all a commercial city; and it was not surprising that the Signoria should resign itself, in its turn, to forbidding the *frate* to preach any more.

Savonarola's fall was decided much less by Rome than by Florence itself. The relatives of the conspirators who had been beheaded swore to avenge themselves. The *arrabbiati* supported them. And the Franciscans, being opposed to the Dominicans, desired the overthrow of the 'Judge' who had rebelled against the Supreme Pontiff. Lastly, and especially, the Florentines were terrified lest their trade should be ruined.

One day Savonarola had offered to establish the truth of his predictions by passing through fire. Francesco of Apulia, a Franciscan who was preaching in Santa Croce, took him at his word and offered to undergo the ordeal by fire at the same time. 'I truly think I shall be burned', he added. 'But if Savonarola is not burned at the same time, then you can believe in him as in a prophet.'

This proposal, in the eyes of the public, was to force Savonarola to face the consequences. He accepted the challenge without enthusiasm, but the more fervent of his disciples declared that they would be overjoyed to undergo the ordeal. 'One is amazed', wrote an eye-witness, 'to see so many lay-folk, even women and young boys, as resolute as the monks to pass through the fire. You would think they were invited to a wedding. But I believe all that will go off in smoke.'

On April 7, 1498, two stakes, drenched with oil and resin and standing about five feet apart, so as to leave room for a man to pass between them, had been set up in the middle of the Piazza della Signoria. The portico now known as the Loggia dei Lanzi had been separated by a partition into two compartments. The Franciscans and their champion on one side, Savonarola and two of his adepts on the other, awaited the ordeal while the judges began to discuss the procedure. As the champions' clothes might be enchanted, they were first stripped naked and then dressed in other clothes; whereupon one of Savonarola's followers declared that he would enter the fire only with a crucifix in his hand.

'Profanation!' cried the Franciscans.

'Then I will carry the Holy Sacrament.'

'A still more horrible profanation.'

Hours were spent in discussion, and meanwhile a 'cruel' rain began to fall, dusk came on, and the Signoria ordered the crowd to disperse.

It was evident that neither side was anxious to undergo the famous ordeal; but Savonarola and the Dominicans came worst out of the adventure. Why should the Judge be afraid of risking his skin when it was a question of proving the divine character of his mission? From that moment his cause was lost. The Florentines had been deprived of a great spectacle and were furious that their credulity should have been turned to ridicule. They called down curses on the excommunicated hypocrite and described him as a *gabbadeo* (one who deceives God); while the irreconcilable faction and the debauchees organized a riot which cost the lives of three *piagnoni*, and invaded the convent of San Marco with cries of: 'At the monk! At him!'

Savonarola had had a presentiment of his end. 'All who have prophesied', he said, 'have suffered and been hewn in pieces.' He was on his knees before the altar, chanting the holy offices with the last of his adherents, when the order came that he was to appear before the Signoria. He took leave of his brethren, received the Communion and surrendered himself to the officers. On his appearing in the Palazzo, with his hands bound, he was stoned. One man struck him behind, crying: 'Prophet, who struck you?' Another said: 'His spirit of prophecy resides in the place where he was struck.'

Once the prisoner was secured, the Signoria hastened to seek from the Pope absolution from all the sentences pronounced against Florence, permission to put the monk on trial and at the same time leave to raise a tax of three-tenths on the secular clergy and the religious. The Signoria obtained satisfaction all along the line and there was general rejoicing, except among those who remained faithful to Savonarola. 'The *frate* has been sold for thirty pieces of silver, like Our Lord; for three times ten makes thirty.'

The trial was scandalous. Torture was applied,[1] the record of the examination, and the answers given, were falsified, while a succession of manœuvres, in which cruelty was allied with falsehood, impressed the public. Here are some fragments of the confessions which were alleged to have been extracted: that for twenty years past Savonarola had not confessed to a single mortal sin although he had frequently fallen into the sin of incontinence; he had used imposture to make people believe his prophecies; he had spied on private families; he had persuaded the monks of his order

---

[1] Savonarola had one arm put out of joint.

to divulge the secrets of the confessional; he had administered Communion without consecrating the host.

Landucci, who was no fanatic, was filled with sadness when he read of this. 'My soul was sorrowful when I saw such an edifice crumble in ruins. . . . Florence was awaiting a new Jerusalem, the coming of a new splendour, the example of an upright life, the renovation of the Church, the conversion of the Infidels. . . .' And all that was founded on lies! 'I took the medicine', the apothecary wrote resignedly.

On May 22, 1498, in view of the enormity of their alleged crimes and pestiferous sedition, Savonarola and his two stalwart adherents were condemned to degradation as schismatics and contemners of the Holy See, and were handed over to the secular arm. On the 23rd in the Piazza della Signoria three gibbets were set up; when however it was seen that one of them had the shape of a cross, the branch was sawn off. Savonarola was first stripped of his sacerdotal vestments:

'I separate you from the Church militant and triumphant.'

'Not triumphant', was the reply. 'That is not in your power.'

After seeing his friends put to death, Savonarola himself mounted the scaffold. 'Prophet,' someone cried, 'now is the moment. Perform a miracle.' The bodies were now hanging from the gallows, and fire was put to the keg of powder beneath them. For a moment the flames blew sideways, and the multitude cried: 'A miracle!' But the fire soon mounted vertically. Gradually the bodies which looked 'black as rats' lost their arms and legs, and nothing remained but the torsos suspended by chains. Stones were thrown to bring them down since it was feared that adherents of the *frate* would carry them off. The executioner felled the gibbets and took care to see that everything was burned; then the ashes were carted away and thrown into the Arno.

All that remained of the 'son of perdition', his writings, the red crosses he had distributed, was to be handed over to the authorities and purified by fire. Nevertheless, certain of the faithful made a patient search for relics; some, taking every precaution for fear of being denounced, went by night to gather up the incinerated fragments that were floating down the river; and three days after the martyr's execution women were to be seen kneeling on the spot where he had been burned.

Formerly, in the time of St John Gualbert, in 1068, a young monk named Pietro had passed between two flaming pyres without being burnt. It had been a question of proving the guilt of a Bishop accused of simony, and after the miracle Pietro, surnamed Igneo, was carried in triumph and made a Cardinal. But those times had passed away. Savonarola died and his adherents were persecuted.

The *compagnacci* and *arrabbiati* now threw off all restraint and indulged in 'indescribable horrors'. They let loose in the Cathderal a wornout old hack, tormented and excited it with their shouts until the beast collapsed half-dead on the steps of the porch. They burned asafeotida in place of incense, threw filth into the pulpit, poured ink into the holy-water stoups. From the convent of San Marco they took the crown of the Virgin and set it on the head of a courtesan. At the fireworks on Midsummer Day—the Feast of St John—a number of dogs were displayed along with a pig; the dogs were the *piagnoni* and the pig was that 'pig of a *frate*'. After nightfall the rioters armed themselves with weapons and torches and danced madly under the covered portion of the Mercato Nuovo. 'It was Hell.'

But these very excesses threw into relief the noble image of the Judge, as men recalled it. One winter's night, by the fireside in his studio, Sandro Botticelli was asking a relentless *arrabbiato* why so ignominious a death had been inflicted on the prophet. He himself had remained his follower.

'Sandro,' replied the other, 'must I tell you the truth? We never discovered that the man had committed even a venial sin. But if we had sent him back to San Marco, the populace would have cut us in pieces. We decided to put him to death in order to save ourselves. Do not the Scriptures say: "It is needful that one man should die for the people"?' Thus the astute *arrabbiato* justified his instinct for self-preservation by quoting a sacred text.

Machiavelli had at first regarded Savonarola as a clever rogue;

F*

later on however he praised him for denouncing the corruption of the Vatican and the clergy. As regards his prophecies, he said: 'I do not wish to judge whether he spoke truly or falsely, for one should speak only with respect of a man so extraordinary.' Gradually the prophet was transformed into a herald of Virtue and a witness to the Truth. As early as 1500 people in Rome were buying medals which had been struck in his honour: the words 'Blessed Martyr' were engraved on them. And on the anniversaries of May 23rd, as late as the eighteenth century, flowers were strewn over the place where he had been put to death.

It is true that the first people to weary of the theocratic system he had established had been his own fellow-citizens. They were temperamentally less interested in religion than in politics and found little pleasure in seeing their town transformed into a monastery. And yet the flame of piety and mysticism he had kindled was to leave traces which we shall come upon again in the most tragic hours of Florentine history.

CHAPTER XIII

UNCERTAINTY OF THE TIMES

Vicissitudes of war – Florence and the sack of Prato – Return
of the Medici and restoration of the principate – Florence
once again a city of festivities and merry-making

A BLOW most humiliating to the Republic had been the
loss of Pisa, which had been liberated by the French. A
condottiere was engaged to recapture it, Pagolo Vitelli;
and he, with 16,000 men and 'a great and fair artillery-train', now
laid siege to the rival city. A breach had been made in the ramparts
and victory seemed certain when Pagolo gave orders for a retreat.
It was a clear case of treason. Pagolo was arrested and beheaded on
the night of October 2, 1499, in front of the Palazzo della Signoria.
Under the light of a single torch, an officer raised the traitor's head
by the hair and displayed it to the crowd, 'more than 10,000
people who were awaiting his death'.

And now came the threat of war and rapine. The Republic was
certainly not in luck. The son of the Borgia Pope, the terrible
Cesare Borgia, Duc de Valentinois, was at this time carving out a
kingdom for himself. At the suggestion of the exiled Piero de'
Medici and of Vitellozzo Vitelli, who thirsted to avenge the death
of his brother Pagolo, Cesare marched from Romagna towards
Florence, though not as an open enemy, for he knew that Louis
XII of France was favourable to the Florentines. He simply asked
for free passage for his troops.

But the Republic knew its man and prepared for the worst.
Landucci and Masi now noted day by day the depredations of the
invader; how he pillaged the farms or set them on fire, and seized
oxen from the peasants to drag his artillery-train. On May 13,
1501, Cesare Borgia's mercenaries were reported to be drawing
near, and the Signoria now ordered the citizens to appear in arms
under their gonfalon as soon as they heard the bell begin to toll.

The order was not well received. 'What have we to do with this Valentinois? We are not at war with him. If the Signoria was not afraid of Charles VIII's 30,000 men, why should it now humiliate itself, with the patience "of an ass", to the point of negotiating with this intruder who is not worth three farthings, this bastard whose army is no more than a barefooted rabble? One is ashamed of being a Florentine.'

But the Signoria negotiated all the same. Florence was weak, exhausted also by the war against Pisa, and it was feared that the Medici might be restored by force. On May 15, 1501, an agreement was made by which the Republic engaged Borgia as its *condottiere* for a sum of 36,000 florins. In return for this he agreed to evacuate the territory.

To receive payment was one thing, to leave the country another; and the Borgia was in no hurry. He now asked the Florentines to give him half their artillery, while his mercenaries redoubled their depredations. They cut the corn for their horses, 'squeezed' the peasants' heads or hung them up in the most painful positions to make them confess where they had hidden their money. Worse than devils out of Hell, they violated women and young boys— such horrors as had not been known in the time of Charles VIII. Vitellozzo seized girls and women and took them on pack-animals to Rome, perhaps to sell them as the Turks sold Christians. He stabbed a child who was begging for mercy on his knees; he set fire to a tower full of refugees, and 'they perished amid howls and cries, not one escaped alive.' Such were the deeds of this bandit and his master, the Valentinois, vile wretches who feared not the Lord!

The Florentines thought now only of hoarding bread. The city 'had drunk so much of melancholy that it was like to be drowning'. And, to make things worse, Cesare proclaimed that he would go only on condition of receiving an advance of 8,000 florins. The Signoria nevertheless continued to humour him. No injury was to be done to him or to his mercenaries, under pain of the gallows: and to obviate nocturnal rioting, every window was to be lit up.

Good news came at last. Louis XII of France declared it was contrary to his will that the Valentinois should 'do harm to Florence or impose any levy upon her'. If he did not remove himself, French troops would march against him. The Signoria drew breath—and at once thought of how it could break its promises to Cesare. But the latter was compelled to obey, 'devouring his vexation', and to depart without receiving money or artillery.

The merchants had suffered least from the ordeal, but they were bound to recognize that the situation was not brilliant. Commodities were expensive, taxes heavy, and the Great Council, in which the majority was constantly shifting, was in a state of confusion. All this would have to be changed; as a wise observer remarked: 'Since the Republic has no one to take care of the public weal, let us establish a long-term magistrature.'

So a popular government was set up under the direction of Pietro Soderini, who was appointed gonfaloniere for life. He was a wealthy burgher married to a lady of the nobility, and well-versed in public business as had been his brothers in the time of Lorenzo the Magnificent. He had a yellowish face and a big bald head with a few wisps of black hair. A clever and sometimes eloquent speaker, he was pious in his way, and 'economical although rich'. But his work was cut out for him. Cesare Borgia, who had just seized the Duchy of Urbino, bore the Florentines a deep grudge; and though he cared little about the restoration of the Medici, he played with them and used them as a kind of scarecrow to terrify the Republic. His condottiere Vitellozzo had seized Arezzo, a subject city, amid cries of Marzocco,[1] which meant 'Medici'! and immediately, as Landucci put it, 'it seemed to the Florentines that their bowels were in the frying-pan'.[2]

Reduced to these extremities, they dispatched Soderini and Machiavelli to Urbino where, on June 24, 1502, a little before midnight, Cesare Borgia received them. He did not mince his words. 'Florence is ill-disposed to me', he told them. 'If you don't

[1] The lion.
[2] An apothecary's metaphor. (Translator)

want me for a friend you will have me for an enemy'. It was no use talking. 'Talk and cleverness are cheap'; what was needed was cash down, for a renewal of the *condotta* which had been agreed to the year before. Cesare knew that in time of peril the Florentines had been in the habit of buying their safety with money, full weight; intimidation was his weapon, and while Soderini trembled, Machiavelli admired.

Had Cesare enjoyed freedom of action the outlook for Florence would have been grim. But the Republic appealed once more to the King of France; and as Louis considered the Borgias' ambitions excessive, he ordered Cesare and Vitellozzo to leave the Florentines in peace and to restore Arezzo. Simultaneously 'the bowels came out of the frying-pan'.

Meanwhile, the siege of Pisa was still being prosecuted, but the mercenaries were half-hearted about it. Knowing as they did that Spaniards were defending the city, they refused to go into the trenches and their craven attitude was contagious. The popular government in Florence had hitherto been tacking about among the reefs, and had not fallen foul of the wars that were then ravaging Italy, wars in which Frenchmen, Germans, Spaniards and Swiss were at grips; but Machiavelli, one of the most clear-sighted observers of the age, guessed that such good fortune would scarcely last. His own country, compared with others, appeared very weak, and he wanted to reorganize its military forces.

Mercenary soldiers he had seen at work, and he had a horror of these bands of ruffians carrying standards, these ribald soldiers who were always gambling until the moment for action, when they would take good care not to be killed. They had corrupted the art of war, they were a State within the State. Only a national army, he believed, could really protect the country; and it should be an infantry militia. Owing to recent changes in modes of fighting, cavalry brigades had lost their former pre-eminence. So Machiavelli turned recruiting-officer, and in February 1506 there marched through the streets of Florence 400 militia-men, dressed in white doublets, blue and red trunk-hose, blue berets, and iron breastplates, and armed each with a spear and a carbine.[1] 'That is what's called a battalion. They are led by a constable, who teaches them the drill.' They received regular pay, were required to report as soon as they were summoned, and were subject to punishment if they blasphemed when playing cards or dice.

Florence was proud of this innovation, 'the finest array of men that was ever seen in our city'. In December the 'Nine of the Militia' were appointed, and Machiavelli became their 'chancellor'. He counted on increasing the ranks of this embryo so as to withstand the Spaniards whom he feared more than the French; and he hoped that these trained peasants would conduct themselves better than mercenaries.

Soderini was now favoured by good fortune. Cesare Borgia had departed from the scene after his father the Pope; Piero de' Medici had been drowned in the Garigliano; and on June 2, 1509, after an agreement with Louis XII, Pisa was given back. What an event! Everyone in Florence 'is mad with joy, bonfires are blazing all over the city. You can imagine what it will be at night.' Hatred between the two cities had been intense, as one may judge from the following example. A Pisan had ventured into the Florentine camp to beg bread for his dying mother. They gave him some. But when the dying woman saw it was white bread, and heard where it had come from, she cried: 'Take it away. Take away the bread of those accursed Florentines. I would rather die.'

But once victorious, the accursed Florentines displayed good sense and generosity. There was no violence, no cries of *Marzocco*! Offences were pardoned and property restored. The Pisans could hardly believe their eyes. Wrote Masi:

They greatly feared that Pisa would be sacked. They never believed they would escape. They said: 'If we had thought you would pardon us in this way, you may be sure we should never have come to the point of being ready to die of hunger, as we were.' And they also said: 'We were accustomed to being the greatest and most cruel enemies of Florence. Now we wish to be the best and most affectionate friends whom the Florentines have under their jurisdiction.'

---

[1] Italian *schioppetto*, a sort of blunderbuss. (Translator)

Soderini was now at the zenith of his reputation; he had established peace, restored the finances and recovered Pisa. This newly won prosperity was however accompanied by a relaxation of morals which shocked the disciples of Savonarola. The courtesans emerged from the quarters that had been assigned to them and openly walked the streets, dressed as nuns or escorted by a respectable-looking widow; they were taken for honest women. But they adopted a haughty air and threatened the authorities by means of their hired bullies.[1] Young men, for their part, were displaying a more and more pronounced taste for celibacy; or, if they agreed to marry, they demanded a dowry so enormous that the number of marriageable girls was constantly increasing. But how could one remedy this state of affairs when, apart from the gonfaloniere, the government changed every two months?

The Florentines, on the other hand, were beginning to have had enough of this 'Great Council' and of a gonfaloniere who had been appointed for life and who thus barred the way to advancement. They told themselves they would be happier under a single master; many regretted the Medici; the lower classes remembered that under Lorenzo they had had more food and had enjoyed themselves; and in time of dearth women were heard crying out in the public squares: '*Palle e Pane*'—the balls (of the Medici arms) and bread.

Everything was moving toward a new crisis. After their Pyrrhic victory at Ravenna, in April 1512, the French had been obliged to abandon Lombardy under pressure of the Papal, Spanish and German armies, and Florence was to be the first victim of this reversal of the situation. She had refused to join the Holy League against France and had persisted in a pro-French attitude, which was unendurable. She would have to do penitence.

For the Medici, this was an excellent opportunity to return to their city, to take up the reins of government, and to recover their banking-business. The Spanish general Cardona now advanced

---

[1] *Ruffiano* (Italian)—whence our word—strictly means a procurer. But French *Ruffian* can mean either a rake, a debauchee, or a ruffian or bully— and usually the latter.   (Translator)

towards Tuscany, and with him Cardinal Giovanni, the one who had fled at the time of Charles VIII's arrival. At first the Florentines were beguiled with fair words; then they were ordered to get rid of the gonfaloniere Soderini and to recall the Medici, simply as citizens.

Florence refused to submit. Her forces had cut off Cardona's supply-lines, so that 'before three or four days were out, his troops must have died of hunger or been taken prisoners'. And the Florentine militia were ready.

The enemy was approaching Prato, the exquisite city whose cathedral now evokes the names of Donatello and Filippo Lippi; but, although superior in numbers, the Florentine militia, on whom Machiavelli pinned such hopes, broke and fled. The city was taken in a day, almost without a blow being struck. The sack, which began on August 30, 1512, went on for three weeks. Four thousand people perished. The inhabitants, not merely men but small babies, were burned alive like pigs. The barbarians who, it was said, included Moslems and infidels, 'did not spare the young girls who were sheltering in sacred places: churches and convents witnessed scenes of lechery and sacrilege'. Those fugitives who had escaped came pouring into Florence, 'poor women with girls and boys, staggering under their poverty'; and there was no house that was not lodging from eight to twenty peasants who had fled from the fury of the soldiers.

Giovanni's cousin, Cardinal Giulio de' Medici, felt obliged to confess that victory had not been won without some cruelty and slaughter; but he added: 'The taking of Prato, a rough and speedy business which has caused me some grief, will have had the good effect of serving as an example and of inspiring terror.'

Meanwhile panic reigned in Florence. There were omens of catastrophe. When the Prato gate was struck by lightning the golden lilies of the arms of France were shattered, which proved that the city was to pass under another master. The Palazzo della Signoria was abandoned and the prison-gates opened. And now the partisans of the Medici, together with the nobles who had been sedulouly courted by the Medici Bank, demanded Soderini's deposition. And he, treated even by his fellow-citizens as responsible for the defeat, left the city.

The Medici had triumphed. Escorted by a thousand lances, the whole family made its formal entry into Florence. At the head of the procession rode Cardinal Giovanni, and beside him his brother Giuliano, his nephew the young Lorenzo and his cousin Cardinal Giulio; behind them, two other nephews, Giuliano's bastard Ippolito and Cardinal Giulio's bastard Alessandro. It was like seeing a genealogical tree. The Medici Bank, arrayed in scarlet, took possession of its old quarters, and Florence paid for the loss of her independence with 150,000 ducats.

The Palazzo della Signoria was thrown open to the condottieri and the mercenaries who pillaged it and defiled the hall of the Great Council which Savonarola had built. In the piazza of Santa Maria del Fiore, the Spaniards, 'those white Moors, those renegades, more cruel than the Devil', sold the booty they had seized at Prato. But they did not always profit from this ill-acquired wealth. Sometimes the goods were stolen or even recovered by the rightful owners; sometimes the soldiers were killed. On September 12th twenty Spaniards were struck down and rifled near Florence by masked men; and it was found that they had on them several thousand florins and letters of exchange for Spain.

These were the last stirrings of independence. A Republic of a popular complexion seemed an anomaly among a number of monarchical states which were struggling for predominance in Italy. When the great bell of the Palazzo summoned the people 'to parliament', scarcely one twenty-fifth of the population is said to have presented itself. The exits from the square were guarded by Mediceans, and the new régime now inaugurated was merely a restoration of the old tyranny accompanied by the caricature of a constitution. Twelve citizens from each quarter, annually elected, were supposed to represent Florence. Actual authority was exercised by Giulio de' Medici, who obeyed the instructions of Cardinal Giovanni.

One must recognize that the latter, while expressing regret for the massacre of Prato,[1] treated his country without tenderness; but, after all, he and his family had been expelled eighteen years before; and, as he was no saint, he meant to show who was master. So the Medici 'came back like foxes', and the Florentines prepared to fall again under the yoke. Some even congratulated themselves. Business would no doubt prosper; and the cry of *Palle* went up as in former times.[2]

*   *   *   *

[1] We were told above that it was Giulio who had expressed these regrets. Perhaps Giovanni had as well? But it scarcely seems to matter.   (Translator)

[2] The Republicans did not, however, regard themselves as beaten. In February 1513 Pietro-Paolo Boscoli, a Florentine of good family, conspired against the Medici. The plot failed; and the last hours of Boscoli, who had been condemned to death, are a revelation of the state of mind and disquiet of a cultured Florentine of the Renaissance who had undergone both the mystical influence of Savonarola and the influence of pagan Humanism.

'Ah!' said he to his friend Luca della Robbia (a member of the famous family of artists, although himself a philologist), ah! drive from my head the image of Roman Brutus, so that I may follow the way of a Christian!'

Luca replied that the characters of the old Romans have come down to us, not as they truly were, but idealized. Boscoli strove to bend his reason to belief, but, as he knew only the Lord's Prayer and the Ave Maria, he wanted to spend a month with good monks in order to become a good Christian. A Dominican of Savonarola's convent explained to him the ideas of Aquinas on tyrannicide. 'Father,' replied Boscoli, 'do not waste your time. The philosophers can give me courage to die: do you aid me to suffer death for the love of Christ.'

Although he could conceive the divinity of Our Lord, he could not manage to understand His humanity; he wished especially to see the Man in the God, 'as if Jesus Christ were coming out of a forest to meet him'. Before his execution he was served with a solid meal, which he did not refrain from; but then he lamented over it like a child. 'I have eaten salted meats so that it now seems impossible to unite my spirit with God. . . . God have pity on me, for these people have loaded me with food. . . .'

When the executioner was preparing to wield the axe, Boscoli asked him to wait a moment, because, since his sentence had been read to him, he had not ceased to aspire to complete reconciliation with God; but at this moment he hoped to devote himself entirely. Then the axe fell.

He was thirty-two years of age; short-sighted, but admired for his handsome fair hair.

In March 1513 a great piece of news arrived by the telegraph of those days, a chain of beacons. Cardinal Giovanni had just been elected Pope and had assumed the name of Leo X.

Florence went mad with joy. This was the first Medici Pope. 'People played the fool without respect of age or sex.' The cry of *Palle* was louder than ever, bells rang and bonfires were lit on every side. 'In the Mercato Nuovo the young fellows tore boards and planks from the establishments of the silk-merchants and the bankers, so that by next morning not a single roof belonging to the Vaccheraccia and the Calimala was not broken and burned. And if the authorities had not intervened, no doors or roofs would have remained. This went on for three days.'

The shops were empty, church bells rang for *gloria*, carbines were discharged and trumpets sounded, while fires burned on the summits of the towers and on the campanile of Santa Maria del Fiore. The whole city was topsy-turvy with noise and smoke. Every evening a triumphal car was drawn by oxen from the Medici gardens in the Piazza San Marco to the Via Larga; the praises of the new pontiff were sung, and then the car and garlands were set on fire.

The Medici had wisely shut their palace, but from the upper windows they scattered ducats by the hundred. These had been contained in napkins of cloth of silver; when each one was empty, it was dropped too, and the people disputed the fragments among themselves. Masi says that over 10,000 ducats were distributed, and more than twelve silver cloths, not counting berets, cloaks, etc. For three days barrels of red and white wine, and baskets of bread, stood in the street, and people took what they wanted. Florence seemed to be mad with joy. Condemned prisoners were pardoned, and everyone lauded his Holiness Leo X, 'our Florentine', for his goodness and civility. Far away was the time when young Cardinal Giovanni had prayed on his knees, on the balcony of his palace, trembling with fear.

But now the frenzy of delight was over, and Florence settled down to enjoy the amenities of Medicean supremacy. This was represented first by Giuliano, the Pope's brother, a melancholy man of thirty-four whose poor constitution was further weakened by debauchery. He was however a witty person and a friend of writers and artists.[1] And after him came Lorenzo, the Pope's nephew, a young fellow of twenty; swarthy and rather fierce-eyed, fond of hunting and something of a libertine.

The Pope entertained few illusions about these two kinsmen. 'I have', he said, 'appointed two inexperienced captains; if they encounter any great difficulty, I don't know how they will manage.'

Lorenzo had however received good advice as to the most opportune way of treating the Florentines. It was advisable in the first place to organize a number of gracious ceremonies; next, to invite people to dinner in the city or the country. Graciousness and generous entertaining would win him sympathy. Then, in accordance with time-honoured procedure, Lorenzo went every morning to the Palazzo, accompanied by young nobles and armed attendants, and kept up the comedy of a 'Republican' government. He assisted ambitious Florentines to advance their interests in Rome, in civil or ecclesiastical careers. To have a fellow-citizen as Pope was a great advantage.

No longer was Florence the city of the 'weepers'. Gay mascarades were organized, like that of the Diamond with Giuliano, and that of the *Broncone*[2] with Lorenzo. Although the Pope governed from a distance, he treated Florence as his private estate, and his tyranny was absolute. But, as a philosophical contemporary observed, what could one do? All kingdoms and communities now have a savour of tyranny, and one can live decently under them, provided that the ruler who has usurped power is a good sort of man. Now Leo X is a rich lord, still young and notoriously generous. The merchants saw a prospect of good business under his pontificate.

Optimism prevailed; but Machiavelli was right when he said: 'They will cry: "Peace! Peace!"; but there will be no peace.'

In 1515, after their victory at Marignano, the French reappeared

---

[1] He had known Da Vinci.

[2] A *Broncone* is a large vine trained up a stout wooden prop. (Translator)

on the horizon; and to prevent their coming into Tuscany, where they were too popular, Leo X went to meet their king, François I, at Bologna. On November 30th he passed through Florence, where the *festaiuoli* surpassed themselves in organizing a reception. The Porta San Pietro Gattolini and the Porta Santa Trinità were adorned with columns 'in such fair array that never could any architect in the world have made the like'. There was also an obelisk like the one in Rome. Four triumphal arches stood in the Piazza della Signoria, and everywhere were porticoes and columns which looked as though made of marble. 'You feasted your eyes on them all day long, you could not take your eyes off them.'

Received by the whole body of the clergy and the religious, and escorted by sixty young men wearing a livery of purple cloth brocaded with gold, the Pope appeared under a superb canopy adorned with his coat-of-arms. Under another canopy the Holy Sacrament was borne by a beautiful white mare which, it was said, had never carried a rider and whose blanket and bridle were embroidered with pearls and gold. Behind the Pope eighteen Cardinals, mounted on mules, rode two by two; then came Bishops and Prelates, and the Swiss Guard, 150 strong.

After passing under the triumphal arches by the Signoria, Leo reached Santa Maria del Fiore, where the architect Jacopo Sansovino had built a special façade which Andrea del Sarto had adorned with 'stories in chiaroscuro'. The population gaped in wonder at this masterpiece. On the processional route, at street corners and by gateways where girls and children were looking on, the Pope's friends scattered money far and wide. In the Cathedral Square, a gilt horse had been set up, trampling under foot a giant armed with a shield and gilded like the horse. It was here that Leo dismounted and took up his quarters in 'the Pope's Room', which had been hung with tapestries, while a vast blue canopy, decorated with his arms, had been stretched overhead.

The scene after dark was fairylike. Chinese lanterns lit with tallow candles, shone from the loopholes in the towers and from all the windows in the campaniles and galleries ('which is prettier than torches and lasts longer'). It seemed as though the whole of Florence was alight, with smoke and flames; and in fact the trades-men's tents near the Baptistery were destroyed by fire. Over 2,000 workmen had been employed to construct 'these things that pass like a shadow and with which one might have raised a temple to the glory of God; however, it means money for the poor artisans, and the spectacle is such that no city could ever have organised the like'. Leo X was not niggardly, especially with other people's money. The Signoria was out of pocket to the tune of 50,000 ducats, and more.

When in December 1515, after signing an agreement with François I, the Pope returned to Florence, the festivities consisted mainly of races that were run along the Via Larga, not only the traditional *palio*, but races in the Roman manner, between boys, or girls, or old men, sometimes on horseback, sometimes on donkeys. All this amused the populace. And the new rulers con-trived many ingenious entertainments. One day, the car of Bacchus would advance along the street, the god himself bestrid-ing a cask of wine, while this cask and a huge pot of macaroni were surrounded by buffoons who kept dipping in both of them, while making friendly gestures to the crowd. On another day, a tourney was held in the Piazza Santa Croce, which was intersected by a diagonal palisade. Or again there was bull-fighting, the bulls being attacked with short swords or spears; and sometimes a great procession of the kind that Savonarola had organized, for example, when the Pope proclaimed a Holy War against the Infidel. Then Florence would fast, butchers and greengrocers would be idle, and the Mercato Vecchio deserted; but such austerities were not of long duration.

Giuliano de' Medici had married a Frenchwoman. The young Lorenzo, following his example, obtained the hand of Madeleine de la Tour d'Auvergne, and thus the family of the old merchant Cosimo lost its homely and civic character. Allied with royal dynasties and surrounded by a brilliant court, it had acquired a demeanour truly princely. There was no more of hail-fellow-well-met simplicity as in the days of Lorenzo the Magnificent.

At a cost of 500,000 florins Leo X carved out a principality for his nephew Lorenzo, who thus became Duke of Urbino. But the Medici of that time seemed fated to die young. After the passing of Giuliano, who died of consumption in 1516, and then of Lorenzo, the government passed into the hands of Cardinal Giulio,[1] who had already played an active part in the restoration of the Medici.

This new head of the Republic was a patient and affable man who lived unostentatiously in the midst of his notables. He appeared to leave the magistrates in the full enjoyment of liberty and not, like his predecessors, to be making use of arbitrary elections. He reorganized the State finances, and built new fortifications. 'Our city', observed a contemporary, 'was never governed with a greater appearance of courtesy and freedom, and never was the Principate so well concealed.'

But everything passes away, and this was especially true of Florence. Twelve years later the fortifications which had been built by Cardinal Giulio were to serve against the same Giulio, who was now Pope Clement VII.

[1] An illegitimate son of the Giuliano de' Medici who had been murdered in 1478 at the time of the conspiracy of the Pazzi.

CHAPTER XIV

THE INTELLECTUALS

The educational system – Petrarch eclipses Dante – Opposition of the humanists to the vernacular – That there were not two renaissances – The superstition of antiquity – Some portraits of literary men: Poggio, Filelfo, Poliziano and Pico della Mirandola

L ET us now turn our backs on wars and rumours of wars and seek out a quieter atmosphere—if that is possible—in the garden of the letters and the arts.

'All men by nature desire knowledge and, as St Jerome saith, the learned and the lettered are like stars in the firmament.' This opinion of Bisticci the bookseller was shared by his compatriots, and the organization of teaching was one of their concerns. Bologna had preceded Florence in the matter of University education,[1] and it was only in the fourteenth century that we find a Florentine university, based on compulsory education and supported by an annual subsidy of 2,500 florins.

The Readers, whose terms of appointment were temporary, led a wandering life like that of actors, passing from one *Studio* to another: they were pedlars of knowledge, although they sometimes settled in one place. In 1402 the Florentine *Studio* had a staff of twenty Readers. A good half of them lectured on Law (could it be otherwise in a city devoted to trade and politics?); some six, on Medicine, Surgery and Anatomy (and for them were reserved the corpses taken down from the gallows); and others on Logic and Philosophy. But the most sought-after chair was that of Rhetoric. The Readers were ill-paid. It is worth noting that

[1] And so had Padua. By the end of the fifteenth century Padua had taken the lead and was to become, between about 1590 and 1640, the leading University in western Europe. (Translator)

they depended wholly on the civic government and not on the Church.

Thanks to the Carnival, Midsummer Day, the sixty Church festivals, not to speak of Sundays and the autumn vacation, the students were not overworked. They wore the regulation gowns, of a common black cloth, and sat in the great Hall of the *Studio*, not on straw as in other Universities but on benches. When examinations were due they rode on horseback to invite their friends and acquaintances to attend the oral tests, and in the event of passing, they left the *Studio* to the sound of fifes and trumpets, and distributed wine and sweetmeats. Never would a Florentine neglect an opportunity for rejoicing.

What spirit presided over this educational system? Renaissance Italy, owing to her advanced culture, was then regarded as the queen of nations. Heir and descendant of the Romans, she waxed great in pride and held in low esteem the barbarians beyond the Alps. Petrarch, for instance, barely agreed to consider the French as slightly less barbarous than the other nations, who were no more than a horde of Scythians.

Swollen with their learning, proud that they could think and write in the atmosphere of Antiquity, the 'Humanists' strutted about among its vestiges as through the streets of a vast Pompeii. 'We', they proclaimed, 'are bringing the dead to life.' Florence contained the best known of these humanists who professed a kind of scorn for Dante and reproached him with having written his poem in everyday Italian, instead of using the noble idiom of Virgil. One of them, it is said, tried to translate the *Divine Comedy* into Latin hexameters[1] without suspecting that this would condemn it to rot in the cemetery of dead epics.

[1] This may be an allusion to Giovanni da Serravalle, Bishop of Fermo, who actually did translate Dante's poem into Latin, at the instance of the Bishops of Bath and Salisbury. Monsieur Dubreton calls him an 'insondable sot'; but it must be remembered that in the fourteenth century few Englishmen or Frenchmen knew Italian, whereas all learned men knew Latin. And a Latin version was therefore the only reasonable way of spreading a knowledge of the *Divine Comedy* outside Italy. See the present translator's *Italian Influence in English Poetry*, 1955, p. 103.   (Translator)

In their serene self-confidence these learned fogies neglected the incomparable poem that touches Heaven and Earth, the marvellous fountainhead of mystical heroism; they abandoned it to bakers, cobblers and people of that description; yet, after all, Dante had wished to be their familiar because he spoke like them and—at least in his poetry—appeared to turn up his nose at the cult of Latin. But the people, who were wiser than the pedants, accepted the gift. They adopted Dante, they sang his *canzoni*, they liked those passages in the *Commedia* that reflected their own daily life; such as the verse about the bell which seems to weep over the dying day:

Che paia 'l giorno pianger che si muore.

But the writer whose fame then eclipsed Dante's was Petrarch, the complete Roman living in the fourteenth century and yet appearing to relive the life of the ancient world which he had unearthed. The ancient Roman; and yet the first modern man, according to Renan; and he was modern in this sense that he knew how to make his way in the world, to win favour as well as money, and to gain personal prestige. He succeeded so well indeed that he was crowned with laurel and that all the fanatics of Rome bowed humbly before him. But here is the beauty of it. Petrarch's Latin works are now only known to scholars and historians. It is only his poems, written in the 'vulgar' tongue and on which he appeared to set little value, that are familiar to posterity; for this epicurean who liked his ease and comfort was an artist; he sang his verses to the lute, and they were so moving that he inoculated Italian literature with a chronic malady, 'a kind of recurrent fever', which is called Petrarchism.

Another and more attractive writer, the Tuscan Boccaccio, exemplifies the same phenomenon. He also wished to live the life of the ancient world. Setting out ardently in quest of manuscripts, he made his way to Monte Cassino and there asked to see the Library. A Benedictine Father showed him a frail ladder which led up to an attic that did not even boast a door. Inside lay piles of mutilated manuscripts; sometimes the margins had been cut off, sometimes sections had been removed. He asked the reasons for such vandalism. 'Two of my brethren,' replied the monk, 'wishing to earn a little money, have used this torn parchment to make psalters and breviaries which they sell to women and children.'

Weeping with indignation, Boccaccio pieced together the fragments and continued his search. Full of enthusiasm for all that pertained to ancient Rome, he wrote learned treatises. But a day came when he felt tired and then, tempted to give rein to his fantasy, he composed the *Decameron* in Italian—the book that was to bring him fame.

One of the humanists said: 'We use Italian for writings which we do not want to transmit to future ages.' It was the exact contrary that took place.

Greek was unknown in the fourteenth century. 'My Homer', wrote Petrarch, 'lies voiceless beside me, and I am deaf beside him. Yet I rejoice at the sight of him, I often embrace him.'

This devotion was rewarded in the following century by the Greeks who had emigrated to Italy. Old Gemisto, whom they called 'Plato', lectured and indoctrinated his pupils with the ardour of a youth of twenty—wonderful in a greybeard of eighty-three. To Chrysoloras of Byzantium, Florentine church-men and patricians, old and young, listened as one might listen to a being from another planet. And great was the prestige surrounding the learned Argyropoulos, a violent and cross-grained eccentric who ate and drank like a trooper. Finally, after these notable pioneers, came a whole proletariat of scholars driven out by the Turks after the taking of Constantinople in 1453, poor devils who found jobs as scribes, copyists and school-masters. 'After the foundering of Greece,' wrote a contemporary, 'all the learned men of that country took refuge in Florence as in a sheltered haven.'

Very soon the children of the nobility were speaking the idiom of Sophocles so correctly that you would not believe Athens had been destroyed and occupied by the barbarians. 'Athens has emigrated to Florence, bringing all her baggage and her very soil; Florence has totally absorbed her.' The words are those of a humanist obsessed by the literary point of view; but they are relatively correct.

After the true Aristotle—not Aristotle adulterated by Arabic commentators—had been discovered, it was the turn of the 'divine Plato'. He was regarded as a herald of the Christ. We have already encountered his high priest, Marsilio Ficino, in the entourage of Lorenzo the Magnificent. Ficino was a puny little man with a slight stammer, a gentle and melancholy creature who explained and dilated on the master's words from the pulpit of the church of which he was a canon. Thus it was that Plato became Christianized. Lamps burned before his bust, he was depicted side by side with the Apostles, festivals were celebrated in his honour, and his bust was crowned amid the chanting of *Lauds* and *canzoni*. There was even, later on, a question of including extracts from his work among the passages prescribed to be read on Sundays. Canon Ficino would begin his discourse, not with 'My very dear brethern in Jesus Christ', but with 'My very dear ones in Plato'. Pagan thought was adapted in this way to the requirements of Christian dogma, and the mystical soul of Ficino found satisafaction in the result.

*   *   *   *

Historians have told us there were two Renaissances, the pagan and the Christian, but the distinction seems rather theoretical. In the Middle Ages it was the Church that had preserved the patrimony of the ancient world, and even in Florence there was no lack of monks who were humanists. Such were the Dominicans of Santa Maria Novella and the Franciscans of Santa Croce. What is true is that between the humanists and the Church there was, if not overt opposition, at least a tacit aversion. The champions of Antiquity imagined that they had renewed the face of the world and rescued philosophy from the divagations of the Scholastics. In reality they were merely turning in a circle of their own. They strung words together, apostrophized their masters, quoted them on every pretext, imitated the periods of Cicero: they in fact thought only of the form and counted the substance for nought. Anything was good provided it smacked of Greek or Latin. 'They have made themselves so entirely the slaves of the Ancients and have so utterly subjugated the freedom of their minds that they are not only averse to stating anything that is contrary to the views of the Ancients but they dare advance nothing that has not already been said by them.' So Savonarola informs us, and it was true.

For the use of the Florentines who had to speak in the civic councils or at public meetings, the rules of declamation, with the appropriate attitudes and gestures, were fixed in accordance with ancient models. You might hear the announcement of an engagement beginning with: 'Aristotle, the celebrated Peripatetic, says . . .' Another kind of speech would open with: 'Publius Cornelius Scipio . . .' It was a pellmell of literary reminiscences and commonplaces which were thought rarities because they had been dug up out of an ancient writer. There was not an image but had a learned source. 'We, Cicero and ourselves . . .' There was nothing further to add.

All these rhetoricians were wearing blinkers which separated them from life and nature. Originality in their eyes lay in not being original, in copying a model so accurately that, from a certain angle, humanism looked like the occupation of literary undertakers. Sincerity, a sense of the picturesque, a taste for colour, all the richest elements that we find in the chronicles and the *novelle*, counted for nothing with these fanatics. What they wrote was in contradiction with the facts of life, their works tell us nothing about the age they lived in and so contribute nothing to history.

Possessed of a measureless vanity, completely out of touch with the *profanum vulgus* and persuaded that he and his like were the élite, the humanist became a sort of literary condottiere, prepared to serve those who would pay him the highest wage. He was indifferent to all questions of politics, religion and morals, and his own morals were usually depraved (with a view to imitating the Ancients). His main object was to win favour and money.

Deeply jealous of his colleagues, he disparaged and slandered them when he could, and he and they bandied ferocious insults and even blows on occasion. You would think you were in a badly run boarding-school, and there was in fact among these scholars so much childishness that you might have taken them for ill-bred schoolboys.

The passion for recovering the smallest vestiges of the ancient world had one curious effect: it prevented the Florentines from being the pioneers of printing. They revered Greek and Roman manuscripts as their great ancestors had revered the relics of the Holy Land. They too were Crusaders in their way, pilgrims in quest of the Holy Grail of ancient learning. One recalls the experience of Boccaccio on Monte Cassino. But while two German monks were introducing printing at Subiaco, the Florentines seemed to take no interest in this revolutionary invention. It was not until 1471 that a goldsmith and engraver named Bernardo Cennini, when examining some books that had come from beyond the Alps, had an intuition as to the methods and technique of this new art. He cut his own type, and in the first book he published, the *Commentaries on Virgil*, printed these words, instinct with ingenuous pride: 'To the mind of a Florentine, nothing is difficult.' Later, in the middle of the sixteenth century, the Dutchman Lawrence Torrens, known as Torrentino, was invited to Florence by the Grand Duke Cosimo de' Medici, and it was he who printed Vasari, Guicciardini, Villani and others.

The old humanists ended by forming a class apart. Later still, when their fame had evaporated, they ceased to be poets and orators in princely courts to become overseers in printing establishments. But the taste for culture in Florence remained as lively as ever. It was a merchant who wrote: 'There is as much difference between a man with literary culture and a man without it as between a real man and a painting of one.' We read in a banker's diary: 'I recall today, this 14th of May 1503, how I promised our brother Andrea that I would give him a new pair of hose if, every morning and also in the evening at table, he would read to me some lesson in Latin and in verse, and now, after two months, I have to give him the said hose, and thus I have concluded my bargain with him.' In the eyes of this Florentine attention to business should not be allowed to prejudice the adorning of one's mind.

*   *   *   *

Let us now evoke the memory of a few literary men who played an important part in the daily life of Florence.

Leonardo Bruni had been an almost penniless student before becoming a private coach and tutor. But he attained something like glory by perpetrating a history of the Florentine Republic in Latin (1439). He had honoured his country, and was rewarded by exemption from tolls and taxes, both for himself and his heirs. Henceforth he was to be seen conversing with other luminaries and discussing questions of grammar and literature in the Piazza della Signoria, under the Loggia of the Pisans or in some bookshop. People waited for his arrival and hung on his words as on an oracle. A Spaniard once went down on his knees before Bruni and was only with difficulty induced to stand up.

Though rather small, Bruni made the most of his stature. Clad in a scarlet cloak, open at one side, and falling to his heels; with fur-trimmed sleeves, and a pinkish hood round which the *foggia* was rolled, he passed slowly and majestically through the streets. As his early life had been difficult, he was churlish, laconic, touchy and avaricious; but he knew Greek, and Florentines and foreigners alike revered him as a new Socrates. When he died, in 1444, he received honours befitting an ancient sage. His body was covered with a cloth of black silk; on this was placed a copy of the History of Florence; and from a nearby rostrum his colleague Manetti delivered a Ciceronian discourse in which he saluted 'the luminous star of Latinity'. Then in presence of the assembled notables and people, the head of Leonardo Bruni (that head which had given birth to seventy-four books) was crowned with a laurel wreath.

Bruni represents the pontifical type of humanist. There were

(*above*) Festival in the Piazza della Signoria

10. Frescoes by the school of Vasari in the Palazzo Vecchio

(*below*) Jousting in the Piazza S. Croce

(*above*) Procession in the Piazza del Duomo

11. Frescoes by the school of Vasari

(*right*) Mercato Vecchio (the old Market)

volcanic types, and among these Poggio[1] occupies the first rank.

His parents who came from near Florence had been ruined by the money-lenders, and he himself made a living by copying books, as he had a beautiful hand. He learned Latin and Greek almost without a master and created such an impression that the Papal Curia employed him as secretary for official correspondence. His passion for Antiquity was sincere. When he sat on a fragment of marble from the Tarpeian Rock and gazed on the ruins of the Capitol and the broken columns half-buried under brushwood or piles of refuse, he would be seized by a sort of vertigo and such thoughts possessed him that he spoke of Rome in accents that make one think of Montaigne and Chateaubriand.

Before entering the offices of the Curia this robust and impetuous young man had travelled in search of manuscripts; he had pushed his enquiries as far as England. Life here seemed very painful. The islanders would spend four hours at table; they did nothing but eat and drink, and Poggio was obliged to bathe his eyes in cold water so as not to fall asleep. But he discovered ten of Cicero's discourses in a monastery.

Although a Papal official, he was definitely anticlerical; to make people laugh he did not hesitate to ridicule the ceremonies of the Church. He had no gift for pretence or diplomacy. But all this did not prevent him, in his will, from asking that a hundred masses should be said for his soul, and a chapel served by monks founded for the purpose.

He was a great woman-hunter and boasted of his 'contraband' exploits. His bastards were conspicuously numerous about town, and when Cardinal Cesarini—who was however a very broad-minded man—reproached him, he replied: 'I have sons, which is very respectable in a layman; and I live without a wife according

---

[1] Poggio Bracciolini (1380-1459) came to London in 1418, at the invitation of Cardinal Henry Beaufort, Bishop of Winchester, who had held out the hope of considerable emoluments. He returned to Italy early in 1423. There are scattered, through his writings, a few interesting remarks on English social customs. (Translator)

G

to the general custom of the clergy.' By his mistress Lucia he had twelve sons and two daughters. Cosimo de' Medici exempted him from taxation on account of his merits! But Poggio got tired of concubinage and in 1435 married the Vaggia, a Florentine of eighteen. 'As God was merciful to me when I departed from the straight path,' he wrote to Cesarini, 'He will pour out His mercy more abundantly now that I have returned to it.' He was fifty-five at this time. At the age of seventy-three he returned to Florence and lived there as a philosopher surrounded by his progeny.

This patriarch was violently abusive, ever ready to attack any who contradicted him with invective or obscenity. 'Stinking, blear-eyed satyr, ass on two legs', he would shout; and the other would pay him back in the same coin. It made no matter: Poggio was gay, one was not bored in his company. While in the Vatican he had devised the *Bugiale*, full of hoaxes and humbug, and here too he had written the *Facetiae*, which alone have survived from the wreckage of his other writings.

These humanists were colourful enough, and Francesco Filelfo not less so than the others. He had been born near Ancona in 1398, his father a monk, his mother a tripe-seller—according to Poggio. He had studied at Padua, then gone to Greece; and from Greece he brought back manuscripts and also a wife, Teodora, the daughter of the learned Chrysoloras. On his appearance in Florence he was regarded as the most elegant of Latinists and the best of Greek scholars. People stopped in the street to admire his young wife and his magnificent beard. The most fashionable ladies stood aside for him: he was one of the marvels of the world. Though still young, he accepted such homage as his rightful due; had he been crowned with laurel, he could not have made a braver show. He thought that if the stones of Florence could speak, they would proclaim his glory.

His colleagues were unwilling to tolerate such conceit. They taunted him, they worked also to prejudice Cosimo de' Medici against him. One morning as Filelfo was on his way to the *Studio*, where he was a professor, a bravo disguised as a tradesman attacked him with a naked sword; but Filelfo dealt him such a buffet that he drew off. Enquiries revealed that he was a well-known bandit named Filippo and that he had been hired by Girolamo Broccardo, a student who hated Filelfo; but the latter believed that the Medici were at the back of it all. It was at this time (1438) that, as we have seen, Cosimo was exiled in consequence of a revolution. Filelfo was jubilant. A year later Cosimo returned, and Filelfo fled. 'Ah! if I had remained', he said, 'it would have been good-bye to the Muses! good-bye to Filelfo!'

To Siena, where he had taken refuge, he was followed by Filippo, who kept shadowing him but so clumsily that he was arrested and tortured, and he ended by confessing that he had meant to murder Filelfo. His right hand was cut off.

Filelfo now conspired with a number of Florentine exiles and they hired a Greek named Antonio Maria of Athens to get rid of Cosimo, of the student Girolamo and of Carlo Marsuppini, a humanist whom Filelfo loathed. The Greek excused himself as regards Cosimo, who was too well guarded, but he undertook to tackle the other two. He proceeded to Florence and met them; but as the opportunity for killing them was unfavourable, he calmly proposed that they should kill Filelfo. As a result of this he was arrested and tortured, and his hand was cut off; but his confession enabled the authorities to condemn Filelfo, who was to have his tongue cut out, if he was unlucky enough to be caught.

Filelfo, to keep face, now composed *The Book of Exile*, in which he described the Medici as tavern-keepers, promoters of gambling, usurers, traitors, foxes, tigers, etc. . . . . In reality he was living in terror of poison and the stiletto. Poggio, hired to attack him, loaded him with abuse and alleged horrors about his private life. But the exile knew the game and did not worry. Two years later he made his peace with Cosimo, because he preferred calm and luxury. He needed four maids, two serving-men, a comfortable house, choice food and wine, silk raiment and fine furs. He also maintained a number of courtesans whom he called his Muses.

But for all this money was needed, and Filelfo sold his pen to the highest bidder. His prose and verse were no more than commodities, and he traded on that thirst for immortality which was felt then by all the Italian tyrants, great or small.

After the death of his wife Teodora, Filelfo wondered whether it would not be expedient to renounce the world and embrace an ecclesiastical career. He raised the matter with the then Pope, Eugenius IV, who however regarded him as mad and did not trouble to reply. Having therefore to remain in the world, Filelfo married Orsina Orsaga, of a noble family of Milan, and she added three daughters and a son to the already considerable brood sprung from the first marriage—not to mention the bastards. On Orsina's death, Filelfo's thoughts turned once again to the Church; but the question was now more complicated. According to canon law a second marriage constituted a bar to the taking of orders, unless one obtained an apostolic dispensation. Now the new Pope, Nicholas V, was a friend of the humanists, and Filelfo besought him in Latin verse to grant the dispensation.

'From my tenderest years', he wrote, 'I have longed to renounce the vanities of this world and to dedicate my person to Christ, great Pilot of Olympus, and my Muse to the glory of Pope Nicholas.' After that, he thought, the Pope can scarcely do less than make me a Cardinal. 'I will always be heartily on his side.'

The notion of this Cardinal-Poet with his swarm of children no doubt appeared comical to Nicholas V, who, like his predecessor, remained silent. Filelfo waited, lost patience, and then, abandoning all hope of the purple, married for the third time. He wandered from Rome to Milan; he was not happy; he regretted Florence; and finally, after bestowing the warmest eulogies on Lorenzo de' Medici, the grandson of his old enemy, he received permission to return and was given a professorial appointment (1481). It was too late. He died almost as soon as he reached the city he had once adorned, leaving as his successor the humanist Giorgio Merula, whom he was kind enough to refer to as Merdula. He was eighty-three.

Coming now to Angelo Poliziano, we leave the band of the patriarchs.

He had been born in the charming Montepulciano, perched on

the hill above Lake Trasimene. As a poor student in Florence he was lucky enough to catch the eye of Lorenzo the Magnificent, who appointed him tutor to his sons, gave him a *studio* near the Cathedral and a villa at Fiesole. The half-famished student now put on flesh. He had a pronounced squint and was graced with an enormous hooked nose, the lips of a gourmand and the chin of a prelate. But his mind was of the keenest; he was 'subtly ambitious', severe in his judgment of other writers, not scrupling to plagiarize them on occasion, and astounding his listeners with stories from Herodotus which he passed off 'as fruits from his own garden'. He was always pretending to be poverty-stricken. But of all the humanists, this mountebank had the most exquisite feeling for poetry.[1] The popular festivals, the showy games of these burghers dressed up as paladins, he commemorated in Italian verse—in stanzas of which the form is charming and the content of small account. Spring, night, country-life, hunting, the house of Venus, the garden of love, and the tournament are his favourite subjects. Each stanza presents a little static world, posed like a model; and, as Francesco de' Sanctis has observed, the form is a description that melts away in notes of music. One can understand why artists were inspired by him.

Poliziano no more underestimated his talents than did Filelfo his. He let it be understood that thanks to him Florence had become a new Athens. But one day in 1494—he was then forty—when he had taken up his lute to sing the praises of a young man, he had a sudden attack of fever. Delirium followed, and he quickly passed away.

The noble Pico della Mirandola[2] was also mown down in the flower of his age. At the time of his birth, in 1463, a circular flame

---

[1] He used to say to Marsilio Ficino: 'Among the works of the Classics you seek for the true; I seek for the beautiful.' He wandered round Tuscany collecting popular turns of speech. He had a real feeling for classical beauty. It took him only a few days to improvise and compose the *Orfeo*, which was the first Italian drama (cf. Schillman, *History of Tuscan Civilisation*, p. 170).

[2] A well-known painting of the time is supposed to represent Ficino, Poliziano and Pico standing together.   (Translator)

had appeared above his head; it quickly vanished—a presage, people supposed, that the young Giovanni's life would be brilliant but transitory.

Moving from university to university, from Bologna to Paris, he early acquired a knowledge of Latin, Greek and Law. By the age of sixteen he was the most precocious of scholars; and the most voracious. A Jewish philosopher named Elias del Medigo taught him Hebrew and Arabic, and introduced him to the mysteries of the Cabbala. He defended at least nine hundred theses. When some of these involved him in charges of heresy, he fled to France. There he was arrested and spent some time in the fortress at Vincennes. Finally, after his release, he returned to Florence to resume his oriental studies.

People admired his great piety and his continence, for he appeared to be unmoved by the charms of the fair sex; and yet this semi-divine being, as Machiavelli described him, did not remain wholly exempt from human weakness. He became secretly involved with the wife of a grocer at Arezzo. On the grocer's death, the widow's kinsfolk married her to a very poor member of the Medici family. But Pico could not endure this misfortune and decided, in agreement with his mistress, to abduct her.

He set out for Arezzo accompanied by his secretary and a score of companions. On reaching the city he found his beloved waiting for him at the gate, took her up behind him and galloped off for Florence. But the town-guard, believing that the lady had been abducted without her consent, raised the alarm. The bells rang and the constables rode in pursuit and came up with the fugitives. The battle that followed left fifteen men on the field; but Pico escaped with his mistress and his secretary. They were however imprudent enought to halt at Marciano, where the authorities incarcerated them and sent the news to Florence.

Fortunately Lorenzo, who was ever magnificent, now saved the situation. He decided in his wisdom that the young lady could not have been unfaithful to a Medici—such a theory was untenable. It was only the secretary who had hatched the plot and Count Pico, who really knew nothing about it, had acted in all innocence.

Arezzo and Marciano would be free to punish the secretary if they wished, and the husband was to recover his wife.

This adventure cooled the young scholar's ardour. He punished himself with the scourge, thought of entering the order of St Dominic, became a devotee of Savonarola and plunged into Greek and cabbalistic speculations with such fervour that he died before he was thirty-two.

Many other men deserve a place in this gallery of scholars and bibliophiles. Such, for example, was Gianozzo Manetti, a former accountant in a bank. He had gradually become obsessed with books that were not accounts and had come to give his whole time to study. He rarely left his garden except to confer with colleagues at Santo Spirito. A great Hebrew scholar, he engaged the Jews in endless controversies. 'Take care, he told them, 'and look to your weapons, for I wish to attack you only with your own.' Unfortunately his enemies contrived to have him exorbitantly taxed, and though he tried not to take tragically 'this infirmity which is not mortal', he was obliged to go into exile. But, as Bisticci says, the more he was persecuted, the higher rose his fame. His son Agnolo was a prodigy, a marvellous polyglot and mathematician whom the merchants when in disagreement would come to consult.

To this list of highly endowed Florentines one should add others, such as Piero di Pazzi who was not merely a shrewd ambassador, but devoted himself to learning Petrarch by heart and who, while on the way to Fiesole or strolling round his estate at Trebbia, could recite to you the *Aeneid* in strong and musical accents. Another remarkable man was the astronomer Paolo Toscanelli, who set up a *gnomon* or sun-dial, which remained famous, on the cupola of Santa Maria del Fiore; and who contributed to Columbus's notion of undertaking his great voyage.

Is it surprising that strangers regarded Florence as the Mecca of learning?

One day a very dignified ecclesiastic wearing a violet cloak came into Bisticci's bookshop. It was John, Bishop of the Five Churches.

'Welcome!' cried Bisticci. 'Are you a Hungarian?'

Whereupon the Bishop embraced him warmly and declared that before returning home he was especially anxious to see the illustrious men of Florence. Bisticci therefore took him to Careggi where Cosimo de' Medici received him kindly and introduced Poggio and the celebrated intellectuals. The Bishop then visited the city and the Library, purchased Latin and Greek books without regard to the price and left money so that others could be procured for him. 'If', he said on leaving, 'if you wish to know what the Bishop of the Five Churches in Hungary is doing, know that he is translating Plotinus the Platonist.'

Another, and less well-to-do, Hungarian Bishop spent so much money on manuscripts that he found he had none left and was in despair. Fortunately Bisticci was at hand. The good bookseller busied himself with the matter, collected 200 ducats—for 'we must show that there are no lack of good men in Florence'—and brought the money to the Hungarian, who thus recovered his cheerfulness.

Before leaving the society of writers and scholars we should note that if Florence was the first city to adopt Latin, she was also the first to return to Italian, to the 'volgare' as it was called. The humanists had in the end wearied the public with their presumption, with their mania for posing as superior beings who had a monopoly of true culture. Alberti, it will be remembered, had already founded an academy which restored popular literature to the place it deserved. Lorenzo the Magnificent boasted of writing in *volgare*, 'in that language in which he had been born and nurtured'. And as the vogue of humanism declined, the star of Dante rose in the firmament. In 1481 he was illustrated by Botticelli, commented on in the *Studio*, and printed. His tomb at Ravenna was restored; and the Signoria, after raising the ban of exile which had darkened his memory, caused his effigy to be crowned in the baptistery of San Giovanni.

CHAPTER XV

LIVES OF THE ARTISTS

Professional training – Conscientiousness and simplicity –
Manners and morals – The painters: from Masaccio to
Gozzoli – Adventures of Filippo Lippi – Fra Angelico –
Botticelli and poetry – Andrea del Sarto – The sculptors:
Verrocchio, Donatello – The architects: Ghiberti, Brunel-
leschi – The universal quality of Florentine art

THE Renaissance, it has been said, aspired to become 'the
glory that was Greece and the grandeur that was Rome'.
This was especially true of the Florentine Renaissance. In
the fourteenth century, when the merchant Giovanni Villani was
standing one day before the ruins of Rome, he felt himself
'inspired to write the history of her daughter Florence, in honour
of God and of St John and to the glory of his city'. His nephew
Filippo, son of Matteo, found a pious consolation in recalling the
antiquities of Florence and the doings of her great men with a
view to purifying his own generation which seemed to him so
corrupt. These men played, in some sort, the part of a Herodotus.

A century later Matteo Palmieri extols the happiness of being
born in an age when the arts are more flourishing than has been
seen for a thousand years. In the sixteenth century Varchi boasts
of the excellence of these same arts which have enabled the
Florentines 'to adorn not only their own city but many others, for
their greater glory and profit'. All these chroniclers were proud
of their country.

The Florentines, like the Athenians before them, were merchants, and miserly ones; but this did not destroy the loftiness of
their conceptions. Accustomed as they were to live among bales
of wool and silk, they could, when they wanted, follow less
mundane instincts and apply themselves to great enterprises. The
Florentine had no mind for half-measures, and when it was a

G*

question of learning, and still more of beauty, the miser was ready to spend money, whether to pay a teacher or to buy a picture.

The art honoured in Florence was a trade; the artist, like the workman, had to undergo a long apprenticeship, and it took some time to pass from the status of *discepolo* to that of *ragazzo*, and from *ragazzo* to *maestro*.

When he was nearly eighty, the painter Cennino Cennini was imprisoned as a debtor in the *Stinche* and he occupied his time by writing a treatise on painting which is full of personal experiences (1437). The apprentice, as a very young boy, becomes a servant in the studio of a master who, for a year, teaches him the art of 'correct drawing on tablets', and then how to pick the colours, to make the sizing,[1] mix the paste, prepare and polish the panels. This goes on for six years. Six more years, even feast days, are devoted to learning all the varieties of colour, such as cinnabar, *minio*, *amatite*, dragon's blood; how to lay gold on fabrics, how to work in fresco. He must also learn a whole series of recipes, and Cennini is lavish of them. Nine chapters of his book deal with the way of laying on gold, seven tell you how to imitate velvet, how to make iridescent colours, and ultra-marine, and how to paint rivers and fishes. The old prisoner explains all this at great length and in meticulous detail, and ends by commending his soul to God, to the blessed Virgin and the Saints.

Most of the great Florentine artists passed through these grades. When they became masters they were treated as artisans; they received orders which they had to complete on a fixed day. They did not scorn to paint coffers or trays. Botticelli painted fabrics and standards in such a way that the colours would not run or fade.

The same conscientious simplicity is to be noted in the sculptors, who, even when their reputation was established, would make chandeliers or crests for helmets, or produce silver enamel-work. And the same applies to the architects. When the cupola of Santa Maria del Fiore was being built, Brunelleschi concerned himself

---

[1] Or 'size', i.e. the substance that is applied to the canvas, or other surface, before the paint is laid on. (Translator)

with the smallest detail, examining every brick to make sure it had been properly baked. He fussed about the oven and even supervised the mixing of sand and lime.

These artists whose names are now immortal were nearly all men of the people. They wore a long tunic with a leather belt and a cloak that came half-way down the leg. Their 'mechanical' trade was deemed hardly fitting for a gentleman. Nor were they very well paid. Fra Angelico received sixteen ducats a month, Gozzoli only seven. Frescoes were sometimes paid for by the yard. But most of the artists made a tolerable living, thanks to the fidelity of their patrons; and they gradually rose in the public estimation, because a Florentine, whether *grasso* or *minuto*, liked pictures and had a feeling for plastic beauty.

* * * *

Giotto, whose work in painting is equivalent to that of his friend Dante in poetry, was the true founder of the Florentine school. This little shepherd whose genius invented the pathetic was the first, as Berenson says, to satisfy the tactile imagination without which a painting cannot exercise the fascination of a reality that is intensified. But Giotto had died in 1336, and it was sixty years before his teaching came to flower. But what a flowering followed!

The corporation of artists did not forget the name of their great founder, and his sayings were collected and repeated like Dante's.

One Sunday Giotto, who was gay and talkative, was relating a story to his friends in the Via del Cocomero when a great herd of swine rushed past, and one of them struck his legs so violently that he fell. Assisted to his feet, Giotto shook himself, refrained from abusing the pigs and remarked with a half-smile: 'But are they not right? I have made thousands of *lire* in my time with their bristles, and I have never even given them a bowl of soup in return.'

This tradition of a gay and rather childish good humour was maintained by the artists. They were anything but pedants, as

may be seen from the following anecdotes. Nanni Grosso, a
pupil of Verrocchio, had lived so imprudently that he had to
spend some time in the hospital of Santa Maria Novella. On being
discharged, he was asked by his friends how he felt. 'I'm not well',
he replied—'And you have been cured!'—'Yes, but I'm not well.
I need a little fever so as to be maintained comfortably and looked
after in the hospital.'

But the story which Florentines never tired of repeating was
the one about Manetto Ammanati. Although only twenty-eight
he was a fat and dumpy fellow: and, for the rest, good-natured,
rather simple, but an excellent master in marquetry. His friends
Brunelleschi and Donatello amused themselves at the expense of
'fat Manetto'. Brunelleschi thought it would be a joke to persuade
Manetto that he was no longer 'il Grasso', but Matteo, another
of their friends. He therefore, towards nightfall, shut himself in
Grasso's workshop near Santa Maria del Fiore, and when Grasso
knocked at the door, he was amazed at hearing a reply in what was
apparently his own voice. 'What is this?' he asked himself. 'It
seems to me this fellow is myself.' Then Donatello, 'a maker of
figures in marble', came up and said to Grasso: 'Matteo, if you are
looking for Grasso, he has just returned home.' And the jest
continued. At the request of a creditor of Matteo, Grasso was
arrested by the bailiff's officers. He struggled violently, was put
under lock and key, and felt terror-stricken. 'Yet it seems to me
I am still Grasso!' he reflected; and after further reflection he sent
word to his friends that he had been imprisoned but that he feared
if he confessed the truth, he would be taken for a madman. Finally
Matteo's two brothers paid the imaginary debt and took Grasso
home with them. At supper they gave him a little opium; then,
taking him to his own house, put him to bed with his head where
his feet should have been, and turned his workroom topsy-turvy.
Poor Manetto ended by thinking he was really mad; and when one
one day he met a companion who was looking for a master in
marquetry-work with a view to practising the art in Hungary, he
went abroad. Fortune smiled on him, he became a rich man and
sometimes revisited Florence. When Brunelleschi asked him why

he had left, he related his story which was known as that of Grasso the carpenter.

In later years artists' clubs were founded, such as the Company of the Cauldron and the Company of the Saucepan, principally for merry-making. In the hall where they met for gala-suppers, near Santa Maria Nuova, the young daubers vied with each other in amusing and ingenious entertainments. To a shrill accompaniment of fifes, the cook would set on the table buildings that were entirely edible: first, perhaps, a temple with foundations of Parmesan cheese, columns made of tripe and capitals consisting of roast chicken. The entrance was shaped like a serpent's mouth and the rotunda represented Hell with its pits. Then would follow a number of dishes frightful to behold but delicious to devour; and the evening would end with a comedy. The subjects were always taken from Dante.

*   *   *   *

The artist who took up the torch that Giotto long before had laid down, was not a gay fellow. He was not spiteful or ill-natured, but simply a man with one object in life, a man who was devoted heart and soul to art, and who paid little heed to himself and still less to others. Masaccio was indeed so little appreciated in his lifetime that no inscription was placed above his tomb. He was twenty-seven in 1428 when he died—perhaps of poison, because people were jealous of him; but his trail was like that of lightning.

Leonardo da Vinci, who scarcely names any artists in his *Treatise on Painting*, wrote: 'He who takes as an absolute model the works of other painters will produce only mediocre work; but if, as the goal of his study, he sets Nature before him, he will bring forth good fruit.' And he cites Masaccio, who 'by the perfection of his works proved that all who do not take as their model Nature, that instructress of all masters, will strive in vain to produce art'. It has even been said that Masaccio gave birth to the whole of the Renaissance; and it is true that the frescoes in the Carmine were an open book for successive generations of painters. Vinci as a young man copied them, as did Michelangelo and

Raphael. Masaccio was the first to discover the deeper meaning of things; he grasped them at the highest point of emotional intensity. To realize this, one has only to study his picture of Eve driven from Paradise and howling with sorrow.

What a wonderful era, when Masaccio was painting the frescoes in the Carmine and Ghiberti casting in bronze the doors for the Baptistery of San Giovanni, doors whose warm pristine glow has but recently been restored!

After Masaccio came other and picturesque artists, drawn like him to reality, but to a reality more violent or more rugged. Paolo Uccello, who had once been an assistant of Ghiberti's, was a bizarre and melancholy soul, of subtle and 'sophisticated' outlook, whose only joy was to grapple with difficult problems of perspective. At night he would spend hours in his studio solving these problems, and when his wife called him to go to bed, he would sigh: 'Ah, what a sweet thing is perspective!' Sometimes people would not see him for months together.

'Ah! Paolo,' said Donatello, 'by your study of perspective you are exchanging the certain for the uncertain. All this is only helpful to marquetry-workers.'

But Paolo refused to listen. He indulged his mania until he fell into poverty, and agreed at last to work for the Abbot of San Miniato, who fed him only on cheese. This was too much. I fear I shall 'become nothing but cheese', he cried, 'and be used as putty'. And he ran away. But once more he was reduced to poverty. His income-tax statement is a long lamentation: 'I am now old, and without business, and I cannot work, and my wife is ill.' He died towards 1479.

Yet this strange monomaniac produced a great number of works in the most varied genres. He was much interested in animals, whence his name Uccello.[1] He even tried to draw those he had not seen, and sometimes of course he fell into error. Thus when he wanted to paint a chameleon, which symbolized air and light, he drew a camel, open-mouthed and filling itself with air. But his great joy was in depicting battle-scenes, which are full of

[1] The Bird.

perspectives: the horses seen from various angles, the forest of lances and the tangle of swords, shields and helmets. There was a virtuoso as well as a visionary in Paolo Uccello.[1] And then suddenly, after painting a scene of violence, he would produce a quiet and restful little picture in the Flemish manner. It will be recalled that the Flemings played an essential part in the evolution of fifteenth-century painting and that Florence was in constant relations with Flanders.

Andrea del Castagno, whose roughness borders on the brutal, may be described as a condottiere of painting. He had been a shepherd-boy like Giotto and was discovered by one of the Medici scrawling figures on a wall with a piece of charcoal. 'Do you want to be a painter?' he was asked—'Nothing would please me more.' And he soon rose to fame thanks to his 'terrible' talent and his speciality for painting men's and women's heads larger than life.

In Sant' Apollonia, on behalf of Pandolfo Pandolfini, he painted a Last Supper, and also a gallery of famous men, excellently marshalled and arranged. Conspicuous among these was Filippo Scolari, known as Pippo Spano, one of those Renaissance figures who are not easily forgotten. A man of good family but poor, Pippo settled at Pesth, in Hungary, where he founded a business and became a favourite of the King. In consequence of a revolution he was condemned to death, but he escaped, restored the monarchy, was appointed Captain-General and defeated the Infidels in several battles. It was in his home in Hungary that poor Grasso rediscovered his own identity. Pippo, now that he was great and glorious, returned to Florence, where, though the Signoria was afraid of him, he was conspicuous only by the splendour of his manners. Now Andrea del Castagno was exactly the man to bring Pippo to life before our eyes: we see him, in Sant' Apollonia, holding his sword with both hands, his feet firmly planted beneath him and his head proudly, almost insolently thrown back.

[1] He is the artist of the equestrian portrait of the famous condottiere, Sir John Hawkwood, on one of the inner walls of the Duomo. Hawkwood had been in the service of Florence in the later fourteenth century. (Translator)

From the more violent type of painting we enter quieter regions with Ghirlandajo and Gozzoli. Some critics regard them as pure illustrators, interested in general effects, but this makes them the more valuable to the historian.

Ghirlandajo was the son of a goldsmith and was brought up as one. As he used to sketch the customers who came into the shop, and as his drawings were very life-like, he became the society-painter of Florence. The flower of the city lives again in his frescoes, from the timid young lady in her silk skirt to the haughty patrician in heavy brocade. Thanks to him, we can look on the misshapen profile of Lorenzo the Magnificent, surrounded by notables, including the big Poliziano, a whole society depicted in all its spontaneity and easy charm.

Ghirlandajo is recorded as saying to his brother: 'Do you look after the money and our means of livelihood. Now that I am beginning to understand this sublime art, I should like to be commissioned to cover all the walls of Florence with pictures.' But his great facility did not prevent his being a careful craftsman. He knew how to place the groups, to distribute light and shade, to arrange perspectives and open distant views. The general effect of his pictures is nearly always agreeable; they appeal to the imagination and sometimes to the heart. It was in his studio that the Podestà of Chiusi's son, the young scion of the Counts of Canossa, Michelangelo Buonarotti, began his apprenticeship at the age of thirteen. This was on April 1, 1488, when Ghirlandajo was decorating the choir of Santa Maria Novella. The master's admiration for the pupil was soon to turn to jealousy.

If Ghirlandajo evokes for us the high society of Florence, the good Gozzoli, whose placid countenance under its red bonnet looks out from the fresco of the Riccardi palace, brings before our eyes other aspects of Florentine life, especially those crafty burghers who could handle with equal dexterity the business of the State, of the wool-trade and of the banking-house: miniature copies of old Cosimo de' Medici.

Whatever the scene he is depicting, one guesses that the actors have been painted simply and truthfully from life; yet there is no

platitude and the impression is that of a well-told story. When one
thinks of his frescoes at Pisa, Florence and Montefalco, one realizes
what a tireless worker he was, and how conscientious. Once,
when Piero de' Medici declared he was not satisfied with certain
seraphim who figured in the sky of a fresco, Gozzoli replied that
one could scarcely see them, that this caused no distortion but was
rather a beauty; but, still, he would do what he was ordered. Then
he added: 'I should have come to speak to you, but this morning
I began to put on the blue and that work cannot be left. The
weather is very hot and the sizing spoils after a few moments'
(July 10, 1459). This upright and talented man lived as a true
Christian, 'spending his whole life in an honourable profession',
and died in old age in his small house at Pisa.

Compared with this peaceful existence, the career of Filippo
Lippi reads like an adventure story. As an orphan child he had
been brought up by an aunt and then, while still young, became
a monk in the Carmine convent, where he was Masaccio's best
pupil. But he was of an amorous turn and Cosimo de' Medici,
after engaging him to work in his palace, locked him in so that he
would not waste his time. After two days of imprisonment
Filippo tied his sheets together, let himself down into the street
and decamped. Cosimo soon had him recaptured and brought
back to work; but he now allowed him complete freedom. 'Men
of such rare genius', he said, 'are an emanation of celestial beings
and not donkeys to be pack-saddled.'

But our monk did not sober down. After a troublesome case of
forgery he emigrated to Prato, where the nuns in one of the convents engaged him to paint a St Margaret. On his asking for a
model, the Mother Superior sent him a charming young nun,
Lucrezia, the daughter of a Florentine named Francesco Buti;
and on the day when the girdle of Our Lady, a relic greatly
honoured at Prato, was to be displayed, Filippo carried off
Lucrezia. Great then was the flutter in the convent and in the
Buti household. Lucrezia was recovered, but she declared she
would never abandon her lover. Pope Eugenius IV tried to
arrange matters by offering to release Filippo from his vows, so

that he could marry Lucrezia; but Filippo would not listen to this, and things remained as they were. The child of this union was the amiable Filippino, a painter like his father.

This was not Lippi's only adventure. One day at Ancona he was out in a sailing-boat with a friend when a corsair-ship belonging to Abdul Maumen hove into sight, captured them both and took them as slaves to Barbary. Filippo remained there for a year, handling the oar instead of the brush. But he was amusing himself one day by drawing on a wall, with charcoal, the picture of his master in Moorish costume, so brilliantly that you would have thought it alive. Abdul happened to come up, admired the picture and took Lippi into his favour. Once again he was able to exercise his art; the Moor gave him presents, and finally dispatched him and his companion to Naples.

This was freedom, no doubt, but not wealth. On August 13, 1439, Lippi appealed for aid to the miserly Piero de' Medici: 'It is clear', he wrote, 'that I am one of the poorest *frati* of Florence. God has left me six nieces to be married, all useless and infirm, and the little they have, though it is much for them, is I. If you would arrange for me to receive from your house a little corn and wine that you would sell me, it would give me great joy. Set it down to my account, I beg of you with tears in my eyes; for if I depart, I leave it to these poor children.' But Piero refused him even a *quattrino*.

In spite of all this, Filippo was still subject to his *beati amori*, and when he died in 1469, at the age of fifty-seven, it was said that he had been poisoned by the family of a woman he was courting.

Now this abductor of a nun, this slave in Africa, this monk sinking under the burden of his unmarried nieces, knew how to depict the most innocent and virginal Madonnas, and he saw them not as great ladies but as gentle peasant-girls. To him had been given, with the art of pleasing, the charm of the intimate and the domestic. He had been working at Spoleto when he died, and Lorenzo de' Medici went in person to ask for the mortal remains of Fra Filippo which he wished to have buried in the Duomo in Florence. But the men of Spoleto replied that their city suffered from a dearth of distinguished men and they begged him not to press his request. Lorenzo had to be satisfied with a cenotaph.

Though few signs of true piety have been discernible among the artists we have studied, it triumphs in Fra Angelico, the St Francis of painting, the illuminator of the *Golden Legend*.

His secular name had been Guido. Entering the order of preaching Friars, he led a life that was consistently quiet, modest and pious. When Nicholas V, who appreciated his merits, wished to make him Archbishop of Florence, he begged the Pope to appoint someone else, since he felt himself little fitted for government. When dining on one occasion with His Holiness, he was offered meat but dared not eat it without permission of his Prior. When asked to paint a picture, he referred you to his Prior for permission. In fact, he was always *in manus*—dependent. He would never draw from the nude. When depicting the Christ he wept; and he refused to add after-touches to his pictures because he said that they had come into being by the will of God.

His frescoes display reminiscences of Antiquity, but these are secondary. It was above all the world of his dreams and visions that was painted by the gentle monk of San Marco, the pure-hearted mystic whom the Florentines surnamed Angelico and of whom Michelangelo was to say that he must have visited the Earthly Paradise with permission to choose his models there. There is something etherial about his paintings, with their hosts of seraphim and their quiet and smiling landscapes. From them arises a hymn of praise in which the world seems pierced through and through by the golden rays of the love of God; and these scenes are simple, wordless, tender, yet free of insipidity—very remote from the violence of Savonarola, who was to live in the same convent of San Marco.

Berenson quotes, apropos of Fra Angelico, the words of Browning, which might serve as an epitaph for the tomb of Fra Angelico in the church of the Minerva in Rome[1]:

> God's in His Heaven—All's right with the world!

[1] Fra Angelico had been born at Fiesole in 1397. He died in Rome at the age of sixty-eight.

If one had to give examples of the great diversity of Florentine genius, one might compare Fra Angelico with Sandro Filipepi. Born in 1444, Sandro had been ailing and restless in his youth. His father put him in the charge of a goldsmith named Botticelli, whose name he afterwards adopted; and it was here that he learned how to plait gold and silver filigree, engrave ladies' ornaments and reliquaries, and carve the daisies and roses with which, in later years, he would adorn his pictures.

In Florence the goldsmith's art led inevitably to painting. For a time Sandro was a pupil of Filippo Lippi, who took a fancy to him. Then he followed his own bent, dabbled in literature and selected from the Classics and Boccaccio subjects for painting. They were always tragic.[1] And he illustrated Dante. But there was nothing sombre or ascetic about the man himself. His neighbour was a weaver whose looms shook Botticelli's studio and who was deaf to all complaints. Botticelli retorted at last by setting a large stone on the top of the dividing wall, poised insecurely but in such a way that it would inevitably fall into the weaver's workshop. The latter's protests were met with the remark: 'As for me, I do what I like at home'; and so matters were arranged. Botticelli's trick was greatly admired in a society still rather simple-minded.

He had little notion of economy and spent his money at random. Hoping to teach him sense, Tomaso Soderini, one of his protectors, advised him to marry. 'My Lord,' replied Botticelli, 'I want to tell you what happened to me one night. I dreamed I had a wife, and such was my anguish that I awoke. And I was so much afraid of having a similar dream once more that I spent the rest of the night striding about Florence like a madman.' Soderini did not insist further.

This dreamer's art is primarily intellectual. Consider these lines of Poliziano's: 'Pure white is she, and pure and white her robe, but painted also with roses and flowers and grass; her golden curls fall over her brow.... Around her the forest smiles.' Is not

---

[1] As for example the legend of Nastagio degli Onesti: the story of the woman pursued by mastiffs and the Black Knight.

this Botticelli's allegory of *Spring*? Poliziano wrote elsewhere: 'So the goddess rose from the waves, pressing her hair with one hand and with the other the apple of her breast . . . the sand, smitten by her divine foot, is clothed with flowers and grasses.' Here is the *Birth of Venus*. All this is replete with *morbidezza*, and from a certain angle makes one think of Far-Eastern art. The lines and forms are harmoniously balanced as in a symphony, and one can understand how generations of poets have drawn inspiration from these pictures.[1] It was only just, for Botticelli had drawn his from poetry.

But these Florentines always have a surprise in store. After the death of Lorenzo the Magnificent, Botticelli became a fervent adept of Savonarola. Terrified by apocalyptic visions and sincerely repentant, he gradually gave up his painting; then he became 'old and poor and useless, walking with the aid of two sticks, for he could not stand upright'; so at last he died, over seventy years of age. But we must not think of this aged and stooping figure when we stand in front of the *Primavera*.

One of Botticelli's pupils had been Filippo Lippi's son, Filippino, whose life was as modest and orderly as his father's had been undisciplined. The thing happens fairly often. Filippino was always courteous and affable. The ingenuity and inventiveness he displayed in the organization of festivities explain his popularity among the youth of Florence; but connoisseurs also appreciated the artist who completed the wall-paintings in the Carmine in a manner not unworthy of Masaccio, and admired the painter of so many exquisite canvases and frescoes with delicately drawn architecture. Like his father, Filippino had the art of pleasing.

Of the painters who all played a part in the daily life of Florence one did scarcely more than cross the stage. Born in 1452 Leonardo da Vinci was the son of the notary Piero and a peasant girl named

---

[1] There has been a constant connection between poetry and the plastic arts in Italy. Dante makes one think of the bas-reliefs of Jacopo della Quercia, Donatello and Ghiberti; he as it were foresees some of them. See, e.g. the description of the Angel carved in white marble: *Purgatorio*, X, vv. 28-45. (Cf. J. A. Symonds, *Dante*, 1891, p. 254.)

Caterina, in the small town of Vinci near Empoli, a country of vineyards and olive-groves. He was so handsome and agreeable a youth that people compared him to Hermes; but he had the rarer qualities of unbounded curiosity and fantasy. He lived from hand to mouth, heedless of preparing a career, but constantly engaged in meditation or research or the solution of problems which his contemporaries thought fantastic, such as the invention of a flying-machine, the piercing of a tunnel or the transport of enormous weights. At the same time he was learning how to model and draw in the studio of his master Verocchio, acquiring a love of plastic beauty, admiring Masaccio, reproaching *Nostro Botticelli* with his neglect of landscape, and generally taking his place in the life of the city.

It was he who, after the conspiracy of the Pazzi, was commissioned to paint Bandini on the walls of the Palazzo—that Bandini who had been handed over by the Sultan and put to death. Here are the notes he wrote on the rough sketch: 'Tan-coloured cap, a black, lined tunic, a blue cloak lined with fox-skin, black hose.' He represented the corpse dangling by a rope, with loose-fitting clothes and the hands tied behind the back. And soon after this he painted the *Virgin of the Rocks*.

This new edition of Leone Battista Alberti, endowed now with genius and universal in his talents, had studied ancient art without being conquered by it. The humanists could not deceive him. Swollen with pride and pomposity, they are clad and decked out, he said, not with their own works but with those of others: 'a stupid breed'. Vinci himself remained loyal to the common tongue and recalled the ancient only when it was a question of architecture. For he knew everything. We think we know him, but we do not; his strange curiosities seem to have led him to stand deliberately in a half-light, half-shadow of mystery. Fortune was not always kind to him. After losing his protector, Ludovico il Moro, and then Cesare Borgia whom he had served as military engineer, he returned to Florence. Here, in 1504, he met Michel-angelo. The contact produced a spark, but not a friendly one. A discussion regarding a verse in Dante degenerated into a dispute

—or so it was said—and then into hostility. And yet Leonardo must have been capable of appreciating the sombre genius of his junior. With Raphael, on the other hand, he was on terms of confidence. He became the respected master of the young Umbrian, who followed his counsels and learned from him not only the value of landscape but what artists call *sfumato*, the art of giving an aerial and indefinable softness to contours. Berence says that Vinci was the spiritual father of Raphael.

A disagreement with the gonfaloniere Soderini led Vinci to leave Florence; and in 1507 Louis XII of France obtained permission from the Signoria for '*Léonard Avince, Painctre de votre cité de Fleurance*' to become painter to the King of France.

As to Michelangelo, Pope Julius II invited him to Rome, where he arrived in 1505; and now began that strange dialogue between the 'terrible' Pontiff and the 'terrible artist', a dialogue interspersed with quarrels and reconciliations. We shall again encounter the sculptor of the Tomb of the Medici at the most moving crises in the life of Florence.

*   *   *   *

In the fifteenth century Italian art had been dominated by Florence and 'Rome was one of her suburbs'. At the beginning of the sixteenth the situation seemed to be reversed. Rome 'imported' the Florentine artists for her greater glory; and yet, despite the political shocks which caused the City of the Flower to oscillate between Republic and Tyranny—despite the exodus of her painters and sculptors—she remained a brilliant artistic centre. The name of Andrea del Sarto alone (1488-1530) is enough to prove it.

The life of the tailor's son is steeped in a sort of mediocrity which however enhances the glory of his work. Beginning like so many as a goldsmith and then passing over to pictorial art, he figured in the little society of the Scalzo which met near the gardens of San Marco; and here he painted frescoes of astonishing charm and grace. But he fell in love with a hosier's wife, a pretty, conceited creature named Lucrezia, and neglected his work. The hosier, however, died; and forthwith Andrea, without advising anyone, married the young widow who brought him, as a dowry, the whole of her family, her father and sisters. In vain did Andrea's friends deplore the situation. Andrea had drunk the love-potion. He was jealous of Lucrezia, who held him easily at her beck and call; and so he remained under the yoke of this pretty shrew, forsook his own relatives and friends—who sent him to Coventry—and despite torments of jealousy considered himself a happy man.

Two of his pictures had been admired in France; and François I, who wished to attach him to his service, sent money with the invitation. As he was not perhaps sorry to see the world and, for a time, to slip the chain of conjugal servitude, Andrea went. He had been poor hitherto (Lucrezia and her family had taken care to drain his resources), now he was loaded with presents. After a life of bourgeois economy, he enjoyed more than comfort and well-being; and his smiling *Charity*, in the Louvre, probably reveals the tone of his mind at that time. He was in any case, with Cellini, Rosso and Primaticcio, one of the eminent members of the Italian colony in France.

But Lucrezia had not forgotten him. Her letters plunged him into sadness, they awakened his memories of home; so much so that he sought leave to return and swore upon the Gospel that he would come back in a few months' time with his wife; and King François, trusting to his word, gave him leave—and a well-filled purse.

But on his return to Florence he fell once more into the power of Lucrezia, spent all the money and forgot his oath. He was never more seen in France; but some of his finest works in that country were to keep his memory alive. Such was this slave of love, condemned by his passion to a kind of solitude and yet free in the world he had made his own—a world he coloured with an art that is refined while appearing simple. He knew how to invest his saints and Madonnas with an extraordinary charm and distinction. One could only wish that he displayed more warmth and had a greater range; if he had not, it was perhaps Lucrezia's fault.

*   *   *   *

We have mentioned how, in May 1483, the apothecary Landucci had admired the Christ and St Thomas of Andrea di Verrocchio. This goldsmith, 'perspectivist', sculptor, engraver, architect, painter and musician, was now over fifty and had reached the zenith of his fame. And what could have been more just? He was the first in Florence to divine the importance of landscape, of atmosphere, of the play of light in a picture; that is, of the means of giving rein to the imagination. His *Annunciation* would not be what it is without the cypresses which form a kind of escort. As a sculptor he has left the *Child with the Dolphin*, and the *David*, whose graceful posture, whose almond-eyes under the clustering curls and whose air of merry triumph over the success he has achieved reveal him for what he is—a Florentine youngster not yet even adolescent. Verrocchio has been reproached for a hard and dry manner, which is regarded as a mark of effort. But such a criticism is not valid for the *David* who, with that smile which Da Vinci was to remember, seems to have sprung spontaneously into being. Nor is it valid for the *Colleone*, one of the most perfect specimens of equestrian statuary, and one of the jewels of Venice.

Verrocchio's name naturally evokes Donatello's. The latter was the son of a wool-carder, and, though not rich, was lucky enough to have been distinguished by Cosimo de' Medici. The *Pater patriae* gave him numerous orders and paid him well, but was always dissatisfied with his dress. One fête-day he sent Donatello some new clothes, a pink cloak, a hood and a cape. The sculptor consented to put them on, but at the end of two days he declared he could wear them no longer: 'They are too fine for me.' He was a man of the people and looked for his models among the people, even when he wished to represent the Saviour. Brunelleschi, whose meals he used to share, said to him one day: 'You have put a peasant on the Cross, not the body of Christ.'—'Well,' replied Donatello, 'do you take wood and carve a Crucifixion.' Some time later when Donatello, who had been to market, reached Brunelleschi's house with a basket of eggs for their meal, he saw the carving of Christ which had been made by his friend. He was so overcome with its beauty that he dropped the basket—and the eggs. 'What's wrong?' cried the other. 'And how are we going to dine now?'—'As for me.' rejoined Donatello, 'I'm satisfied. It is for you to carve the Christ and for me to carve peasants.'

But he was not, in fact, so limited. His own *David* is not a little peasant but a handsome Greek youth as seen through the eyes of a Florentine realist who has not been blinded by reverence for ancient art, although indeed Donatello had been to Rome. After 'throwing to the four winds of heaven the old arsenal of the Middle Ages', he had looked on Nature as she is, and applied himself to reproducing individual types without being burdened by any tradition, whether classical or medieval. Hence the *joie de vivre*, the air of expansiveness and eternal youthfulness which animate his work. And his love of Florence accompanied him everywhere. When he was in Padua,[1] he declared: 'I can learn nothing here. I need the criticism of the Florentines, not the compliments of the Paduans.'

He continued to work even as an elderly man. Towards the age of eighty he became paralysed and was slowly dying in his small house in the Via del Cocomero when some relatives, who hoped to inherit a little property he owned at Prato, came to see him. 'I cannot content you', he said, 'because it seems reasonable to leave this land to the peasant who has always worked hard in cultivating it, rather than leave it to you who have done nothing and simply wish to inherit it by coming to see me. Go your ways, and with God's blessing.' He was still the man who had said to Brunelleschi that the peasants were his province.

Once the initial impulse had been given, a whole company of artists sprang into being; but to classify them as sculptors, painters and architects would be to ignore their true nature. They cannot be placed in separate categories. Antonio and Piero Pollajuolo, who were sons of a poultry-dealer, began as goldsmiths in the Mercato Nuovo. Then they made wax bas-reliefs and other

---

[1] The splendid equestrian statue of the mercenary 'Gattamelata', which stands in front of the great church of St Anthony in Padua, is one of Donatello's masterpieces.   (Translator)

'fantasies'. When Piero began to paint, Antonio followed his example. But Antonio also carved the tomb of Pope Innocent VIII. All these Florentines were prodigiously gifted, and untrammelled too in their mode of self-expression.

In the mid-fifteenth century the realism of the earlier period was modified: it ceased to be 'terrible' and acquired a kind of grace which did not yet degenerate into dainty affectation. This was true of Rossellino, who, according to Vasari, displayed such gentleness, refinement and delicacy that his art may really be called modern. It was true also of Desiderio da Settignano, who fashioned Marsuppini's tomb in Santa Croce; and of his pupil Mino da Fiesole, who carved the Madonna and the pretty children who adorn Count Ugo's tomb in the Badia; though Mino's facility was already showing signs of mannerism.

In the organ-loft of the Duomo other children might be seen singing, playing and joining in dance. These were the sons of an emulator of Mino, Luca della Robbia, who possessed more than any other artist a sense of charming innocence in movement. But Luca was also an inventor. Terra cotta had been used for decoration before his time[1]; but he conceived the notion of making it more resistant by applying enamel to the clay; and thanks to this new art, he brought into being a world full of charm, ever young and ingenuous, which seems to mark a period of repose in the tormented life of the city. Now this mode of inexpensive decoration was accessible to persons of modest condition and even of the common people. Luca had a large family and his descendants continued to exercise the art. The children in swaddling-clothes who adorn the porch of the Hospital of the Innocents were the work of his nephew Andrea.

Distinguished architects figure also in the Pantheon of Florentine art; although, as we have said, the various 'trades' overlap in this land of privilege. Ghiberti, Brunelleschi and Michelozzo were sculptors as well as architects. When the two former visited Rome they spent whole days measuring the ruins, watching the

[1] The Pisans had imported this art from Majorca, after their conquest of the island: hence the name of Majolica.

excavations, and looking for medallions with such pertinacity that people supposed they were in search of treasure. In this instance the ancient world was to exert an undeniable influence on Italian architecture; and yet Florentine inventiveness was not warped by it. Thus Brunelleschi thought of adorning Santa Maria del Fiore with a double cupola, with an inner vault and an outer vault, so that one could climb between them. Ghiberti himself thought the project so chimerical that Brunelleschi dared not walk abroad, because people had been pointing at him and saying 'There goes the madman.' But the madman was right.

Lorenzo Ghiberti's fame rests principally on the doors of the Baptistery of San Giovanni; but he was very near to not being the sculptor for one of them. On April 29, 1444, it was proclaimed in the streets that he could not exercise the function with which the Signoria had commissioned him, because he was not the child of a legitimate union. His mother, Mona Fiore, had been the wife of a half-stupid creature named Cione Paltani. She had fled the domestic roof and had 'fallen into the hands' of Bartolo Ghiberti, by whom she had two children, one of whom was Lorenzo. Later on, when Bartolo was 'reproved' for 'living in adultery', he, after the death of Cione, married Mona Fiore. It was none the less true that Lorenzo was illegitimate. The denunciation—which throws a curious light on the daily life of the times—was probably due to some rival who had suddenly turned moralist. But he might have spared his pains. Ghiberti was allowed to carve 'the gates of Paradise.'

He had a high notion of his art and of learning in general. 'He who has learned everything', he used to say, 'will be a stranger nowhere. Even without money or friends, he will be a citizen of every country and can disdain the vicissitudes of fortune.'

What distinguishes the great fifteenth-century artists is their freedom and the sincerity and clear-sightedness of their outlook. They traced out their own way, remained themselves, and owed nothing to others. Florence was like a crucible in which every artist took his own bearings, followed various routes as his nature dictated, sought out and essayed new directions and vied with his compeers in untiring inventiveness. There was as yet no question of 'schools'. One had been the *ragazzo* of such and such a *maestro*, but one remained oneself.

Things were to change in later years. The advent of great masters and a fuller knowledge of Antiquity were to weigh heavily on art; and a day was coming when the artist would be trained to study fixed patterns and ready-made methods. He would draw from memory, and spontaneity would be stifled. Vasari, in the sixteenth century, wrote: 'Art today has been carried to such perfection that, whereas our predecessors produced a picture in six years, we produce six in one year.' And that, precisely, was what was seriously wrong.

CHAPTER XVI

FEMINISM

Evolution in the attitude to woman – Feminism as a product
of the renaissance – Agnolo Firenzuola as a theorist of beauty
– Advice to ladies regarding charm and good manners – The
emancipation of women – Platonic love – Disparagement of
marriage – The various categories of courtesans

In Italy, as elsewhere in the Middle Ages, invectives against
woman had been the rule. Her morals and rationality were
those of a child; her glory should lie in submission to the will
of man and especially in holding her tongue. Petrarch—Laura's
lover!—says that woman is usually a devil incarnate. A Siennese
writer calls her a devourer of patrimonies and an instrument of
Hell. What was required of woman was not to be graceful but to
be physically capable of bearing fine children. Her virtue lay in
not walking in the streets or going into shops, in not meddling in
business, in not gazing out of the window, but in feeding the
babies, telling her beads, mending the linen and looking after the
keys.

The Renaissance destroyed this narrow outlook, and freed and
raised the dignity of woman. She now had warm advocates, and
the old-fashioned type of husband was thoroughly well trounced.

'You regard women as slaves and servants rather than companions, which is what justice requires; and this is so impious and
contrary to the natural order of things that no other animal than
man has the audacity to do it.' This opinion of the Florentine
Gelli was shared by most of the Italian writers of the sixteenth
century. 'A husband', wrote the novelist Matteo Bandello, 'should
bear his wife company at all times, dress her according to his
means and grant her that decent liberty which befits her rank.'
And here is the even warmer defence of Castiglione, author of the
Cortigiano, that breviary for gentlemen:

Who knoweth not that without woman we could experience no pleasure in life, that life, in her absence, would be rough, bereft of all gentleness and harder than that of wild beasts? Who knoweth not that women banish from our hearts all vile and base thoughts, griefs, misfortunes and those dull sorrows that accompany them? Women raise our minds to the knowledge of great things, rather than turning us from them; in time of war they render men fearless. . . .

We are not to suppose that this is sentimental verbiage, or a reminiscence of the Courts of Love. The enlightened Italian of that time was a resolute feminist, and was not even shocked when someone argued that it would not perhaps be a bad thing to let women govern cities, make laws and control armies. Did they not attain excellence in all the arts to which they applied themselves?

Even the less determined feminists admitted that the progress in the education of girls was tending to establish equality among young people, and a grave author quoted *Genesis* and Aristotle to demonstrate that woman possesses the same moral dignity as man.

'It is very cruel of you', wrote Bandello, 'to wish to do everything that comes into your head and not recognize that women have the same right. If they venture to do something that displeases us, we very quickly have recourse to rope, dagger or poison.' Such barbarism was no longer fitting in a civilized community, where, at least among the well-to-do classes, woman was being emancipated and asserting her personality. The highest praise one could bestow on a woman was to say that she had the mind and soul of a man. Old people were still amazed at the change that had taken place.

'I should never have believed', said a jurist when talking with a lady, 'that the ladies of Florence were so conversant with moral and natural philosophy, and with logic and rhetoric.'

'Master,' replied the other, 'Florentine ladies do not like to be deluded. Hence the activity of their minds and the way they conduct their lives.'

It was not merely a question of philosophy and rhetoric. These ladies read Petrarch, Ariosto and even such light-minded authors as Aretino. But beauty was their principal interest, and on this matter they had first-rate advisers in Florence itself. Boccaccio had already given his opinion as to what constitutes feminine beauty. The head should be fairly large, the eyebrows should not form two curves but a single line; a slightly aquiline nose, a broad bosom, a white hand which looks well against a scarlet cloak, a smooth, straight forehead (not bulging, as had once been fashionable), brown, almond-shaped eyes with a gaze that could be serious, or lively, or even roguish, a round neck and small feet— such were the constituents of a beautiful woman. But in the sixteenth century Boccaccio was to be outdone by another Tuscan, who became a sort of professional theorist of beauty. Agnolo Firenzuola (1493-1545) was an ex-Benedictine who had retired to Prato. 'Inspired by the smiles and graces of the women of this country', he wrote discourses on love and beauty in which he strove to lay down principles and provide definitions which make his work a sort of canon of aesthetics. And it was to play an important part in the daily life of the ladies of Florence.

Charm, in the eyes of Firenzuola, is a woman's gift for bearing herself, or moving, or acting, harmoniously. Grace is like a hidden light, an indefinable gift conferred by some secret privilege and arising out of a harmony of the whole person. Here are the characteristics of a beautiful countenance: the hair should be fair but golden-tinted and verging on brown ('Blonde' is the queen of colours and can be obtained by artifice. Venetian women are expert in the matter.) The skin should be bright, not dull; the eyebrows, full in the middle and tapering off towards the nose and the ears; the eyes large, slightly protuberant, the eyelids white and marked with scarcely perceptible red veins. The white of the eye should be slightly bluish, the eyelashes not too long or too thick or too dark. The brow should be white, rather like a mirror but not so shining as to reflect objects. The borders of the eye must be red and shining, like a pomegranate seed. The pink on the cheeks is more marked round the curves. The nose becomes more slender, but by insensible degrees, towards the top. The mouth should be rather small, and should not display more than six teeth when the lips (which should have a dimple and not be too thin) are half open. The gums should remind one of red velvet: they should not be too dark.

As for the body—the neck should be white, round, and too long rather than too short. The leg should be long and slender, and firm at the calf; the foot small but not thin. A white hand large and fairly broad, a pink palm not too deeply marked with lines, shining finger-nails, pink also, and 'not extending beyond the fingers by more than the breadth of the back of a knife'. The bosom must be ample and shining, and not show any bones.

Italian possesses a whole vocabulary for beauty. *Vaghezza* is that attractiveness which awakens desire; *leggiadria* is charm; *venustà* denotes the rhythm of pure contours; *morbidezza* is the exquisite delicacy and pallor of the skin and the physiognomy in general; *snellezza* is the airy lightness due to slender limbs, and so on. Ladies might choose, when they could.

There were means of remedying imperfections. As women who sleep on their right side often find that the right temple is slightly depressed, they should use flowers to conceal the defect. The long-stemmed cornflower may be suggested for this purpose. To keep your hands soft and white, heat a little lemon, with white sugar, or take some mustard mixed with apple and bitter almonds, and rub the mixture on your hands at night, and then put on tight-fitting chamois-leather gloves. In the morning wash your hands in water mixed with a little benzoin-oil, and you will be satisfied.

Many women, unfortunately, imagine they can acquire or increase beauty by the use of paint and other ingredients. In the morning they plaster their faces with make-up so that they seem to be wearing a mask, and they refrain from laughter (laughter, which Firenzuola calls 'the radiance of the soul') for fear of cracking it; and so they remain all day like wooden statues. They cover their brows, cheeks and bosoms with white paint and their lips with rouge to make them look like coral, they curl their hair with a hot iron and keep the curls in position all night, and they

H

'also pluck their eyebrows so as to leave only a thin line like a bow.'

According to Ariosto, a lady's toilet table resembles a laboratory. 'How many little knives and scissors for the nails; and little cakes of soap, and slices of lemon for the hands! They need an hour to wash them and another hour to anoint and rub them until they are perfect. And how many powders and how much work are needed to clean the teeth! I could not count the number of boxes, phials, little bottles and other trifles that they use. One could fit out a ship from stem to stern in less time.'

Wise matrons recommended moderation. Leave these sublimates and ceruses alone, they said. To keep the skin white, limit yourself to sweet-almond oil with white wax and a little camphor; and think rather of hygiene. Certain Renaissance handbooks deal particularly with this subject. A well-bred lady should wash herself completely every day with warm pump-water in which some sweet-smelling herbs have been boiled. 'Cleanliness is what enhances beauty.' A lady should attend to her person for her own satisfaction and for her husbands.' 'There is nothing worse than to look clean where you are visible, and cross yourself as regards the rest.'

Pay heed also to the laundry. Mix some pine-resin and laurel leaves in the water to make it smell sweet; and wash shirts separately. To maintain your health and complexion, pay heed to your diet. If for example you suffer from obstruction, you should avoid cheese, fish and very sweet wines. Rub yourself every morning, and take more exercise than you are accustomed to. 'I don't suggest that you should hunt like Diana, but I should not blame you if you played at ball every day.'

As regards manners, a woman should cultivate a reserved and not a provocative attitude; in her movements she should display what is beautiful and conceal what is less so. By wearing gloves, or playing chess or cards, or again at table, she may display her hand, if it is pretty, to advantage. She may give a glimpse of her leg, skilfully and in moderation, when walking, fishing, hunting or leaping some small ditch; and in a salon too she may show 'just a little of her leg, especially if she has pretty velvet slippers and very clean stockings'. It is all a matter of skill and moderation. One should not wear too many jewels. A necklace of white pearls, a tastefully enamelled collar worth fifteen crowns or so, and a diamond ring on the left-hand finger, will be enough. Scents should not be too strong, nor should they be mixed.

Do not display too keen a taste for balls, fêtes, games and other social functions, which might disquiet your husband, but simply a natural and innocent inclination. When amusing yourself, preserve your usual outer demeanour. Do not talk too much, and think before you speak. 'One needs a hundred eyes, a hundred ears, but only one mouth.' In this way you will refrain from slanderous gossip and avoid many worries. Do not on the other hand display excessive timidity or prudishness; and do not withdraw if the conversation becomes a little broad, because people may suppose that there is something behind this pretence of austerity. 'Such uncivilized ways are always objectionable.' And do not give yourself such airs as to allow people to say: 'Do you think that the flies buzzing round are in love with you?' Avoid affectation, be smiling and gracious and, especially, charming. 'If Italian ladies do not surpass the French for their figures, charm at least makes them queens of the world.'

*   *   *   *

Beauty, personal merit, balls, games and society functions are all nothing without love. They are like 'a fine house in winter where there is no fire'. Renaissance literature is full of hymns to love. 'From love spring all good things, all virtues and all pleasant customs. Love is the sweetest condiment of existence and without it everything would be insipid.' To doubt this would be as absurd as to look for the whiteness of snow in the middle of a fire: such was the creed of these lords and ladies whose breviaries were Petrarch's *Canzoniere* and treatises like Mario Equicola's which appeared in 1525 and immediately ran through nine editions.

In former days a notary named Francesco da Barberino had

warned young women to distrust the pitfalls of love and had advised them as to how they might preserve their modesty:

Beware of those long-bearded pilgrims who come with their begging bowls and sit beside the women and prophesy things that ensnare young fools. Beware of the physician who pays less heed to the sickness than to the charms of the patient. Be on your guard against the tailor who offers his services free and, while taking your measurements, walks round you and admires you. Do not go to Church or to the baths at night; be prudent. If you want to go to a ball where there will be young men ready to dance, let it be by daylight or at least when the lights are bright enough for you to see those who are tickling the palm of your hand.

To the girl who had been placed when very young in a convent and who was now proud of her emancipation, all this seemed like dusty and out-of-date verbiage. Let us now hear what advice was given by that experienced matron Raffaella, whom we have already encountered, to young Margherita. The latter's husband is 'the best fellow in the world' but, being very busy, is often away from home. Margherita, being left a good deal to herself, to her sewing and embroidery, dreams of another kind of life; and Raffaella gives her very different instructions from those of old Barberino:

One must not waste the years of one's youth and, to avoid greater scandal, you should consent to some small backsliding, because, if you do not yield a little to the attraction of pleasure, despair will deliver you bodily to the devil. Honour rests only on public esteem, and that is why a woman should use all her ability to prevent people from talking scandal of her. Honour, in fact, does not consist in what one does or does not do, but in the impression one gives of oneself, advantageous or otherwise. Sin if you can't resist, but maintain your good reputation.

This was already Tartuffe's principle:

> Le scandale du monde est ce qui fait l'offense
> Et ce n'est pas pécher que pécher en silence.

Raffaella now passes on to the choice of a lover.

Avoid young men of twenty like the devil. They are inexperienced and do not know how to keep an affair secret; they even boast of it. Distrust old men too. No longer having the grace of youth, they burst with spite when they see others enjoying the sweets of love, and so they grow envious and back-biting. Avoid also falling in love with a married man. Be prudent and choose an honest and discreet fellow whom you have opportunities of meeting secretly.

Naturally Raffaella has such a fellow at hand.

The story of Margherita confirms the following observation by a novelist: 'Florentine husbands give their wives great freedom to be unfaithful because, winter and summer, they sometimes remain in the Council as late as the third or fourth hour of the night.' One of the inconveniences of a democratic régime.

Wives who were imbued with Raffaella's maxims might readily enough look for illicit love, and their infidelities rarely ended in catastrophe. People even came to regard them as legitimate when they were provoked by a husband's faithlessness. It was the law of tit for tat, and when the vengeance was in proportion to the outrage, the public did not hesitate to applaud. Crimes of passion, especially those for which a third party had paid, were more rare in Florence than in other parts of Italy, and this was doubtless due to the existence of a regular judicial system which gave redress to the complaints of those who were wronged. But after the disappearance of free institutions and with the coming of dictatorship, as we shall see, murders of a particularly atrocious character, committed by hired assassins, became more numerous.

*   *   *   *

The cultured and emancipated Florentine was not always interested in physical passion. The learned scholars and commentators had told her about the spiritual kind of love associated with Platonism, and this opened new horizons, as we shall see from the example of Costanza Amaretta.

During the Easter festivities of 1523 in Florence, this amiable young lady met a refined and cultured young man named Celso. He was her ideal. They appealed to each other and lived under the same roof in perfect chastity. After Easter they, with two other couples who had formed similar unions, left for Celso's country-house, and here they led the most delightful existence that could be imagined. During meals they chatted or listened to music; then they would walk or ride out to some agreeable spot, where the view was charming, and improvise verses on a subject proposed by Costanza, the queen of the cénacle. On one such occasion she told the story of her life.

She had been married 'for reasons of money and convenience' to a Roman whose only talk was of increasing his fortune and whose tastes were wholly coarse. It was in vain she had tried to love him. 'If this man had not desired to have a child by me, which led him to treat me with a certain benevolence, I am sure that there would have been nothing but hatred and quarrelling between us.' With Celso, on the other hand, she had discovered the meaning of true love. 'Our souls are in accord and we listen to their harmony. This love has shown me that the way to virtue is not barren and strewn with thorns as I had supposed; and so I have climbed it with joy.' Costanza went on to explain the Platonic distinction between the two kinds of love. The one which is bestial and a source of crimes and adulteries, is born of a false Venus, of mortal origin; the other, born of the heavenly Venus, is redolent of celestial things; it leaves the body aside and delights the soul.

It appears that the Constanza-Celso couple continued to live on a wholly Platonic footing. One of the other couples only managed to maintain this etherial relationship for six months, after which they succumbed.

Matrons like Raffaella represented marriage as a risky enterprise requiring minute precautions. Here is the advice for maintaining domestic peace with which they regaled young married woman: 'Just as a musician does not sever those strings which are dissonant but patiently and little by little attunes them to harmony; so the good wife should, without sourness, endure her husband's ill humour until she has brought him round *piano piano* to that domestic harmony which is not too often encountered nowadays.'

Marriage was not in fact highly thought of at that time, and, as we have seen, celibacy was becoming fashionable. People wrote against marriage, made mock of it, and nearly all literary men agreed with Aretino that a wife was a burden best left to an Atlas to bear up. Machiavelli, however, drew distinctions: 'Women', he wrote, 'are the most charitable beings in the world, and the most tiresome. Those who repel them escape troubles but also what is beneficial. Those who frequent or maintain them have both the beneficial and the troublesome. So true it is that there is always a fly in the ointment.'[1]

* * * *

One result, in any case, of the decrial of marriage was the success of the courtesans. It had begun in the second half of the fifteenth century and increased at the beginning of the sixteenth. These persons were of course of different types. There was the low-class kind, the intermediate kind known as the *cortigiana di candela* (because she generally lodged in the house of a candle-maker), and lastly the 'honest' courtesan who was held in honour and who alone played a part in social life.

When the terrible Savonarola described them as 'pieces of meat with eyes', this was just medieval invective. The high-class courtesan was a well-bred and cultured woman, sometimes a poetess too and a musician; she was witty, knew how to receive in a courteous manner, and was in short a woman of the world. Florence contained fewer of such women than Rome, Venice and Naples, but the names of some have been recorded.

Nannina Zingera, for example, had a voice so sweet and gentle that it might, people thought, move mountains and calm the wind. Her manners were those of a great lady, and 'as shadows vanish before the sun, so everything base and vile flees from her approach'. Zafolina was sharp-witted, gay and piquant; 'both by nature and experience' she was redolent of the Tuscan land, and appreciated by the nobility. When the honest courtesan paid a visit or went to a fête or to the baths, she was taken for a lady of quality. She had the bearing and reserve of one. She attended

[1] '. . . qu'il n'y a pas de miel sans mouches.'

Mass and Vespers, gave her opinion on the preacher's eloquence, observed Lent and the Ember-Days by remaining quiet or at home. She could be invited to dinner without anxiety. She ate and drank slowly, delicately and in moderation, with no sign of greed. Her air was pleasant and smiling, she never whispered in people's ears or paid attention to anyone but her host. If by chance he pressed her foot or touched her hand, she merely smiled.

Her hair was always of that Venetian blonde which she obtained by dyeing it liberally and exposing it for long periods to the sun. At home she was surrounded with little lap-dogs and handsome cats, talkative parrots and mischievous apes which filled the house with their cries and greeted their mistress joyfully whenever she appeared. The air however was saturated with perfumes, such as rose water, orange-flower water, civet, amber and 'mirabolan'.

The Zingera and her sisters were usually fond of good food; people extolled the delicacy and elegance of their tables. They took particular care of their wine-cellars where Trebbiano, Malmsey and other delicate vintages were stored. Their apartments were luxuriously appointed, the walls, seats and chests being covered with tapestries and rare fabrics; while the sideboard might be adorned with chased silver, and here and there stood vases of alabaster, porphyry or wavy-patterned marble. An honest courtesan described her wardrobe as follows:

My dresses are made of velvet or silk, interwoven with gold and adorned with pearls and precious stones. I have more than a hundred silk chemises, gold-fringed, and a profusion of dancing-shoes, half-boots and slippers. I wear a necklace worth at least two hundred gold ducats. My linen is whiter than snow and I have such quantities that anyone who sees it is amazed. It is impregnated with rare scents, and I myself like to be perfumed. . . . There can be no harmful miasma or infection where I am, for I fill the air with so many sweet-smelling odours.

The wise courtesan avoided any display of anger or contempt, and she sought the company of literary men, not for their money, because they rarely had much, but because they could celebrate her beauty and advertise her charms. She contrived in this way to acquire a clientèle, and sometimes she would decide to regularize her position. Such was the case with a certain courtesan who was formally married by her lover. He took her to his home and treated her with every kind of respect. She attended social functions like the other ladies of the city and went to church. One day, however, when she was kneeling beside a patrician dame, and the latter took offence and got up to move elsewhere, the one-time sinner said, loudly enough to be heard: 'Do not move away from me, Madam. I assure you that my infirmity only attacks those who wish to be attacked.'

One of the notable events of 1531 was the arrival in Florence of the famous courtesan Tullia d'Aragon, daughter of the no less celebrated Giulia. She had come from Rome where her culture and taste for poetry and music were so well known that her departure had been deplored. No sooner had she appeared in Florence than six young knights declared themselves ready to maintain, armed in the lists against all comers, that there was no woman in the world of greater worth and talent than Tullia. She in fact spent most of her time with writers or historians like Varchi, and do you know what they talked about—at least according to a certain wag? How to prove that the Etruscans are not Arameans, and that frogs are toads. Some years later a decree of the then reigning Grand Duke forbade courtesans to wear cloth or silk dresses and required them to be covered with a yellow veil to distinguish them from honest women. But public opinion could not allow Tullia to be subjected to so degrading an obligation. Her admirers agitated in high quarters and won their case. Tullia d'Aragon might dress as she liked and should not be obliged to wear the 'yellow sign', and that, in consideration of the rare poetical and philosophical talents 'which are found in her to the great joy of noble minds'. This learned person ended her days very respectably in the bonds of holy wedlock.

For the rest, a statute so insulting to the weaker sex was so remote from Florentine manners that it was not strictly observed, and the women in question went about much as they liked and advertised themselves more than ever. 'Is it not the habit of great

H*

cities', someone asked, 'not to persevere in their declarations but to do one thing today and undo it tomorrow?'

The courtesan, however, had her little troubles. She had to pay the tax on the date appointed. Sometimes the Signoria would have a fit of morality and take measures to see that the professionals did not leave the quarter reserved to them. And, lastly, there were blunderers among them who lost any sense of proportion and gave themselves airs—and then they would be lampooned, and young men, especially during the Carnival, would go about the streets singing of the infamy of 'those who had plucked them'.

The courtesan was surrounded with a little circle of shady persons whom she could not do without unless she were in a well-established position. First there was the procuress whom you might see trotting down the street and mumbling 'like a she-monkey'; and after her the witch, often a Jewess, who prepared love-philtres and charms, cast spells, pronounced incantations, and practised the art of rejuvenating feminine charm. According to a connoisseur the cupboards of a courtesan contained human skulls, bones, teeth and skin, soles from old shoes, and clothing stolen from graves; and beside the cupboard was a kind of devil's laboratory in which, like an ancient sorceress, the courtesan formed a heart out of hot ashes and then pierced it with a needle, chanting these lines:

> Ere the fire be dead and drear,
> Let him at my door appear.
> Love to him may I impart,
> As I now transfix this heart.

From the Zingera to the amorous witch was a big step downward; a further step takes us to the girl who lived in a supposed registry for servants, or *mammazuole*, where she worked under the eye of a housekeeper. The name of one of the latter has come down to us. She was known simply as Conscienza, and was an orderly and meticulous woman. These houses which stood in distant quarters of the city served as meeting-places for men of letters, poor officials and employees, the flotsam and jetsam of life; they served as an office, a restaurant and a sort of salon where one conversed in company with the 'servants'. Machiavelli, after he had been dismissed from his post and had fallen into poverty, was acquainted with such places.

CHAPTER XVII

STORIES AND ANECDOTES

The Florentine taste for stories – The fable-singers and their repertory – Songs – Legends – The story of Ginevra degli Amieri – 'Cercar Maria per Ravenna' – News items: miracles, accidents, misfortunes, plague – The paradise of men of letters – Conversation in a country retreat

THE stormy days of Florentine democracy were at least characterized by something lively, original and spontaneous. Wars, exiles and party-struggles were interspersed with gay festivities under the sign of Lord Cupid, and every domestic happening was shared in, not merely by the family and their friends but by the citizens as a whole. From birth to marriage, and from marriage to burial, each episode of one's life gave rise to rejoicing or to sorrowing in common.

These Florentines were never tired of gossiping and relating anecdotes. They had a passion for stories, and such novelists as Boccaccio, Sacchetti and Giovanni Fiorentino, author of *Il Pecorone*, were their favourites: they possessed a sense of the burlesque, the strange, the tragic—a whole gamut of emotions—which delighted the reader. Now this inveterate love of a well-told tale could be satisfied in the street, thanks to the professional 'fable-singers'.

In some public square, such as the Piazza San Martino in the working-class quarter, a crowd of curriers, tanners, porters, donkey-men, dyers, second-hand-clothes dealers, armourers and blacksmiths would be crowding round a little platform. No women would be present. The fable-singer mounted the platform, called upon the Lord Jesus and the Holy Trinity to direct his words and complimented the august assembly whose mere presence dignified the paving-stones on which they stood; then, proposing a certain number of themes, concluded by saying:

'Choose the one that best pleases you.' The audience having chosen a subject, he began with a slow melody and then recited the story to the accompaniment of lute or violin, hurrying or slackening the cadence according to the nature of the action he was describing; then suddenly he would stop in the middle of an episode and adjourn the sequel to the next recitation. 'I exhort you to return on such-and-such a day.' After which, cap in hand, he would made a collection.

A labourer who had toiled all day in the sun or the workshop would not care to miss such entertainments; a case is even recorded of one giving the singer money to persuade him not to let Hector die in the next episode. With a public of this kind the most varied themes, ancient, modern or even contemporary, could be treated. Short stories or *novelette* alternated with the long *storie* which were divided into *cantari*, but the main substance of the repertory was furnished by the '*matière de France*'[1]—the stories of Renaud de Montauban, Ogier le Danois and Fierabras, which were adapted and naturalized. Charlemagne was celebrated because he had reconstituted the Holy Roman Empire, Roland because he had been born among the Etruscan ruins of Fiesole!

The 'story-singer', an itinerant bard who had the ear not only of the people but of the middle classes and even the Signoria, whom he entertained at meal times, drew largely from a collection of tales dating from the later fourteenth century: *I Reali di Francia*.[2] This volume, which summarized several French poems and also furnished the outline of Italian poems still to be written, is not distinguished for any qualities of composition, but it is full of tragic scenes and episodes embellished and romanticized, which restore to the dusty old parchments something of the

[1] The '*matière de Bretagne*' was also known, as witness the episode of Paolo and Francesca in Dante, and some of the Church-sculpture in northern Italy; but it apparently exercised less popular appeal.   (Translator)

[2] This was the work of Andrea di Jacopo da Barberino in Valdelsa. It has been frequently rehandled, modernized and adapted to contemporary taste, and popular editions are still current in Italy. It is favourite reading for country-folk and at least as good as most serial novels.

vividness and movement of life itself. The *Reali* became really popular, and they are the source of the famous heroi-comic narrative poems of the Renaissance, in eleven-syllable verses arranged in rhymed octaves.

The singers who quickened the daily life of Florence—if one admits that it needed any quickening—recited more than epic fragments. They also sang pious lauds, and *capitoli* of a descriptive or satirical turn. Some of them could improvise with remarkable ability: such were Cristoforo Fiorentino, known as *l'Altissimo*, and Antonio di Guido who sang of Orlando's campaigns so eloquently that people almost thought they were listening to Petrarch. Landucci deplored the passing of this gifted artist.

On a lower level blind men, beggars and even young apprentices sang the Tuscan refrains in which it might be a question of Nero, Constantine, Charlemagne or some holy legend or miracle, and even more of woman's beauty, an inexhaustible source of songs to which Lorenzo the Magnificent made a notable contribution. Let us imagine ourselves among the merchants, shop-keepers, and shopping-crowds in the Mercato Vecchio, and listen to these voices in which there is no sign of effort:

'O thou of the milk-white face, the winds are hushed as thou passest by. All the stars caress thee with their beams. Thou art the fair rose of the garden. O orange-blossom plucked in Paradise, O leaf of the olive whose leaves are so lovely, thy loveliness is faring to France. . . .'

And other voices would strike up in chorus: 'Beautiful, O dear and beautiful, who made thy eyes? Who made them so amorous? White as the mountain snow, O rose from Naples, why do they call thee Neapolitan when thou wast born in Florence and baptized with clear spring water?'

Or again: 'I went my way, seeking a flower, but thou hast such fair flowers on thy milk-white face. . . . Thou hast so many flowers in thy fair tresses that they seem like a garden of fresh-blown roses. So many flowers are intertwined in thy hair that they seem like a garden. . . . And I see such lovely flowers in those white hands that they appear as a garden of pomegranates. . . .'

N'avete tanti in quelle bianche mani
Che paion un giardin di melagrani.[1]

These rustic songs, full of pretty speeches, would quickly grow monotonous without the accent of the country, the *canto fiorentino*.

In quite another key, the anecdotes of oriental inspiration, apologues suggested by the *Arabian Nights* and related by the Seven Sages whose names were Bancilasso, Ansile, Lentulus, Innachindas and so on, appealed to the Florentines because they treated of the deceitful tricks of woman. In quite another genre they liked the tragic story of a King of Dacia's daughter who, when pursued by her father's incestuous love, cut off her hands in order to disgust him. But her virtue was rewarded, for her hands were restored whole as before, by the grace of Heaven.

Another legend which had a lasting success and which illustrates the old Florentine piety and taste for the supernatural, was the legend of Sant' Albano.

A certain hermit, wishing to make sure of salvation, swore that he would abstain from all lust, murder or perjury. Now one night the Devil brought into his hut the pretty daughter of a king, who had lost her way when hunting the deer. Overcome by sensuality, the hermit violated the royal maiden and then, terrified by his sin and dreading also that he would be discovered, he decided to remove the only person who could bear witness against him, that is, to kill the innocent victim of his lust. When the men whom the king had dispatched in search of the princess arrived, he swore that for long, long past no one had come to disturb his solitude. Thus, in one night, he lost the reward of so many years spent in prayer and mortification. After that, in order to regain the way of salvation, he imposed fearful penances on himself and took an oath that he would henceforth proceed only on hands and feet, and never speak again until God, by some manifest sign, should signify that he was once more in a state of grace and that his crimes were forgiven.

Years passed by; but one day the king happened to be hunting in the region where his daughter had disappeared, and his barons

[1] Tigri, *Canti popolari toscani.*

found the hermit, a hairy creature on all fours and looking more like a beast than a man. When brought before the king, who regarded him as a monstrosity and plied him with questions, he at last confessed to the murder which, Christian though he was, he had committed. The king then asked him where he had buried his very dear daughter. The bones were discovered. The king placed them against his heart, and besought God, if he pardoned the murderer, to bring back to life his pure and innocent child. The hermit begged the king not to force him to raise his eyes to Heaven, which was contrary to his vow, but to put him to death.

'Look up to Heaven,' ordered the king, 'and pray to God with all thy heart.'

The hermit obeyed. He raised his eyes for the first time for years, and after craving mercy, 'O Lord God', he cried, 'if you forgive me, deign to release me from the dark prison of this world, so full, for me, of misfortune and anguish.'

Suddenly the king's daughter came back to life just as she was on the day when she had arrived at the hermit's hut, and in the same instant the hermit's soul left his body and was carried up by angels into Heaven amid songs of ineffable sweetness.

The king caused Sant' Albano's body to be buried in the fair and noble church of his city, and from the tomb arose an odour so pleasant that twenty-thousand nutmegs could not have surpassed it.

*   *   *   *

Another and even more popular story was the legend of Ginevra degli Amieri,[1] a notable 'example of love' which took place in Florence about 1400 at a time when the plague was raging. Being vouched for by contemporary witnesses, the story came at last to be regarded as authentic. The Amieri belonged to the aristocracy of commerce, but as they resided in the Mercato Vecchio which was the home of such minor 'arts' as those of butchers and fish-mongers, they were said to be affiliated to the pork-butchers' association. This was a great error: Ginevra belonged to a good

[1] And not 'Almieri', according to Alessandro d'Ancona.

family. Her lover, Antonio Rondinelli, on the other hand, was a *popolano* and hostile to the wealthy class. After these preliminaries, here is the story, told in verse for the greater joy of the Florentines:

Ginevra, whose speech was so sweet and gentle that she might have been born in Paradise, had been married to the rich Francesco Agolanti; and from that day onward the man who loved her, Antonio Rondinelli, had felt as though a knife had pierced his heart. The plague broke out and Ginevra, who fell sick of it, seemed to have ceased breathing. Her husband, dreading the infection, ordered her to be buried immediately between the two doors of Santa Reparata. And this was done. Now the spirit, which had departed wandering, returned to Ginevra's body and two hours later she came back to life. Finding herself lost, she implored the aid of the Virgin.

The stone covering the tomb contained a fissure through which the moonlight filtered. Steeling her nerves, Ginevra crept towards the moonbeam and found a small ladder by which she reached the tombstone which was not heavy or sealed. She raised it, emerged and prepared to return home, not by the main street but by a narrow alley where the cold and wind were cruel. This alley was afterwards known as the *Chiasso della Morte*. Previously it had had no name, it was simply the place where refuse from the sewers was thrown.

When Ginevra knocked at the door of her house, her husband came to the window. 'Who is knocking there?'—'I am your Ginevra, do you not hear me?' Francesco crossed himself, saying: 'Tomorrow I will go and pray for your salvation.'

Rejected by her husband, Ginevra went to her mother's house, where a similar scene was enacted. 'Go in peace, blessed soul', said the mother, as she closed the window. At her uncle's house Ginevra had no more success.

'O miserable and deceitful world,' she cried, 'unhappy is she who trusts in you! O shame! Mother, uncle and husband all abandon me in my distress.'

She was on the verge of letting herself die in a corner, then thought of seeking refuge in a convent; but the image of Antonio

Rondinelli, whom she had long loved in all modesty, restored her courage. She set out again and at three in the morning knocked at the door of his house. But here she fell exhausted; her fair body, trembling with cold, could no longer stand upright.

'Who is down there' called Antonio.—'I am Ginevra. For the love of Jesus, help this poor creature whom all men abandon.' On hearing her voice Antonio descended, four steps at a time, with a light in his hand, awakened the servant and the groom, and took Ginevra's body, now cold as ice, in his arms. 'Quick, woman, warm this blanket!' With his own hands he laid Ginevra on the bed, covered her warmly with blankets and then sat on the near-by coffer, a prey at once to joy and sorrow.

After half an hour Ginevra opened her eyes. Antonio approached her. 'My love, have no fear. Ask, I am devoted to your service, my dear beloved.'—'*Anton mio*, I place my honour in your hands.' She told him her story, then said: 'Go to the tomb, Anton, and close it so that no one may know of my adventure.'— 'I will do so, dear love.'

After replacing the stone, Antonio went to the market, where he bought a fat pigeon, some marzipan, pistachio-nuts and sugared almonds to comfort his beloved. Ginevra was restored; she slept; and in the morning she declared: 'I have ended all my troubles.' After four days she was completely cured and had recovered the freshness of her complexion. 'What do you intend doing?' asked Antonio. 'Returning to your husband?'—'Anton, don't think of it. That is far from my mind. I am ready, if you wish, to become your wife.'—'Would to God I could marry you. I should deem myself only too happy.'—'Be easy in your mind; I will show you the means. They buried me as a dead woman. Now death ends everything, it breaks every bond and strong attachment. There-fore if you like me, Anton, we will live together until we die. I am going to the notary's; then we will see what the Bishop says, and the officials at the Palazzo.'

Antonio gave her a ring, and Ginevra, now a fiancée, thought next of dressing. 'Go', she said to Antonio, 'and find the wretch who had me buried alive and see if he will sell you my clothes.'—

'To content you, I will make no difficulties about that', said Antonio, who proceeded to buy the clothes and bring them back to Ginevra.

So one Sunday morning, accompanied by Antonio and his mother and the servant, 'this fair, charming, noble and gallant morning star' proceeded to the Nunziata. She was recognized by many people, and Ginevra's mother, who happened to be coming from the direction of the Servi, cried out: 'Oh Heaven! she is like my daughter. Tell me, how did you come back to life?' Ginevra answered not a word. And now came Francesco, the husband. 'Where have you been? Who brought you out of the tomb?' Now Ginevra spoke: 'Certainly not you, because you had buried me alive. After that, I returned to our house and you drove me away.' And she added: 'Leave me alone. Never shall I return under your roof.'

Francesco then addressed Antonio. 'Why are you holding back my wife?' he asked.—'You know', was the reply, 'that I have never played you a foul trick, nor ever will. The marriage will not take place before this evening. Defend yourself in Ginevra's eyes, if you are right, because I would do you no wrong.'—'We shall see what the Bishop says.'—'That contents me.'

And Francesco set off for the Bishop's palace, to accuse his wife. This did not disturb Ginevra. 'I would rather take the veil than come once more under his authority', she said. When in her turn she appeared before the Bishop, she made a bow so noble, modest and decent 'that she appeared like a divine spirit, created in Heaven'. The Bishop treated her with courtesy and asked her to explain her case. She replied that her husband could have had very little affection for her since he had declared her dead and as such had had her placed in the tomb. 'I found myself buried, when I was still in this world. Everyone rejected me, and this would have been the end for me, if I had not remembered Antonio who had been in love with me for four years. But for him I should be dead; thanks to him I am alive.'

Francesco could find no answer, and the Bishop pronounced against him. 'If', he said, 'death terminates everything, go then, my daughter. I cannot but decide in your favour. Go with your Anton and be happy. And you, Francesco, go in peace, and think over my sentence. You have lost wife and dowry together.'

You can imagine how dolefully Francesco returned to his house. The whole city was informed of the affair. Ginevra, who had won her case at the Bishop's palace, and Antonio were married in all due solemnity and lived long in happiness and glory. 'Here ends the story I have told in your honour.'

The Bishop's judgment leaves us wondering; but the Florentines accepted it without more ado and even applauded it as the triumph in noble spirits of love over death. Ginevra's adventure was handed down from generation to generation, thanks to the public singers; it even furnished material for a play which was performed before the Grand-Duke Cosimo in 1546. As for ourselves, we cannot but admire, in this daughter of well-to-do Florentine merchants, such presence of mind that she had hardly returned to life before she thought of raising the tombstone, recovering her trousseau, and bringing an action against her husband.

Another and different Ginevra, whose home was Ravenna, is the heroine of a short Florentine poem of the fifteenth century, of unknown authorship. This Ginevra was the daughter of a citizen, not a plebeian, and she loved a handsome young man whom she had seen wearing a fine green silk doublet as he rode past her window on a white horse. His name was Diomed. She would have chosen him for husband, but her father intended her to marry an old man whose 'back was bent like a bow'; and Diomed left the city in his grief.

The marriage took place, and in the evening the women undressed Ginevra. She resembled 'a mountain of snow without a veil, so clean and immaculate as to turn a tiger into a lamb'; but the old husband was no more than a spectator. Now after the lapse of eighteen months he was appointed Podestà of Perugia; and Diomed, on hearing the news, returned hastily to Ravenna. He was so young that he looked like a girl, 'without a hair on his face'; and so he had disguised himself as a woman and offered himself as a serving-maid under the name of Maria.

Now Ginevra's old husband was, in point of fact, looking round for a maid who, during his absence, would keep an eye on his better half; and when he heard that Maria was neither ambitious nor exacting, but would be satisfied with board and lodging, he immediately engaged her. Ginevra agreed, without however being aware of Maria's identity. The consequences may be divined, but the conclusion bears the true Renaissance stamp. The ex-Podestà returned from Perugia, having apparently recovered his vigour. He began to flirt with Maria and discovered that she was a man. Then one day the two lovers sent him rolling down the staircase; he broke his skull at the bottom, Ginevra finished him off, and the murderers inherited his money.

This tragi-comedy gave rise to the popular saying, *Cercar Maria per Ravenna,* to seek Mary through the streets of Ravenna, or, in other words to go in quest of one's own downfall.

* * * *

A Florentine merchant depended a good deal for entertainment on what happened or was talked of in the street; and when he kept a diary in which he recorded any notable doings, we learn something of the news-items which occupied his daily life. Here are a few:

April 1465. A little girl was arrested for killing the daughter of a goldsmith and stealing a pearl necklace and other ornaments she had been wearing. She had then thrown her victim into a well. The child-murderess was beheaded.

April 1475. A peasant of twenty-three, from near Florence, remained in Santa Maria del Fiore after the Cathedral-doors had been shut on Easter night. He had hidden himself under the altar of Our Lady. In the morning he pursued his nefarious 'business, purloined jewels, articles of silver, and arms, legs and eyes (of relics)'. Arrested and hanged from the bell-tower.

August 1497. In the charnel-house near the Church of San Paolo, the undertakers were occupied with an interment. One of them let his keys fall into the trench and went down to recover them; but so terrible was the odour that he died before his companions managed to haul him out.

May 1503. The headsman was to execute a young fellow who had murdered one of his companions from motives of jealousy. At the third attempt he did not succeed in beheading him; and the chief executioner gave him a cudgelling. Now the culprit was only twenty, and the onlookers, overcome with compassion, began to cry out: 'Stone the man, stone him!' The chief executioner only escaped with difficulty from being stoned, by throwing himself on the ground; but the headsman was lynched by the fury of the populace, and children dragged his body as far as Santa Croce. It is said that this was the headsman who had executed Savonarola and his two adherents.[1]

Other entries record acts of profanation and miracles:

July 1501. An unlucky gamester threw filth over a statue of the Virgin which stands near the Canto de' Ricci. He was hanged that night from the window of the Podestà. All Florence went to see him. The Bishop had the dirt removed, and (so many candles were burned that)[2] pounds of wax accumulated at the foot of the statue.

November 1506. A figure of the Virgin above a doorway opposite the entrance to a bathing-establishment closed its eyes as if it did not wish to see the indecent things that were done there. As a consequence of this miracle, a great quantity of candles were set up in front of the figure so as to form a kind of rampart.

A Spaniard goes naked into the heated oven of a baker, and draws out a loaf. He swallows a flaming torch, touches red-hot coals, washes his hands in boiling oil and sells a prayer just as a charlatan would. This prayer makes him invulnerable to fire. 'Never has such a miracle been seen, if it is one.'

Building operations and sewerage could of course give trouble. Near Landucci's shop in July 1489 men were piling up gravel for

[1] This is from Landucci's journal.
[2] I have supplied these words which seem needed to explain what follows. (Translator)

the construction of the Palazzo Strozzi. The foundations were being dug, and pebbles, chalk and building-stone brought up. 'We artisans were living amid clouds of dust and were hampered by the people who would stop to gaze and could not pass on because of the mules and asses laden with building-materials.' There was a furore for building at this time, both in Florence and the environs, especially for building palaces (*cose di signori*). To encourage building, the authorities granted forty years of exemption from taxes to all those who built houses in vacant areas. Immediately everyone rushed into building so that there were no more masons or material left.[1]

News items would be amusing on occasion, or such as to inspire philosophical reflections. Thus on November 17, 1487, the Sultan's ambassador presented the Signoria with a giraffe, a lion and other animals. He sat among the *Signori*, conversing by means of an interpreter, and carpets and armchairs were placed in the gallery to accommodate the leading citizens. The ambassador gave Lorenzo (the Magnificent) sweet-smelling perfumes in Moorish vases.

Less than eight years later all the property of Piero de' Medici was sold by auction at Or San Michele. There were velvet bed-quilts embroidered with gold, paintings, pictures, and so on. 'How transient is Fortune!' reflects the diarist. 'Let not man be puffed up.'

But the bulkiest chapter relates to accidents and calamities. In the evening of December 30, 1500, the roof and ceiling of the Tavern of the She-Apes collapsed and fell on the sixteen people who were drinking there. By a miracle, only three were killed.

[1] Here is another entry from Landucci's journal, this time concerning Michelangelo's David. The gigantic marble statue was taken out of the workshop of Santa Maria del Fiore on May 14, 1504. A part of the wall above the door had to be demolished in order to get it out. Then, during the night, people threw stones at the statue and a guard had to be set. It was drawn very slowly through the streets with cables and strong planks. It reached the Piazza della Signoria on the 18th, and forty men were needed to move it into position, using fourteen greased joists which were changed from hand to hand. It was set up in the loggia on June 8th. . . .

November 1498. Dearth. The cost of flour is prohibitive and the Commune is selling the stocks at a controlled price: two *lire* for a bushel, or two *soldi* for a baked loaf. Only one *lira's* worth is allowed per person. There was such a rush of buyers to the Cornmarket that in the end more than fifty persons were suffocated. 'They climbed over each other, like animals.'

On August 8, 1510, there were three earthquake-shocks. The house of Masi the coppersmith was shaken, the bed and everything in the room trembled. Most of the Florentines spent the night in the public squares, fearing that their houses might collapse; but by the grace of God, none of them fell in ruins. That same year brought a terrible winter. Every drop of water froze as it fell, so that you thought you were walking on diamonds. The Arno was frozen from bank to bank. People ran on the ice as in an open square, whole companies crossed it on horseback, and games of *calcio* were played as in All Saints' meadow. In the meantime artists amused themselves by making fine snow lions, for example at the campanile of Santa Maria del Fiore.

But the great recurrent theme of these Florentine diaries was the *moria*—the plague—especially the one in 1522.

It began in August in a house near San Piero Maggiore. A man had arrived there to escape the epidemic which had broken out in Rome. He had caught it, however, and died two days after his arrival. The householders were so frightened that they removed the body at midnight and buried it with their own hands behind the church. However, they were seen by some baker's boys who informed the authorities. An order was issued in the morning to seek out those responsible for the 'excess'. It was believed that the man had been strangled. The body was then dug up, but no one recognized it as it was a good deal disfigured and, besides, the man was a stranger. Hence a new order to those who had buried him to appear before the Signoria. They obeyed and confessed what they had done; 'it was seen that the thing had happened just like that'. In the same house, a little later, several other people died. This was the beginning of the plague which lasted a year and carried off some 3,500 victims.

Florence appeared like a city which had been taken by the infidels and then abandoned. A good number of the citizens withdrew to the *contado*, the surrounding country, but here too the pestilence was raging. One peasant, crazy with despair, killed all seven members of his family, set fire to his farm and 'departed to God'. In the city all shops were closed; no more elections were held, the tribunals were not sitting, the laws had fallen into disuse. Now there would be theft, now homicide. The public squares and market-places where the citizens had been used to assembling had become graveyards or the haunt of the vilest rogues. People lived alone; instead of friends they saw only persons infected with this mortal disease. One would carry flowers in his hand, another herbs, or sponges, or phials, or other pharmaceutical preparations. They held them constantly under their nose, by way of preservative. Bread was distributed in cellars, and when one collected it, one felt as though one were spreading the plague. You heard people say: So-and-so is dead, the other is sick, this man has fled to the country, that man remains cooped up at home; some are in hospital, some under observation, others have been lost trace of.

These were the darkest times that Florence had known since the famous plague of the fourteenth century which had served as prelude to the tales of Boccaccio.

*　　*　　*　　*

By the grace of God, however, there were sunny days too. All Florentines loved conversation, and those who were most cultured and well-to-do organized parties in agreeable surroundings where they could exchange ideas and sharpen their wits by discussing the most varied subjects.

Towards the end of the fourteenth century Antonio degli Alberti had founded a sort of literary circle in his villa and gardens beyond the Arno. It was to remain famous as the *Paradiso degli Alberti*. Antonio was a cultured merchant, spiritually minded at times and now again immersed in State business. He was often banished, he took part in conspiracies when in exile, and was heavily fined for his attempts to return home in secret. But when

he had at last grown prudent and made his peace with the authorities, he settled down to entertaining his friends. These were
notable persons old and young, professors, literary celebrities,
churchmen and sometimes ladies. The company began by
attending Mass. This was followed by a very choice collation,
with high-class wines, fruit and preserves from distant lands,
while a concert with instruments and voices created an atmosphere
of harmony. Then came the hour for conversation among the
trees and flowers.

  There was no strict programme. These merchant-princes were
not vulgar pedants, and the conversation followed a natural
course, according to the caprice of the speakers and without being
directed by a chairman. Only the persons competent to speak held
the floor. Thus you might hear discourses on the best form of
government, or on autocracy, or on the lawful means of making
money, or as to whether usury is permissible, or whether animals
possess reason. The comparative merits of man and woman were
debated, and also the superiority of the *volgare*, that is of Italian,
'so rich and ductile that it can express any abstract idea, any
thought however complex or involved.'

Not that fantasy was neglected. The guests related stories or
fictions, an art in which our old acquaintance Francesco Sacchetti
was adept. These precursors of the seventeenth-century salons had
no difficulty in varying the entertainment. One of them, a man
blind from birth, very keen-witted and possessed of an exquisite
musical sense, would amaze his friends by his singing and his
playing on the organ. Another had a gift for mimicry and excelled
in making himself unrecognizable even to those who knew him
best. One was never bored at Antonio degli Alberti's.

The *Paradiso degli Alberti* took root and spread. In the second
half of the fifteenth century a rich and lettered nobleman named
Bernardo Rucellai built a magnificent palace in the Via della
Scala near Santa Maria Novella. It was surrounded by a garden
shaded with trees and adorned with grottoes and rare plants; the
hall on the ground-floor was so contrived as to afford protection
from the rain and from the heat of the dog-days. A cool and agree-

able retreat where men could renew the learned discourses of former days, such were the Oricellari gardens, as they were called. Bernardo, who died in 1514, was succeeded by his son Cosimino, a sufferer from gout—crippled by the 'French malady' —whom one was sure to find at home. He could only move about in a litter shaped like a cradle.

Round this afflicted Maecenas there gathered a circle of writers, philosophers and even political thinkers; and among the latter your attention might be drawn to a lean, hungry-looking fellow with keen eyes, a long nose, hollow cheeks and a rather large mouth encircled with deep furrows. There was something rough and tormented about the whole person of Niccolò Machiavelli. 'Being unable', as he admits, 'to speak of the art of silk, or the art of wool, or of profits and losses, it befits me to speak of the State; I must speak of that or resign myself to silence.'

Fortune had dealt harshly with this man of genius who was the founder of political science; yet now, late in life, he had discovered the audience that befitted him, and it was in the gardens of the 'Oricellari' that he read passages from his works, extolling freedom and praising the Roman Republic; and all this without causing the Medici to raise any objection, for they still feigned to be governing Florence as a republic. In 1515 Pope Leo X was well received by Cosimino. But as the government grew more authoritarian, the attitude of the Oricellari circle began to change. They resented having been duped by the Medici and, as so often happened, everything ended in a plot, and the plot failed.

Happily, however, there were oases round Florence which were not contaminated with politics, quiet haunts beside some stream or spring where the shepherdess brought her flock to water, while singing a rustic refrain. From the hill above, which the peasants called 'la scala'—the ladder—you could see Florence outspread in the valley. To such haunts, having left the city in good time, came the wise lovers of peace and the ladies in their loose-swung carriages, piled high with cushions. The company would halt in a little meadow surrounded with earthen walls in which artfully placed orange-trees sheltered the creamy complexion of the ladies from the fierce rays of the sun. Lunch was taken between ten and eleven, while someone played the lute; now *canzoni* were sung; and then came the hour for amusing talk—talk which, as a lady makes clear, 'may still be called suitable for us women and must not seem to have been inspired in you gentlemen by the fumes of wine'. And there was more converse in the evening, as the shadows fell.

CHAPTER XVIII

LIFE IN THE CITY DURING THE SIEGE AND UNDER THE TYRANNY OF ALESSANDRO

Isolation of the Florentines – The plague – Asceticism and
patriotism – The will to resist – Florentines become soldiers
– A duel under the walls – Famine – Treachery: the fall of
the city – Life of the people after the defeat – Crimes of
princes

WITH the death of Lorenzo, Duke of Urbino and father
of the famous Catherine de Médicis, the legitimate
branch of the family descended from old Cosimo
came to an end. Leo X could now say: 'We belong henceforth
no more to the house of Medici but to the house of God.'

In December 1521 Leo X himself died, perhaps of poison, at
the age of forty-seven, and a revival of Republicanism in Florence
appeared possible. But Cardinal Giulio was vigilant. He had
already had executed two young conspirators who had frequented
the Oricellari gardens; and when in 1523 he was elected Pope
under the name of Clement VII, his first step was to ensure the
obedience of his home-city. He therefore sent, as delegate to
Florence, Passerini, Cardinal of Cortona, a greedy and domineering prelate whose servility Clement could count on, and whose
duties were to keep an eye on the two Medici bastards, the young
Cardinal Ippolito, whose father had been Giuliano (Leo X's
brother) and Alessandro, a son of the Pope himself, perhaps by a
Moorish slave-girl: Alessandro had in fact the appearance of an
African with frizzled hair.[1]

To give a notion of the kind of régime to which Florence was
then subject, here is a typical example. At the time of a conclave

[1] It is more probable, however, that Alessandro's mother was a peasant
from the Roman Campagna, in the service of Alfonsina Orsini, the wife of
Piero de' Medici (U. Dorini, *I Medici e i loro tempi*, p. 248).

for the election of a new Pope, it was customary to lay bets as to the candidate who would be chosen. Now a certain Piero Orlandini had wagered against Cardinal Giulio and as, after the latter's success, he was asked to pay down one hundred crowns, he replied that he wished first, in view of Giulio's illegitimate birth, to see whether the election would be regarded as valid. The successful wagerer immediately denounced Orlandini to the magistrates, and they had him executed the same night without form or trial. Such talk could not be permitted.

The rivalry between François I and the Emperor Charles V was then in full swing, and the clouds of war were piling up over Italy. After a good deal of shuffling and evasion Clement VII dragged Florence into the Holy League against the Emperor. To meet expenses the city had to furnish 26,000 gold florins a month. And to what end! When the French had been beaten and driven from the Milanese, the Imperial army, a rabble of hungry Germans and Spaniards commanded by the Constable of Bourbon, descended on Tuscany in April 1527. Torn between fear of the Imperialists and of the troops of the Holy League, both of whom were devastating the countryside, Florence prepared to defend herself.

'One must think only of war', wrote Machiavelli, 'without giving one single thought to peace. There can be no more limping along now. One must act like a madman. Remedies which a free choice never found may be discovered in moments of despair.'

But this outburst of heroism awakened no echoes. It is true that an anti-Medici riot broke out in front of the Palazzo della Signoria, and Michelangelo's David had one of his arms broken; but order was quickly restored, and, to keep the Imperialists away, for they were thinking of pillaging Florence, the city undertook to pay them 250,000 ducats. What days of calamity! of plague, famine and unemployment! The citizens great and small, we read, 'are all sad and weighed down with unutterable melancholy'. More capes than cloaks were to be seen, more soldiers than citizens. People passed each other without daring to raise their eyes, whether from fear or shame; there was self-distrust, and mutual distrust. Shops closed hurriedly and people stayed at home.

Suddenly, about May 12, 1527, came a terrifying piece of news: Rome had been sacked by the Imperialists six days before. The The sanctuary of Christendom had been profaned, its wealth pillaged—and Clement VII was a prisoner! The sack of Prato seemed pale by comparison. The friends of liberty once more raised their heads; but Passerini, who thought that a State's greatness consisted in compelling obedience, 'had neither enough wit to understand Florentine brains nor enough judgment to satisfy them even had he been able to understand them'. A mere creature of the Pope, he stripped people of their money without concern, and they hated this 'peasant of Cortona'.

The opportunity to change the form of government was so favourable that in the rebellion which now broke out Passerini was expelled, trembling with fear, as were the two Medici bastards, Alessandro and Ippolito. As they made their way through the crowd in the Via Larga, men remarked that Florence would repent one day for having let them go free. So this interesting family of bankers, who had previously been expelled in 1443 and 1494, went into exile for the third time. Its arms and escutcheons were broken, while the insignia of the Republic were set up again. Once more Florence acclaimed the recovery of freedom, and the soul of Savonarola rose from his ashes.

On the first Sunday in June 1527 a solemn procession, headed by a picture of the Annunciation, set out from the Duomo, passed in front of the Palazzo, where it was saluted by the members of the Signoria, all arrayed in black; it then proceeded by way of the Mercato Vecchio and ended with the celebration of Mass. It was possible, by putting the workmen on night-shifts, hastily to restore the Hall of the Great Council as it had been before the return of the Medici. On June 21st more than 2,000 citizens assembled in it, the old constitution was re-enacted, and Niccolò Capponi, a disciple of Savonarola, was elected gonfaloniere.

Now that they had re-established a Republic, the Florentines returned to the austere régime of the Judge who had dedicated the city to the service of Christ; they became ascetic, closed the taverns, regulated women's dress, restricted the activity of courtesans, and renewed the old measures against Jews, debauchees, blasphemers and persons given to sodomy. By way of a public demonstration, the wax statues in the Nunziata representing Leo X and Clement VII were destroyed. 'What have these Popes to do here?'

Meanwhile the plague, which as we know had claimed so many victims in 1522-23, was once again raging. People with money applied the maxim: 'Get away early, come back late', and sought refuge as far away as possible. Those who remained took every precaution and avoided communicating with each other, unless it was to call out from a safe distance: 'Stiamo chiaretti', that is, let us keep our distances. They went out only in the late evenings, and then kept sniffing at the drugs they carried, which, so they said, kept the brain healthy. Before getting out of bed in the morning they rubbed themselves with electuaries.

Physicians had unfortunately been the first to take to flight, and the citizens were reduced to the absurd mixtures concocted by charlatans. Nearly all the shops of the major arts, such as those of silk, wool and pharmacy, were closed or, at most, only half-open, with a protecting bar to prevent people from leaning against the door. Money was not taken by hand but received on a wood or metal tray, and it was then not put in the till but in a bowl of water. Most domestic animals, cats and dogs, were sacrificed.

Officials of Public Health were appointed, and they, for the love of God and out of benevolence, kept watch at the city-gates to bar the entry of any travellers from Rome. Citizens suspected of infection were required to display a piece of white material on their shoulder or at their girdle; and the same sign was fastened to the outside door-bell of infected houses. Persons definitely infected were cared for in a special hospital and, when this was full, the Commune built a number of wood and straw cabins outside the walls, from the Porta Santa Croce to the Porta di Prato, and here nearly 600 patients were confided to the care of the Society of Mercy.

"Twas a wretched thing', wrote a witness, 'and deserving of

(right) Florentine
~~ly~~ with her two women
~~by~~ Ghirlandajo. (S. Maria
Novella, Florence)

(below) Birth of the Virgin by Ghirlandajo (S. Maria Novella)
showing Florentine interior

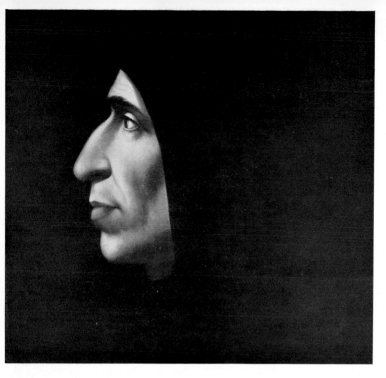

13. (*left*)
Savonarola by
Bartolomeo (S
Marco Museum
Florence)

(*below*)
The martyrdo
of Savonarola i
the Piazza del
Signoria
by Ignoto
Fiorentino (S.
Marco Museum

all compassion, to see this city, once so flourishing, now almost empty and a prey to the lowest scum, folk who thought only of appropriating other people's goods and of enjoying themselves without fear or respect for the law.' Most of the public executioners were missing, and the two who remained could not cope with their task. So great was the insecurity that men made their wills in the street or on the roof-tops; and they even confessed there.[1]

In order to get rid of the 'little ragamuffins' who picked pockets in the Mercato Vecchio and elsewhere, it was decided in the end to maintain them at the expense of the Commune in a room of the *Sala del Papa*, at Santa Maria Novella. Here they were fed and slept together like puppies.

The preachers meanwhile thought only of extolling the new régime and attacking the Pope. People's nerves were more than ever on edge. Coming out of the Council one day, a relative of the gonfaloniere Capponi was annoyed at the sight of the young men mounting guard. 'Thank God', he remarked, 'we shall be freed from all these brats.' His words were overheard by Jacopo

---

[1] People grew accustomed to the epidemic, and their sensibility was not improved by it. Take the example of Benvenuto Cellini on his return to Florence after the plague. When he knocked on the door of the family home—'A furious female humpback appeared at a window and tried to send me away by loading me with abuse and saying that I was infecting her. —"Ah, spiteful humpback," I cried, "is there no face in the house but yours?" —"No, may the Devil throttle you!" she replied.—"That's just what will happen to you in less than two hours from now", I shouted back. All this noise brought out a neighbour, who told me that my father and all the family had died of the plague. As I had already guessed as much, my sorrow was less keen. But the neighbour added that the scourge had only spared my young sister Liperata.'

Cellini found Liperata, who had believed him dead. 'The sight of me, so unexpectedly, threw her into such a transport of joy and amazement that she fell swooning into my arms. After weeping a little over her father, her mother, her husband and a baby she had lost, she thought of preparing supper. During the whole of that evening we spoke no more of death but of a thousand gay and mad things as if we were at a wedding; and so our meal was most agreeable.' Cellini then set up in business in the Mercato Vecchio, where he made a lot of money by mounting jewels.

I

Alamanni, who retorted: 'You will be finished with before this guard departs.' Whereupon Leonardo, another relative of Capponi's, taxed Jacopo with being over touchy. Jacopo took it amiss and, when they were near Donatello's statue of Judith, drew his dagger and attacked Leonardo, who fell. Thinking he had killed him, Jacopo took to his heels and, as he was pursued, cried out 'Guard, to the rescue.' There was no response. He was arrested and hauled off to the Palazzo, where the Signoria then had the doors shut. A vote was taken on the spot and the verdict, but for one white bean, was unanimous. He was condemned for trying to raise a riot and for calling for the guard. He died courageously, and his head was afterwards displayed at a window for the edification of the multitude.

But the plague had made the general situation even more painful than it already was. The chief magistrates, and especially the gonfaloniere who was not the bravest of men, saw only too clearly how dangerous was the isolation of Florence, abandoned as she was by the French and unable to rely on help from Venice, her commercial rival. The Venetians, for their part, did not think that the Florentines would put up a prolonged resistance. 'Even when faced by an armed foe they think not of the general interest of their city but of the particular interest of their group.'

The event however was to prove the contrary.

*   *   *   *

Public feeling was no doubt shaken by the defeats suffered by France, but the resolution to defend the city against all and sundry, against Charles V and his bands and against Clement VII who wanted to regain mastery over Florence, remained intact. All citizens between the ages of eighteen and thirty-six were mobilized. These formed the militia, dear to the heart of Machiavelli,[1] and when they were seen on the march behind their standards, well dressed, well disciplined and in martial array, one of the citizens cried out: 'Without her militia, Florence was limping and as if

---

[1] He had died, neglected and despised, on June 22, 1527, after the restoration of the Republic.

on one leg; with her militia she walks on both feet!' The fury of the plague was diminishing at this time: it had at least served to rid the city of the pusillanimous.

Asceticism favoured patriotism. As Umberto Dorini says, the reawakening of the ancient virtues acted upon the young nobles and intellectuals and so, by a reflex movement, on the people. The uncompromising patriots—those whom one might call the Jacobins of the age—even reproached Capponi with lacking in energy. 'You will be broken in pieces', they told him. 'You have changed the cork but not the wine; now the people want a change of wine.'

But Capponi was not the man to form great resolutions and abide by them. He manœuvred, and one day a letter of his in cipher was discovered, proving beyond a doubt that he was negotiating with the Pope. In Venice he would have been beheaded. The surprising thing is that the Florentine Republicans merely excluded him from the city and appointed in his place a merchant of doubtful probity who had been twice declared bankrupt but who was a notable anti-Papist. His name was Carducci.

The rest of Italy was at peace, but Florence had to prepare for war: she had been excluded from the treaties which Charles V had signed with the French and with the Pope. The Signoria now ordered the city to be fortified under the direction of the 'governor and procurator of military works', the great Michelangelo, who abandoned the Medici chapel where he had been working on the tombs of the 'tyrants', and served his apprenticeship as an engineer and as inspector of the fortresses of Tuscany. And in the meantime an inventory was made of the houses and convents that would have to be demolished, and of their value.

So we see that these artisans, who had been accustomed to working all day and part of the night, carrying bales of cloth and keeping meticulous accounts, could on occasion rise to heights of greatness. The young men who had until recently been unused to arms and had passed their time gossiping on benches and slandering the passers-by, were fired to enthusiasm by the decree on the militia. It seemed as though 'some benevolent Circe had changed them from beasts into men for the salvation of their country.'

But what was lacking was money. The Medici had so thoroughly 'medicined' the country that they had, so to speak, flayed it. Many Florentine merchants had been ruined by the sack of Rome, and there was a budgetary deficit of 450,000 ducats. The government now had recourse to the most drastic fiscal expedients. A forced loan was imposed, and the ten per cent tax was levied on the clergy as well as on the laity. Finally the uncoined silver that was found in churches and convents was sent to the *Zecca* and converted into money bearing the lily on one side and a cross with the crown of thorns on the other.

The militia which had been reinforced by levies of peasants from the surrounding country now numbered 13,000 men, of whom 7,000 were stationed in the city under the command of the condottiere Malatesta Baglione of Perugia. As he was himself the son of a condottiere who had been beheaded by order of Leo X, it was hoped that hostility to the Medici would ensure his remaining loyal.

The general whom Charles V had appointed to subjugate Florence—this Florence whose freedom appeared as a scandal in the midst of an Italy reduced to servitude—was a French refugee, the Prince of Orange; and he was counting for success on the pusillanimity of the inhabitants, and notably of the aristocrats who set so much store by their villas and palaces. But these very men took a foremost part in demolishing any parts of their property which might impede military operations. Apart from this, the convents and churches in the suburbs were also razed to the ground. One day, however, a demolition squad which had reached the convent of San Salvi stood before a painting of the Last Supper by Andrea del Sarto. They had not the courage to destroy it. The same artist, by the way, was commissioned somewhat later to portray on the façade of the Mercatanzia the likeness of a number of traitors and rebels who had been hanged. He dared not refuse; but fearing to be surnamed Andrea of the Gallows, like one of his predecessors, he carried out the work in secret. Later still he caught the plague from a landzknecht and died alone, abandoned by Lucrezia.

The Florentines, meanwhile, seemed like men regenerated. They girded up their loins, exchanged the hood for the military cap, cut their hair short, let their beards grow, lived the life of soldiers and kept an eye on defeatists as well as on the mercenaries. They were prepared to resist until the moment when men could say: 'Here once was Florence.'

In September 1529 the Prince of Orange's army appeared in the Val d'Arno. The Spanish troops took up their position on the hill of Fiesole, while the cavalry overran the countryside. A pack of marauders under an adventurer named Maramaldo now joined the besieging forces. Arezzo and Cortona, strong places which protected Florence, had already fallen. The jaws of the vice were closing. On October 29th the bombardment began, and the morale of the citizens tended to go down.

On the other hand the commissaries who were directing operations remained unshakeable, and their dispatches were full of confidence. 'We are very willing,' they wrote, 'and our courage increases day by day. The only anxiety arises from the great expenses. Everyone feels he is fighting for the honour of Italy. We are ready to employ all our resources rather than fall under the yoke of tyranny. Our citizens are willing to endure anything in order to maintain the liberty which they appreciate the more keenly now that it is threatened. Our infantry has attained such perfection as to numbers and valour that, if it took the field, it would make all Italy tremble.'

This was largely bluster; and yet it was true that these merchants could do far more than measure out cloth or wield the pen in the counting-house. If, as Varchi says, other cities had displayed the same firmness, constancy and courage as Florence did, Italy would have recovered her old-time freedom.

Unfortunately the members of the government did not always agree among themselves. 'One must prefer the certain to the uncertain', argued the peace-party. 'An agreement is a definite advantage, which would save our goods, our lives, perhaps even our freedom. War is of uncertain advantage.' To which the bold spirits replied that there was no question here of a commercial bargain. 'If you try to make terms with the Medici, then either you will cut us to pieces or we shall cut you!'

Nevertheless, a deputation was sent from Florence to wait upon Clement VII. They asked him to grant them liberty and the maintenance of a popular régime. 'Of liberty,' he replied, 'I will give you more than you can imagine, but as for the popular régime, that is an intolerable servitude, imposed by the few on the many, and I will have none of it.' The Pope's temper rose; 'full of rancour', he shouted indignantly at the emissaries: 'You have murdered me in wax, which makes it all the clearer that you would have murdered me in real earnest.' After complaining of the burning of his villa at Careggi and of the sale of Church properties, he shrugged his shoulders and remarked: 'I shall see.'

What people did see, on the front of the Medici palace in the Via Larga, was a painting of Clement wearing the papal tiara and climbing the ladder to a gallows while Charles V brandished a sword on which was written: 'What have you come to now, my friend!' This was the work of a descendant of Ghiberti. Attempts to negotiate directly with the Emperor above the head of the Pope were no more successful. When the Florentines insisted that they would hold out against force, Charles was positively scandalized. 'Ah!' he cried, 'is that how you speak to me? Begone, and let me hear no more of your business.'

All this discouraged the peace-party, and the voice of the bolder spirits prevailed. The enemy's forces, on the other hand, continued to increase; they soon numbered some 40,000 men. The Spaniards, who had reinforced the Imperialists, cried out: 'Get your brocades ready, Madame Florence; we are coming to measure them with our pikes.' But the beleaguered Florentines did not blench. On the night of December 11, 1529, a thousand of them donned white shirts so as to recognize each other in the darkness, and then made a sortie and surprised the enemy's camp. The Imperialists fled in disorder, hustled by the 'white shirts' and demoralized by great herds of swine which had broken out of their lairs. The sortie might have met with even greater success, as 200 of the enemy were lying dead or wounded when Malatesta Baglione unexpectedly sounded the retreat.

His procedure was becoming more and more suspect. He wore the device *Libertas* on his cap, and affected an immense love for the people; but men murmured, here and there, that he was compounding with the enemy and that by continuing the war he was deliberately exhausting and ruining the Florentines. Michelangelo had long been of this opinion. But the people as a whole suspected nothing, any more than did the new gonfaloniere Girolami, an honest man but weak and optimistic, who kept repeating: 'Citizens, you are the masters, I depend on you.' His predecessor, however corrupt, was more of a man.

Morale, however, remained good. Had not brother Savonarola predicted that Florence would be beleaguered for her sins by a Pope, but would be delivered by angels? Prophets now sprang up in numbers, notable among whom was Sister Domenica del Paradiso, a nun; and a wool-carder named Pieruccio who was the oracle of the lower classes and who announced the death of Charles V. Processions of men, and of women separately, threaded the streets. At Santa Maria del Fiore a citizen ended his harangue with the words: 'Liberty or Death!'

Apart from all this, the daily routine went on much as before. The shops were open, everyone went to work, the housewives frequented the market although there was less and less to buy. People no longer quarrelled: 'This is not the moment for fooling', it was said. 'We shall settle these matters later.' The words 'Poor and Free' were written up on the walls; but all night long the sound of bells was replaced by the thunder of cannon.

Even so, the Florentines missed no opportunity for amusement. There existed 'a denunciation-barrel' into which you could drop a card bearing the name of anyone who was suspect and who might risk being declared a rebel; now one day the names of the Pope and four Florentine Cardinals who were his counsellors were found in it. During the carnival of 1530 a great game of *calcio* was organized in the Piazza Santa Croce between twenty-five young men of the white team against twenty-five of the green; and in order to be heard in the enemy's camp and to defy the barbarians, men with trumpets and other instruments were posted on the roof of the church. This provoked a cannonade, but there were fortunately no casualties.

On March 12, 1530, hostilities were interrupted for a short time by the duel between Ludovico Martelli and Giovanni Bandini. They belonged to different parties and both were in love with Marietta de' Ricci, a pretty married woman who was somewhat giddy-pated, to say the least. The two rivals wore red satin jackets, red trunk-hose interwoven with white, and red bonnets with a white plume. They were mounted on Arab horses and accompanied by their seconds. Trumpets went before them, and the captains and soldiers of the militia followed. After crossing the Ponte alla Carraja the procession made its way to the Porta San Friano where physicians, barbers and *restaurateurs* were waiting. The company halted at the outskirts of the enemy's trenches. It was understood that the artillery on either side would not fire that day, and the agreement was strictly observed.

The adversaries entered the lists without helmets and simply armed with a sword and mailed gauntlet; the sleeves of their right arms were tucked up to the elbow. Martelli attacked and Bandini struck him on the head; although blinded with the flow of blood, he rushed forward and was again wounded in the head. 'Yield yourself to me, if you don't wish to die', cried Bandini.—'I yield to the Prince' (the commander of the Spaniards).—'Today, I am the Prince', said Bandini. Martelli yielded. Marietta was allowed by her husband to go and see him lying on the bed where he died soon afterwards, more from chagrin than from his wounds.

Skirmishing meanwhile became more frequent and the Florentines usually had the better of it, but just when an operation was likely to be really successful, Baglione would sound the retreat. It was then that the real hero of the siege appeared, a man whose name was to remain in honour among his countrymen, Francesco

Ferrucci. He was a man of forty-one, an accountant, and had been paymaster to the forces. Enthusiasm for ancient history had reinforced his natural qualities of leadership, his energy and severity in meting out punishment. When commissioned to recapture Volterra, the volcanic hill-town which had been taken by the enemy, he succeeded in driving out the adventurer Mara-maldo. Unfortunately, however, at the end of May 1530 his victory was offset by the fall of Empoli. The only route by which Florence had access to the outer world was thus blockaded, and famine grew more severe. Ass-meat was a delicacy reserved for great occasions, cats had disappeared, and efforts were made to kill swallows, owls and falcons. A rat cost thirteen soldi, an egg ten soldi, a barrel of wine ten crowns; and there was no wheat. The Imperialists jeered at the defenders: 'We shall let you continue to get hungrier and hungrier, until we take you out on leashes like dogs.' One day the Signoria decided to get rid of all useless mouths; then the decree was withdrawn or, rather, applied only to elderly courtesans, a decision of which the public disapproved.

Treason was rife. A certain canon secretly deposited, in the loophole of one of the gates, information which was sent for by Baccio Valori, the Pope's agent in the Imperialist army. Other people made signs from the roof-tops, waving pieces of cloth by day or showing lights after dark. But the arch-traitor was Malatesta Baglione, the commander of the Florentine army.

He hoped that when the citizens, abandoned as they now were by France and Venice, were sufficiently reduced by hunger, they would beg him to treat with the enemy, and that in this way he could not be accused of treason. But the Florentines persisted in defending themselves with a stubbornness which wrung a cry of admiration from that coolest of observers, Guicciardini. 'Truly great', he said, 'is the example of these men who, disunited as they are, without hope of succour and in face of a thousand diffi-culties, have been withstanding for seven months the efforts of an army which it seemed that they could not withstand for seven days.'

Baglione did not admire these madmen. He strove to hold them

I*

back, gave them conflicting advice and so contrived that their enterprises should miscarry. When they spoke of making a sortie —'That's a child's project', he cried. 'To show your face to the enemy is pure madness, it will lead to the ruin of the city.' To which the Signoria replied that he was commanding instead of obeying, prating instead of fighting.

On May 25th Baglione decided to bring matters to a head, to betray the city. He negotiated with the Pope and with the Prince of Orange who was personally in great need of money, as he had lost everything in gambling: during those long days before the walls of Florence time had weighed heavily on his hands. A few weeks earlier Ferrucci had written these words, in the language of an accountant and the spirit of a hero: 'Even if three-quarters of us perish rather than become slaves, the quarter who survive will have such glory as to compensate for the expenditure.'

He was now the last hope of Florence. The city invested him with dictatorial powers, equal to those of the Signoria and the people. He was given the right to make treaties and to hand over cities or money. From Volterra he marched to Pisa, where he contrived to raise troops and obtain horses. His next object was to reach Florence in three days and compel the Imperialists to raise the siege. The latter, commanded by Orange, went to meet him, reassured as to their rear by Baglione's undertaking to make no move.

On July 31st Ferrucci marched towards Pistoia, closely followed by Maramaldo's ruffians. From a hill-top on August 3rd he saw fires raging among the houses below, and the enemy's banners floating from the bell-tower of the little town of Gavinana. He had been forestalled: of this there was no doubt; but he had no thought of shunning the encounter. It would have been cowardice to do so, although he had scarcely 3,500 men as against 8,000 of the enemy. At a crossroads his cavalry worsted those of the Prince of Orange, who was killed as he tried to rally his men. (The peasants used formerly to point out the steep lane where he fell.) Under a heavy rainstorm Ferrucci forced his way into the town. Driven out again by Maramaldo, he took shelter in a small house where, armed with a pike, he defended himself almost single-handed. Finally, when covered with wounds, he was taken prisoner by a Spaniard, who trusted that he could hold him to ransom. Unfortunately Maramaldo came up.

'Vile merchant, you shall die.'

'You are killing a man already dead', was the reply.

Maramaldo plunged his dagger into Ferrucci's throat. Thus perished the man whom the Florentines had named the Gideon who would deliver their country.

*   *   *   *

Baglione, on his side, was trying to prevent a general sortie. For this everything seemed ready. The captains had communicated; an interminable procession of penitents, bare-footed, had marched through the city, Savonarola's disciples were promising victory: God Himself would send His angels. But, except among a few fanatics, there was little enthusiasm, and on August 8th Baglione showed his disapproval by asking for leave, thinking that it would be refused. Instead, he was taken at his word.

His anger was terrible. He was lying down, a prey to 'the French malady', when a messenger from the Signoria brought their reply. On hearing it he sprang from his couch and struck the envoy with his dagger. 'Come to terms with the Pope', he cried, 'or I shall let the Imperialists into the city. Florence is not a stable for mules.[1] I will save her in spite of traitors.' The traitors in his eyes were the Savonarolians and those who were for resistance to the end. Now that the mask was off, he took possession of the gates and turned his cannon against the city.

Such confusion prevailed in the Signoria that some of the members even blamed a little girl of eleven who was accused of

[1] The following words are attributed to Michelangelo: 'Destroy the Medici palace and establish on the site a square that will be called the *Piazza dei Muli*.' Now the word mule, meaning bastard, was aimed at Ippolito, Alessandro and the Pope himself.

spreading discord. Catherine, the daughter of Lorenzo de' Medici and Madeleine de la Tour d'Auvergne, had been living in Florence since 1525. She was a symbol of hope for some, of fear for others. Each party wished to have her in keeping, and while yet so young she learned the meaning of political ambition and passion. In 1527 she had been placed in the convent of the Murate, where her presence provoked argument between those nuns who were for the Pope and those who were for liberty. When the situation deteriorated the Signoria thought it necessary to transfer Catherine to the Convent of Santa Lucia in the Via San Gallo, a safer place; but the gentleman commissioned to arrange the transfer had great difficulty in carrying out his mission. The little girl broke into shrill cries, protested that she wished to remain where she was, and thought she was going to be murdered. She cut off her hair, dressed as a nun and told the gentleman who had requested her to put on her usual dress that she would not do so; she declared she would go as she was, so that everyone could see that a nun was being abducted from the convent; and in fact it was as a nun, on horseback, that she reached Santa Lucia.

When singing of the birth of Catherine, Ariosto makes Florence say: 'One branch is still green with a few leaves; betwixt fear and hope I remain uncertain whether winter will leave it to me or snatch it away.' Catherine de Médicis survived, and this early experience was not lost to her.

The Prince of Orange's death had filled Florence with joy, Ferrucci's plunged her into despair, the treachery of her commander-in-chief was the final blow. Now, the Florentines were 'dying of fear', cursing the Pope and his agent Baglione. Those who still cried: 'Let us fight' were no longer listened to. The Imperialists, in the meantime, were hovering round the city like vultures and already computing the amount of pillage that would fall to them. 'We can do anything', they said, 'since the head of the Church gives us the right to do evil.'

The night of August 8th was dismal. The citizens dared not go down into the streets or the soldiers leave their quarters. On the 9th the Signoria ordered arms to be laid down, on the 10th the prisoners were to be freed. Then the whole city assumed a new appearance, and the cry of *Palle*! went up. Four hundred young nobles, judging that resistance was impossible, went over to Baglione, and the Signoria sent envoys to the enemy's camp to discuss terms. A riot involving the 'obstinate' party nearly broke out in front of the Palazzo, and Florence, according to Varchi, 'was within a hair's breadth of being sacked'.

But wisdom prevailed, and on August 11th, under the direction of the Pope's representative, Valori, the terms of capitulation were drawn up. Florence would pay 80,000 ducats to the besieging army and hand over fifty hostages by way of security. His Holiness would pardon the insults he had received, and within the next four months the Emperor Charles V would fix the form of government, 'always providing for the maintenance of liberty'. A very honourable agreement, said a naïve patriot, delighted with this proviso.

Baglione, who had been responsible for the Papal victory, was somewhat anxious as to the sequel, and he now asked the Pope to confirm the favours he was supposed to have promised, and in particular the title of Duke. But Clement VII took offence at such pretensions. 'If Malatesta had me by the hair or imprisoned in a barrel where he was feeding me through the bung-hole, he would not be asking for more or better!' Treason was agreeable enough, but not the traitor. In December 1530 the man who had sold his brethren 'like lambs in a slaughter-house, yielded up his soul to the Devil, in the place where Judas and other traitors are'. Before dying he had advised his son never to serve the republics.

Florence could now calculate the cost of the siege. Eight thousand persons were dead, and the losses in money, harvests, flocks and herds, houses and cloth were immense. A bitter outlook, indeed, for the merchants. The condition of the city was pitiable, with the nobles furious at having been stripped of so much property and dominated by the plebeians; the peasants dying of hunger; the monks and nuns despised for their false prophecies. 'Everyone went about with lowered head, wild-eyed, pallid and distrustful.' And, overtopping all other misfortunes, the plague which had broken out in the enemy's camp in June, and which, now that the gates were open, once more invaded Florence.

The Imperialists, on their side, had lost 14,000 men, more than the defenders, and they were not satisfied. Frustrated of their hope of sacking the city, they added to their demands, crying out for more and more money. Fortunately they disagreed among themselves. On August 28th the Italian mercenaries in the Imperialist army attacked the Spaniards, after making sure of the neutrality of the German landzknechts—who ended by betraying them. This battle, which went on for two days and cost 600 lives, proved the salvation of Florence. The Spaniards took refuge in the fortresses, while the Italian mercenaries allowed food supplies to enter Florence and then withdrew to Fiesole.

The Pope, who every day during the siege had hoped to hear that his native city had surrendered, was groaning: 'Would to God that Florence had never existed!' He now meant to punish her, but from a distance, without taking a personal hand in the matter; so that, in spite of the pardon that had been granted, repression was inflicted, but by intermediaries. Valori was one, Guicciardini, who displayed 'great cruelty', another. Five persons including the gonfaloniere Carducci were beheaded, while his successor Girolami died, no doubt from poison, in the fortress of Volterra. A Dominican who had preached resistance was to end his days in a dungeon. Great numbers were exiled, not only for reasons of State but on account of private hatred or resentment. 'Men were sold like beasts', and many estates were confiscated, although Valori agreed to spare those who could buy themselves off.

Thus, after resisting for eleven months under a general who frustrated rather than directed her efforts, Florence fell gloriously three years after Rome had been 'assassinated by the same soldiery of Charles V', and, thanks to a Pope who was a bastard of the Medici, the banner of Italian independence was struck down. In the enslaved condition of the peninsula, the siege and the fall of Florence

produced a sensation. Such heroism on the part of a city of merchants had not been expected, and the historian Paolo Giovio,
raising his hands to heaven, admired the prolonged resistance they
had offered more than all the acts of the Ancients or the Moderns.
Stendhal in the early nineteenth century was to write: 'Despite
the treachery of her leaders, all the miracles of which dying liberty
was capable were displayed during this siege. All that Florence
needed, to save herself, was a régime of terror.' Today Umberto
Dorini has summed up the drama in the following words: 'The
siege shed a ray of glory over the fall of the Florentine Republic;
it was an act of epic grandeur that terminated the three centuries
of her marvellous history.'

*   *   *   *

When the capitulation was signed, Michelangelo had hidden in
the belfry of a church near the Porta San Miniato; during this time
his house was being searched. He dared not show himself. And
yet Clement VII was anxious to see him resume his work in the
Medici chapel, he had no thought of punishing and was even
prodigal of kind words. 'His conduct during the siege amazes me',
said the Pope, 'for I have never done him any harm; on the
contrary, I admire him.'

The Pope's words were communicated to Michelangelo in
order to encourage him to go back to work. It was even hoped
that the 'terrible' sculptor would change his whole attitude. What
blindness to the truth! If he once more took up the chisel, as
he did, it was in a mood of dull despair, of lonely rage: he saw
before his eyes the ruin of his country, the end of freedom, a
series of humiliations and of efforts that had proved abortive.
Filled more than ever with the spirit of Dante and Savonarola, he
carved in marble his grief, his disenchantment, even his medita-
tions; and the clearest reply he gave the Pope is contained in the
famous quatrain he wrote on Night:

> *Grato m'è'l sonno e più l'esser di sasso;*
> *Mentre che'l danno e la vergogna dura*

Non veder, non sentir mè' gran ventura;
Però non mi destar; deh! parla basso![1]

Florence now sank little by little into slavery. The period of four months, within which the city was to receive a constitution, was greatly prolonged; but it had served 'like the interval between two acts of a play' to destroy the last hopes of liberty and prepare the transition from republican to monarchical forms of government. It was only in February 1531 that the Pope, in agreement with Charles V, ordered the frizzly haired bastard Alessandro de' Medici to be joined to the *Balia*, or provisional government. The other bastard, Cardinal Ippolito, refused to accept this appointment and rushed to Florence. But he was too late, and although a more likeable man than his rival, he was excluded. Charles V, after antedating the *lodo*,[2] now published the decree appointing Alessandro as Protector of Florence.

Arriving, though without ceremony, on July 5, 1531, he tried at first to create a good impression and even to flatter the people. But distrust was general. The inhabitants were ordered to hand over their weapons at the risk of severe penalties; the police-spies who were sent round to search houses took the opportunity of stealing; private grudges were avenged, and sometimes the police 'planted' weapons on a house by pushing them through the ventilators, and then arrested the householder. This created panic; and everyone tried to get rid of anything that might look like a weapon, larding-pins for example, or any pointed object.

Symptoms of unrest were now to be discerned. It was the cus-

---

[1] The translation cited by Baedeker runs:

> Ah! glad am I to sleep in stone, while woe
> And dire disgrace rage unreproved near—
> A happy chance neither to see nor hear.
> So wake me not! When passing whisper low.

The verses were written by Michelangelo in reply to a complimentary quatrain by G.-B. Strozzi, which also appears on the statue of Night. The statues of Day and Night were made by the great sculptor to adorn the sarcophagus of Giuliano de' Medici, in the New Sacristy which was designed as a last resting-place for members of the Medici family.   (Translator)

[2] *Lodo*—the decision of an arbitrator.   (Translator)

tom on fête-days for the young men, especially the nobles, to come out in disguise and push through the streets a large inflated balloon, which they would throw at open shop-fronts in order to oblige the tradesmen to close them. In wet weather everything was splashed with mud, and so these youths had been in the habit of warning the tradesmen by trumpet, in advance. Now one rainy day towards Christmas two sons of the aristocrat Strozzi, with their companions, all in disguise, invaded the Mercato Vecchio and the Mercato Nuovo without preliminary warning. They turned everything topsy-turvy, and their balloon struck a magistrate whose clothes were badly stained and spotted with dirt. A complaint was lodged with the Signoria, whereupon the rowdies were arrested and taken to the Bargello. Filippo Strozzi contrived to hush up the affair and compensate all who had suffered; but Alessandro saw clearly enough that the intention had been to organize a riot against him.

The truth was that this swarthy ruffian had quickly disgusted the Florentines by his plundering and his debaucheries. Guicciardini himself confessed that 'we have the whole population against us'. The partisans of liberty, now in exile, had sought refuge at Venice and in France, especially at Avignon. The Retz and Mirabeau families are of Florentine origin. But Clement VII was still not easy in his mind and, despite the 'proviso for liberty' contained in the capitulation, he continued to work for the complete abolition of republican institutions. Charles V agreed to this, so that without appearing in the open, 'by throwing the stone without anyone's seeing the hand', he suppressed the Signoria and caused Alessandro to be appointed hereditary Duke of Florence (April 1532). Alessandro was to marry Margaret, a natural daughter of the Emperor; for Charles had need of this son-in-law, undistinguished as he was, to ensure his domination over Tuscany. The 'blackamoor' now threw off all restraint. 'Duke and Lord with the rod'—Doge as he was still called, he proceeded in pomp, amid fanfares of trumpets and salvoes of artillery, to enter into possession of the Palazzo della Signoria. He with his four counsellors took all decisions; the 'Forty-eight' and the 'Two hundred', which were the only surviving assemblies, had now been reduced to the status of registry-offices. To execute his will the 'doge' had a ruffian named Alessandro Vitelli on whom he could rely, this man being a born enemy of the Florentines since they had beheaded his father Paolo at the time of the Pisan war, in 1499; and finally, to establish a firm domination, he followed the suggestion of the aristocrats, and notably of Filippo Strozzi himself, in building a fortress 'on the neck of the people', at the Porta di Faenza. This was something that Florence had not yet known.

The Principate was not distinguished for austerity. Alessandro, a great woman-hunter, passed his nights in carousing and 'after emerging from these orgies, would go masked through the streets with two acolytes in attendance'. His amusements cost from four to six hundred crowns a day, and though the Pope advised him to exercise more reserve, he spared no woman in Florence, not even the nuns.

He had of course somewhat to moderate his behaviour when at the end of April 1535 the Emperor passed through Florence on his way from Rome. The reception was cold, if sumptuous. Forty lords each girt with a silver hilted sword and dagger, and wearing a purple satin doublet, white trunk-hose, a violet beret embroidered with gold and a white plume on the left side of it—the Emperor's livery—bore aloft a canopy of brocade under which Charles V advanced on his white charger. Alessandro presented him with the keys of the city and Charles courteously returned them.

Along the processional route, beginning at the Porta San Pietro Gattolini (now the Porta Romana), a series of triumphal arches had been set up, bearing statues which symbolized—ostensibly—the joy of the Florentines, and which extolled the Emperor's victories. Everywhere appeared his device, '*Plus Oultre*'; and the ladies in gala dress leaned out of the windows that were hung with tapestries.

Severe and distant in mien, and accompanied by only a few gentlemen to show that he had no fear of these former rebels, Charles V spent a week in visiting the sights of Florence, the churches for example, and the Medici chapel, the work of Michelangelo whom he admired. And when he proceeded on his way, he, unlike former emperors, left no privilege or souvenir of his visit. He desired in this way to show his contempt and even hostility toward these Florentines who had been the last to try to escape his domination. He had let the exiles know that they were permitted to return home; but they would not agree, even with the prospect of recovering their property, to reappear as slaves in a city where they had once been free.

On May 31st Alessandro's fiancée, the Emperor's daughter Margaret, a girl of twelve, arrived in Florence. Filippo Strozzi took a conspicuous part in the festivities that were then organized; and it appears that to humour the duke, he behaved in a manner ill-suited to his age. And now began the dramas that accompany despotism. Cardinal Ippolito de' Medici could not tolerate the accession to power of a bastard of mean origin and ignoble habits. He attempted to gain the Emperor's good will with a view to supplanting Alessandro. Now while he was at Itri in the kingdom of Naples in August 1535, he happened one day to feel rather unwell; and in order to restore him his seneschal, a Tuscan named Giovanni Andrea di Borgo San Sepolcro, brought him a bowl of chicken soup, flavoured with pepper. Scarcely had he swallowed it than his malaise became more acute. 'I have been poisoned', he said, 'and it is Giovanni Andrea who has poisoned me.'

He died five days afterwards, at the age of twenty-four. When the seneschal was questioned he simply replied: 'The thing is done.' He had pounded the ingredients for the poison between two stones, but no one knew who had given them to him. Most people ascribed the deed to Alessandro who called the Cardinal an 'evil wasp' and hated him. After being imprisoned for a time in Rome, the seneschal made his way to Florence where he was received in Alessandro's court; but later on his fellow townsmen at Borgo San Sepolcro put him to death.

Under the tutelage of his father-in-law, Doge Alessandro exercised sole authority in Florence. He kept a close watch on the exiles and his spies were everywhere: he distrusted his dear subjects and ground them down with taxation. Nor did he abandon his habits of debauchery. Every night would be marked by some joyous adventure in the company of Lorenzino. This young man was the elder son of a descendant of the junior branch of the Medici; his mother was a Soderini. A creature of poor constitution, dark-featured, restless and melancholy, Lorenzino never laughed, he merely sniggered. He was a poet and humanist, and yet subject to absurd fits of violence. When living in Rome he had broken the heads of the statues that adorn the Arch of Constantine, doubtless in order to make people talk of him. The Pope, not daring to mete out punishment, merely banished him, and Lorenzino settled in Florence where he became the familiar and hired spy of Alessandro. When his friends reproached him with this ignominy, he replied that they would soon have proof that, on the contrary, he was a good man. One day, when talking with Benvenuto Cellini about the device that was to be inscribed on the reverse side of a medal for Alessandro, he said: 'I am thinking of nothing but to furnish you with a reverse worthy of his Excellence.' And as the Duke himself urged Lorenzino to satisfy Cellini—'I will do so as soon as possible', said he, 'and I hope it will be such as to cause the world to marvel.'

Not satisfied with being Alessandro's spy, he was also his procurer: he obtained for the 'blackamoor' the women on whom the latter had cast his eye, and he shared in his nocturnal escapades. Francesco Vettori, an old friend of Machiavelli's, one evening saw the Duke riding across the Ponte Santa Trinità, accompanied by two attendants and with Lorenzino behind him on the same horse. Next day he felt he should put the Duke on his guard. 'What folly is this,' he exclaimed, 'for a prince who has triumphed over Florence by force of arms and is the first to enjoy such authority, to go out alone at night, on horseback with a man behind him, and only two or three attendants! and what is still more perilous, to trust one man only to hold the ladder when he is scaling a wall!' Vettori was alluding to the convent of San Domenico and other convents which the Duke used to enter by means of silk or rope ladders with the help of Lorenzino.

Alessandro was not shocked and he even smiled as he answered:

'Have no fear, Francesco. A man does not escape his destiny. But now that I see you love me truly, I will be more prudent.'

The woman he was then coveting was no other than Lorenzino's aunt, Caterina Soderini, a very handsome, noble and haughty person who was married to a Ginori and lived behind the Medici palace. Was Lorenzino in love with his aunt? If so, it would explain a good deal. In any event, when Alessandro asked him to perform his usual office as an intermediary, he replied that it would be difficult but that, after all, women were always women and that the husband happened at that moment to be on business in Naples.

Lorenzino's acquaintances were not confined to the aristocracy. He now got in touch with a certain Scoroncocolo, a bandit who had been condemned for homicide and to whom Lorenzino complained bitterly of a great lord who, he said, was making sport of him. 'Tell me who he is, and leave him to me', said the other; 'he will trouble you no further.' Without divulging the name Lorenzino said that it was one of the Duke's favourites. 'Let him be anyone he likes, I will kill him', was the reply.

Lorenzino was lodging at that time near the Medici palace in a house where he often sheltered Alessandro in the course of the latter's adventures. At the beginning of January 1537 when he knew that Vitelli, who commanded the army, was away from Florence, he told Alessandro that he had at last persuaded Caterina Ginori to come in great secret to his, Lorenzino's house. A meeting was arranged for January 6th, the Festival of the Epiphany, when the Carnival was to begin.

That evening the Duke was already fatigued with the afternoon's festivities. He threw a long and ample robe round his shoulders and asked gaily whether he was to wear mailed gauntlets or scented gloves. Was it to be war or love?[1] He chose the latter,

---

[1] Alessandro had a remarkable coat of chain-mail which was so convenient that he had no need to go otherwise protected. Now one day when he had forgotten and left it on his bed, Lorenzino had taken it and thrown it down a well. (These curious circumstances, and most of those that follow, are vividly evoked by Musset in his drama of *Lorenzaccio*—Translator).

dismissed his attendants and lay down in the room that Lorenzino had prepared for him. A bright fire was burning in the hearth. Alessandro unbuckled his sword and Lorenzino placed it near the pillow, after taking care to wrap the buckle round the hilt so as to make it more difficult to unsheath. He then went out after advising Alessandro to rest, while awaiting the arrival of the fair aunt. He returned a little later with Scoroncocolo. The door-latch did not open at the first attempt. Softly he approached the couch.

'Are you asleep, my lord?'

At the same moment he struck a furious blow with his short sword at Alessandro's loins. The latter turned round, attempting to evade the attack, but Lorenzino hurled him back and then fell bodily upon him and put his hand over his mouth, so as to prevent him from crying out. 'Have no fear, my lord', he sniggered. Alessandro sank his teeth with rage into his adversary's thumb, and the latter, being unable to use his sword, called to Scoroncocolo, who was running this way and that and finding no place where he could strike, so closely were the antagonists interlocked. He tried first to stab the Duke between Lorenzino's legs, but managed only to poke the mattress. Then, recollecting that he carried a little knife, he drew it, plunged in into Alessandro's throat and so killed him. Up to the last moment the Duke had not loosed his hold on Lorenzino's thumb.

The body rolled on to the floor amid pools of blood. The assassins now replaced it on the bed and concealed it under the blanket which Alessandro had drawn over himself before he had gone to sleep, or pretended to. Lorenzino then opened the window which overlooked the Via Larga. There had been no alarm. It was true that people had heard a noise of stamping, but the Florentines knew that these gentlemen often amused themselves by imitating a riot and crying out: 'Kill him, the traitor!' or 'You have killed me'.

But Lorenzino now failed to profit by his success. Fearing that the people would not follow him, and suffering too from the injury to his thumb, he left everything, abandoned his dreams and decided to join the exiles. At dawn next day he persuaded the guard to open one of the gates on the pretext that he was going to his villa, and fled with his bravo to Bologna. But the exiles who were there received him so distrustfully that he decided to take refuge in Venice. Here he met Filippo Strozzi, who had quarrelled with Alessandro and who ended by admiring Lorenzino's action and described him as a new Brutus.

In Florence it had been some time before the murder was discovered; people supposed the Duke to be resting after the festivities. But Lorenzino's sudden departure aroused suspicion, Vitelli was recalled, and on the night of January 7th to 8th the room was secretly opened. They wrapped the body in a carpet, and carried it to the Sacristy of San Lorenzo.

The festivities, meanwhile, had been continuing as usual; men were tilting at the quintain[1] in front of the palace in the Via Larga; and it was only on the morning of the 8th that the Florentines heard of the assassination of their tyrant. The blackamoor had not been loved, and there were no regrets or disturbance. Lorenzino's house, it is true, was pillaged and partly destroyed so as to make room for a passage which was to be called 'Traitor's Alley'; his effigy too, hanging by one leg, adorned the wall of the fortress. But there was no further movement. The people had no weapons, the most determined foes of the Medici were in exile, and Savonarola's disciples merely said: 'This is what the God-inspired *frate* predicted long ago'; and the affair died away amid gossip. It was observed, for example, that the Duke had been killed on January 6th, at the age of twenty-six, at six o'clock in the evening, that there were six wounds in his body and that he had reigned for six years.

Moralists and political theorists have striven to imagine what were the motives for the murder. In the eyes of some, Lorenzino was a true patriot and lover of liberty, a great-hearted soul after the antique pattern. For others, he was merely a fanatical humanist,

---

[1] The quintain (Italian and Provençal 'Quintana') was a post, or figure of a warrior, with revolving arms. The game consisted in running and striking it with your lance; if you did not hit it in exactly the right place, one of the arms came round and dealt you a buffet. (Translator)

a maniac who wished to make himself a name and who was merely animated by vulgar ambition. It is an open question.[1]

Benvenuto Cellini, who had just set out for Rome, relates that on January 6th, as he was climbing a little hill, he saw what looked like an immense beam of fire glittering in the sky, in the direction of Florence. 'Assuredly', he said, 'we shall hear tomorrow that some extraordinary event has taken place.' The news of the assassination caused him no surprise. He had often seen Alessandro sleeping beside Lorenzino and such confidence appeared to him incredible. In Rome the anti-Medici party were jubilant; one of them, laughing uproariously, said to Cellini: '*There* you have the reverse of the medal that Lorenzino promised you for that infamous tyrant. You wanted to immortalize the Dukes: well, we don't want any more Dukes.' Another added: 'We have unduked them: *li abbiamo sducati*. We shall have no more!' To which Cellini replied:

'In two or three days, you will have another, worse perhaps than the last.'

---

[1] Musset, who of course knew no more than anyone else, took the former view; but he made his drama a penetrating study of the contagious influence of vice. A man who, even from a lofty motive, becomes the companion of a debauchee, will find himself corrupted in the process. The mud will stick. (Translator)

CHAPTER XIX

FLORENCE UNDER THE YOKE

The Principate and the State Police – The last stirrings of liberty – Cosimo puts an end to republican illusions – The Court and business affairs – The academies – Florence pays for the Constitution of the Grand Duchy – Outrages and tragic events – Florentine life loses its picturesqueness

NOT far from Florence there dwelt, in the villa of Trebbio in the Mugello, a young man of eighteen who seemed completely isolated from the vicissitudes of the city. Cosimo de' Medici belonged to that junior branch of the family who, in the time of Savonarola, had declared themselves *Popolani*, and like good demagogues had replaced the Medici balls with the red cross of the people, on their arms.

Young Cosimo's father, Giovanni delle Bande Nere,[1] had won the respect and admiration of the Florentines for a very good reason. In all the family of merchants from which he had sprung, he was the only man of war. An adventurer in the great tradition, he had been 'thrown by his birth, his education and his appetites into the furnace of Italian politics'. When his temper was roused he did not stop short of murder. Once in the Hostelry of the Glove, in the shadow of the Palazzo Vecchio, he had killed an ambassador in his bed, then killed the innkeeper, leapt on his horse, galloped through the city and taken refuge in his lair in the Mugello.

He completely neglected his wife, who was a Salviati, his only real bond with her being the baby Cosimo. One day when returning to the palace in Florence, clad in steel armour, he saw the child in his nurse's arms at one of the windows. 'Throw him to me!' he cried to the peasant-woman. But the window was high,

---

[1] Son of Giovanni de' Medici and the celebrated virago Caterina Sforza, the enemy of Cesare Borgia.

and she did not dare. 'Throw him to me,' he repeated, 'I insist.' Closing her eyes in terror, the nurse dropped the child, and the father received him in his arms and clasped him to his breastplate, delighted to observe that his offspring did not cry out with fear.

Giovanni delle Bande Nere was a great trencher-man, a famous condottiere and the last of the Italian captains who had tried to oppose the invasion of Charles V's savage hordes. His bands of soldiery were celebrated for courage. But at the end of 1526 a bullet lodged in his leg, the leg had to be amputated and he died with the complaint on his lips: 'Must I pass away like this in the midst of plaster casts?'

Now, after the assassination of Alessandro the chief magistrates became involved in fruitless argument, and when the artisans saw these important personages walking past their shops, they remarked, loudly enough to be heard, but without interrupting their work: 'If you don't know how to act, or cannot, call us. We'll act.' Such words were somewhat disquieting, and Cosimo, the last possible member of the Medici family, was summoned in haste. He, with an air of easy-going benevolence heightened by a natural dignity of bearing, declared himself ready to do as the magistrates might decide. The latter went on deliberating, but the crowd outside was restless and someone called through a crack in the door: 'Decide quickly.' As there was some fear that the soldiers might not be able to hold the populace in check, the debate was quickly brought to an end, and on January 9, 1537, Cosimo was elected first magistrate of the Florentine Republic. His house was pillaged, according to time-honoured custom, but Vitelli, who was in command of the forces, brought him the best part of the booty.

'Murder a prince, and others will at once be raised up', said Guicciardini, who was principally responsible for Cosimo's election and imagined that he could easily guide and control this inexperienced youth. But the inexperienced youth now displayed a domineering temper and quickly ridded himself of any kind of tutelage. Being poor, he repaired his fortunes by imposing heavy taxes on the citizens. Besides, how could he doubt of his good fortune? An astrologer had told him that his horoscope was most favourable; he had been born under the sign of Capricorn, like the Emperor Octavius and like Charles V. On June 21st this same Charles V ratified his election and declared him to be the legitimate successor of Alessandro. True, his authority was still subject to certain restrictions, but these were not to last for long. Cellini, who was a sort of prophet, could now pride himself on his foresight:

The Florentines have set a young man astride a marvellous horse, they have strapped spurs to his heels, put the bridle in his hand and finally, after leading him into the middle of a splendid meadow, gay with flowers and rich with fruit, they have forbidden him to go beyond certain limits. Now, just tell me if you can, who will prevent his going beyond them, if he takes it into his head? Can one subject to the laws the man who is master of the laws?

Cosimo in fact was in full control, and nothing was done without his assent. 'There is nothing so great or so small', it was observed, 'to which he does not say yes or no', whatever might be the opinion of his counsellors or of the assemblies. As he had learned to distrust the Florentines who, according to him, were miserly, ambitious, conceited, envious, crafty and so on, he imitated his predecessor by maintaining a system of espionage: but he perfected it. There was not a city, little town or hostelry in the whole of Italy on which he did not receive reports. Piles of letters, extracts and other information reached him in such quantities that Varchi wondered how he ever had time to read them.

The Florentines resigned themselves to the situation, but not so the exiles. When the latter met in Bologna to consider their plans, Cosimo, being informed of it, established a kind of state of siege. It was forbidden to go into the street after sunset under pain of having one's property confiscated and one's hand cut off. House windows must show a light after sundown, under pain of a fine of twenty-five florins. Anyone who took part in an irregular assembly, or in a riot, might be put to death. Now the wealthy Filippo Strozzi, goaded on by the French, by his son Piero and by the continual complaints of the exiles, ended by gathering troops and making open war on Cosimo. But this voluptuous merchant was no general, and he stupidly allowed himself to be caught by surprise by the Spanish and German troops which Charles V had placed at Cosimo's disposal, to defend him—and also to keep an eye on him. At Montemurlo near Prato the rebel forces were crushed. Piero Strozzi managed to escape in disguise, but his father, who was asleep at the time of the attack, was captured along with the most prominent of the exiles; and on August 1, 1537, the Florentines witnessed a procession of these former magnates of commerce, politics and finance, riding along the street on miserable hacks, clad in dirty cloaks, bare-headed and shame-faced in their degradation. It was an example to make the plebeians titter and cause the bourgeois to reflect.

The punishments followed quickly. In the Piazza della Signoria, in front of the tribune of the Marzocco, sixteen of the rebels were beheaded, at the rate of four each morning. Filippo Strozzi, who was the prize capture, was imprisoned in the fort occupied by the Spaniards and placed under the guard of Vitelli, who made himself agreeable and extracted money from his captive. But Cosimo was anxious for this rebellious noble to be convicted of having taken part in the plot to murder Alessandro, and began proceedings against him, despite the intervention of the Vatican and of the French. Strozzi was hoping to get off with a ransom, but in this he was greatly mistaken. He had difficulty in bearing a few strokes of the whip, for his constitution was delicate. One day in December 1538 they found him lying dead between two blood-stained swords; he had apparently, in order to justify his conduct, left a letter in which he declared: 'If I have not hitherto known how to live, I shall know how to die', and, like a good humanist, quoted the following verse from Virgil: *Exoriare aliquis nostris ex ossibus ultor.*[1]

This was probably a staged suicide. Strozzi was one of the richest men in Italy (300,000 crowns in specie were found after his death) and also one of the most dissolute; he had the culture but not the spirit of the ancients; and it is reasonable to suppose that

[1] An avenger will arise from my bones.

he was simply done away with by the orders of Del Vasto, the commander of the Spanish garrison, or of Cosimo himself—murdered in that fortress which he had himself, by giving money to Alessandro, assisted in building; or, as the sententious put it, that 'he had dug his own grave'.

Delighted by his success in dealing with this plutocrat, Cosimo exploited his advantages. He next, though much less roughly, freed himself from his old allies, Vitelli and Guicciardini, to whom however he was under a great obligation. Tyranny now showed itself under a new guise. The better to establish his power, the son of Giovanni delle Bande Nere married Eleonora of Toledo, the daughter of the Viceroy of Naples, an amiable girl of seventeen whom he had met in Naples itself. This was a love-match, and Cosimo, who hitherto had had only one illegitimate child, was to prove a model husband; although, after Eleonora's death, he threw off any restraint. With a view to strengthening his position still more, he left the Medici mansion and took up his residence in the Palazzo della Signoria, the one-time seat of the Republic, which he had ordered to be reconditioned and decorated by Vasari and other artists. It was here that his son Francesco was born in 1541. Finally, as the last step to despotism, he paid Charles V, who was always short of money, to hand over to him the various fortresses of Tuscany: so that, in July 1543, he could sleep 'symbolically' with his family in the fortress that had been built to hold down Florence itself. He was at last freed from his Spanish protectors, though not without expense. It had cost him 200,000 gold crowns.

* * * *

'When the lord Cosimo was raised to power, the city which had been buoyed up by great hopes was now so cast down and degraded in spirit that men dared not look each other in the face. Everyone was sunk in melancholy and went about with lowered head, cursing to himself the evil destiny which had made him a citizen of Florence.' In this way the Republicans chewed the cud of misfortune and defeat, and consigned to the execration of mankind the founders of the tyranny which had allowed Florence to lose her independence and which, besides, had bargained ill enough for itself since despotism had brought the family into disrepute. To all this the political thinkers 'who favoured orderly government' replied that Republic and Democracy had never succeeded in establishing a stable régime; they had served merely as a cloak for the egoism of contending parties. Now one doesn't govern a country by means of *coups-d'état* or conspiracies hatched by exiles; to restore unity, harmony and peace one needs a prince vested with supreme authority. We now have such a prince.

Now that freedom had departed and that the republican mirage had faded away, Florence indeed underwent a transformation. No more were there heard any controversies or arguments as to the best possible form of government. The city was prostrated, wearied of all the changes that had taken place and so distrustful of herself that the citizens lost interest in public business and looked merely to their private concerns. The corporations of the 'arts' had been so reorganized as to bear no trace of their former political functions.

Everything depended on Cosimo who concentrated power in his own hands, took control of the state revenues and increased them enough to enable him to expend 500,000 crowns a year. In this way he financed the building of fortifications and monuments, fitted up the galleries of the Uffizi and built the bridge which, by crossing the Arno, connected the Palazzo Vecchio with the Palazzo Pitti, which he acquired in 1550. Mines for silver and other kinds of ore were established; and all this he organized in accord with his wife Eleonora, a very practical person with a taste for sumptuous living and who, like her husband, was fond of games and races and spent large sums on them.

It is true that after these political upheavals there was a lively renewal of festivities and public spectacles. Cosimo had too keen a feeling for tradition not to pose as a protector of arts and letters, in so far as they gave no offence to the majesty of the State. Thus in 1557 he wrote to *Magnifico nostro carissimo* Michelangelo, who was then eighty-two, inviting him to come and live in peace and freedom under his wing. He similarly encouraged Benvenuto Cellini, on the latter's return from France, to work for him. 'I will pay you better than your King', he told him. But he suddenly seemed to forget his promises, and Cellini, who could not even obtain payment for his famous statue of Perseus, concluded at last that Cosimo's soul was that of a merchant rather than a prince.

And he was not mistaken. Cosimo and his wife were business folk. They traded in sugar, skins, jewels, alum and guano, and maintained two galleys purely for this traffic. Cosimo tried to encourage the manufacture of the fine cloth known as *del garbo* and of silk-stuffs but, as in this field the foreign competition was too severe, he turned his attention to agriculture. By trading in cereals he made considerable profits in time of dearth and he sold grain to neighbouring countries. Furthermore he and his wife, true merchants worthy of the first Cosimo, founded such new industries as the fashioning of articles in coral or crystal and the manufacture of plate glass, Flemish tapestry and pottery of the Chinese type, and thus contributed to an expanding economy.

The intellectuals were favoured but strictly supervised. Young nobles still haunted by the memory of former days sought a new kind of liberty by organizing meetings in which they could talk with a certain degree of freedom under cover of pedantic jargon and obscure formulae. These little academies gave themselves grotesque names. In the Academy of the *Umidi* which had been founded in 1540 by the novelist Grazzini, who was known as the *Lasca*, or roach, each member had to adopt the name of a damp object or being, such as *Ranocchio*, the frog, *Lombrico*, the earthworm, *Fogna*, the drain, and so on. Such clubs, which were organized like little republics behind closed doors, were simply *cicalate*, places for idle chatter.

Although Cosimo was not unduly disquieted by this novelty, he was prudent enough to bring it under control. Thus he turned the *Accademia degli Umidi* into the Florentine Academy and restricted its discussions to matters of language and vocabulary— and certain futilities. This was to give birth in 1587 to the

Accademia della Crusca, the Academy of the bolting-sieve,[1] which legislated on matters of correct usage. These debating clubs, which were a product of servitude, were destined to flourish exceedingly. Fourteen existed in Florence alone, such as the *Infarinato* or *Inferigno* (brown bread), the *Smaccato* (the crushed), the *Stritolato* (the pounded) and many others down to the end of the sixteenth century. Siena possessed twenty-three academies of which the most famous was that of the *Intronati* (the stunned), a circle which the Medici dissolved in 1578. The members of these academies wore expressive devices and tried to be amusing by combining pedantry with obscenity.

While tolerating them, Cosimo kept an eye on them. It was not for nothing that he had founded a police-state: his police were more active than ever. Any action that contained a hint of liberty was repressed by laws of which the mere wording inspired terror. Espionage was rife, and honest men were spied on by those who had the reputation of being honest.

In 1548 Burlamacchi, the gonfaloniere of Lucca, who had been converted to Lutheranism and was being encouraged by the French and by the Florentine exiles, formed the original plan of reviving the old Italian republics and leaguing them together against Charles V and Cosimo. He was a humanist and by temperament a disciple of Savonarola. Having been appointed to lead the militia of Lucca, he prepared for action. His plan was to seize Pisa and then, with the aid of the Pisans who had dreams of liberty, to besiege Florence and drive out the Medici. The whole of Tuscany would then come over to his side.

One of the conspirators, as usually happened, divulged the plot to Cosimo, who asked for Burlamacchi to be handed over to him. Lucca, however, undertook to punish the culprit. As Cosimo was anxious as to the possible outcome of these proceedings, he sought the intervention of a Spanish commissary. This gave rise to a new trial, in which torture was applied. Finally, in September 1548, Burlamacchi was beheaded; and with him died the dream of a confederation of Italian republics.

[1] Which was its emblem.   (Translator)

Pier Francesco de' Medici by Vasari (Palazzo Vecchio)

14. Piero di Lorenzo de' Medici by Bronzino (Palazzo Medici-Riccardi, Florence)

It did not pay to attack the tyrant. A man who had tried to assassinate him in the villa at Poggio had been executed in 1544, and more recently Cosimo had liquidated an affair he had set his heart on, namely the killing of Lorenzino, now known as Lorenzaccio—the evil Lorenzo. The latter had inspired an apologia for his deed, representing tyrannicide as meritorious and citing the example of Timoleon[1] who had slain a relative in order to free his country: but he had since then been leading the life of a hunted animal, in constant dread of the appearance of some hired assassin of Cosimo's or of Charles V's. It was like a death in life. He had wandered from Venice to Constantinople and thence to Paris. But he was imprudent enough to return to Venice, where his family, the Soderini, were living. Cosimo's ambassador now hired a couple of ruffianly soldiers to kill Lorenzino. They made friends with their intended victim and then one day attacked him with daggers which, to make doubly sure, had been dipped in poison. Lorenzaccio died in his mother's arms.[2] Thanks to the ambassador's protection the two ruffians were able in the end to leave Venice and to end their days quietly at Volterra on the proceeds of what they had received.

*   *   *   *

Cosimo possessed the qualities of a despot; he was consistent in his policy, astute in the conduct of public affairs, distrustful on principle of everyone. With his bearded face, his hard mouth and his cold and dubious eye, he was not attractive to look at.[3] But he

[1] Timoleon, who had killed the tyrant of Corinth from motives of patriotism, had then fallen into a state of melancholy from which he was finally roused by an invitation to save Syracuse which was then groaning under tyranny. He became not only the saviour of Syracuse but her ruler and benefactor, and is accounted, no doubt rightly, as one of the heroes of the ancient world.   (Translator)

[2] On February 26, 1648. Lorenzaccio was then thirty-four.

[3] See his portrait by Bronzino in the Galleria dell' Accademia. He is represented as armed from head to foot, and with a powerful hand resting on his helmet.

K

knew how to make his way safely through the jungle of European politics.

Once again indeed the Tuscan exiles, who were supported by France, raised the green banners marked with the word *Libertà* and the verse from Dante: *Libertà vo cercando ch'è si cara*—'I go seeking liberty which is so dear to me.' This was the signal for another rebellion. Led by Piero Strozzi, son of the Filippo who was supposed to have committed suicide, the rebels drove the Spanish garrison from Siena, and at once the whole of Tuscany was in a ferment. Cosimo immediately ordered the gates of Florence to be closed and no one to leave without his permission. This was in order to prevent an exodus of the well-to-do people and of the young men who might be tempted to join Piero Strozzi. It was a sad time in other ways also for Florence. The countryside was being pillaged both by the exiles and by the Spaniards who carried off everything, and notably the grain which had been threshed. In the city corn was unobtainable save at an exorbitant price: it cost eight lire a bushel. Wine, oil and meat were virtually off the market, and people were dying of hunger. Some 18,000 poor folk wandered through the streets and under the walls or hung about the cellar-entrances, although Cosimo caused 8,000 pounds of bread to be distributed every day. Add to this that an epidemic was raging, as in the days of the siege—not the plague, to be sure, but purpura; and also that astonishing signs were observed. An earthquake, more severe than had ever been experienced, overthrew a number of houses; voices and the clash of arms were heard in the sky; trails of fire appeared; and all this struck terror into the hearts of the Florentines who had been 'much roused by new hopes', and were listening for any favourable sign that they might be able to recover their independence.

Such dreams were quite chimerical. When Charles V heard of the revolt of Siena, he said: 'Loose the Duke of Florence upon them.' Cosimo asked for nothing better. Hitherto he had remained on guard and had made no public declaration; now he went ahead. After resisting courageously for fifteen months, Siena capitulated, and this great city, with all its territories and its wealth, passed under the control of the Duke of Florence (July 1557).

Vasari, wishing to glorify the victor, was planning to paint him in the midst of a circle of counsellors, but Cosimo wrote to him as follows: 'This circle of counsellors whom you want to place round me in picturing the deliberations regarding the Siennese war is unnecessary. I was alone. But you might paint a symbolic figure of Silence, with some other Virtue, which would represent the same thing as these counsellors.' Cosimo was not bragging. He alone had brought the history of Florence to a conclusion, he alone had initiated that of Tuscany by founding the state of which Florence was to be the capital. Until that time the subject cities of Volterra, Arezzo and Pistoia 'had been animated with a spirit of separatism which made each of them a hostile power, however small'. They had afforded Florence no help of any kind during the siege, regarding the city with the same hatred which they felt for the invaders. The truth is, that the Republic had shown itself incompetent to establish any community of interests or duties with the vassal-states, any bond of affection which might have enabled them all to unite in resisting the foreigner. Florence, as Antonio Panella remarks, had not been able to create spiritual unity, or political. Now Cosimo killed the spirit of separatism and achieved political unity. Tuscany was his work.

And the work had been costly. The expenditure is estimated to have run to 3,000,000 crowns. To prosecute the war large gifts had to be made, and loans to Charles V who was always short of money and never repaid his debts. The Florentines now groaned under taxation which grew ever more onerous. It is true that the budget was very materially assisted by the confiscation of the property of the rebels and exiles: and already in 1556 Cosimo had concerted with the merchants a new fiscal expedient, namely the State lottery. It was productive from the outset, yielding 30,000 crowns after the first eight draws.

The economic situation was however becoming difficult. The wool-trade indeed was once again prospering, and the Florentines had established a merchant marine and were trading with America,

K*

Brazil, Macao and China; but these outlets were exceptional, and gradually the sources of well-being were exhausted and the spirit of initiative, hampered as it was by controls and suspicion, tended to disappear. These signs of weakness did not however hamper the political ascendancy of Cosimo. He had contrived to secure the favour of the Vatican, and particularly of Pope Pius IV; and when he was received in Rome with a splendid following of 800 horsemen, 'the Florentine nation', that is to say the exiles, applauded him when they had previously insulted him. So great was his success that someone wrote under the statue of Pasquino in the place used for satirical inscriptions: 'Cosimo de' Medici, Supreme Pontiff'—and that the Pope gave him a number of ancient statues which he took back to Tuscany.

Cosimo remained on equally good terms with the Emperor's son, Philip II, king of Spain. The latter conferred on the heir of Giovanni delle Bande Nere the title of Grand-Duke of Tuscany, a new title which implied dominion over a number of states, including Florence and Siena. Other Italian princes might feel jealous and discontented, but, unlike Cosimo, they did not dispose of a navy and a national army in which the young nobles had enrolled; nor had they founded an order of military monks under the patronage of St Stephen and inspired by the Knights of Malta.

Pius V regarded Cosimo with the same benevolence as that of his predecessor. One day he asked the Grand-Duke to hand over a certain dangerous heretic named Carnesecchi, who had placed himself under Cosimo's protection; and rather than fall out with the Supreme Pontiff, Cosimo was weak enought to obey. The heretic was condemned by the Inquisition. Cosimo maintained close relations with the Vatican and the Pope conferred on him, with the Grand-Ducal dignity, the privilege of wearing a special crown adorned in the front with the red lily of the Florentine Republic. The coronation took place with great ceremony in Rome on March 15, 1570, and the Pope embraced Cosimo while the latter was kneeling before him.

Kings and Emperors might judge these honours excessive for the master of so small a territory; but what did that matter? The winds were favourable and Cosimo had set his sails accordingly. He had already married his son Francesco to an Austrian Arch-duchess who in December 1565 had entered Florence in a manner befitting an imperial princess. Whether people liked it or not, Tuscany now had her place on the map of Europe.

*   *   *   *

The birth of a new state was not accompanied by the birth of new morals, but, on the contrary, by a series of outrages and tragedies, as we shall now see.

We have often encountered Benedetto Varchi, the son of a jurist and a former student at Bologna. On his return to the paternal home in the Canto alle Rondini, near San Pietro Maggiore, he was welcomed by Cosimo, who asked him to write the *History of Florence*. Varchi set to work conscientiously, with a concern for impartiality which was not always in keeping with the political régime under which Florence was then living. Now, one night he was attacked, near Santa Maria Nuova, by an unknown ruffian who struck him furiously with a poniard. Varchi, protecting his arm with his *lucco*, defended himself courageously, escaped by a hairbreadth and was healed of his wounds. He knew now, as well as his assailant, what was the motive for the outrage: it was the *History of Florence*. And when the Duke expressed surprise that the book had not yet appeared, Varchi replied: 'You must not be astonished that I am slow in writing it. I value my life, and I run the risk of losing it if I speak the truth.'[1]

Cosimo himself, though for quite different reasons, enjoyed no security against physical assault; and he was so well aware of this that he always wore a coat of mail under his clothing, which for that matter was usually unobtrusive. He had already as we know, in 1544, escaped one plot. In 1559 a certain Pandolfo Pucci, a former familiar of the swarthy Alessandro and who had been imprisoned for offences against morality, conspired with a few associates to get rid of Cosimo. But his was not the manner of a successful bravo, he shuffled instead of going straight to his goal; and so

[1] Varchi was to end his days in 1565, at la Topaia, a villa near Florence.

the plot was discovered and Pandolfo and his accomplices were hanged from the windows of the Bargello.

It was however in the tyrant's own family that tragedies were numerous.

In the autumn of 1562 three of Cosimo's sons, Giovanni, a young Cardinal, Don Garcia and Piero happened to be hunting in the Maremma. They contracted pernicious fever, as a result of which the Cardinal died on November 21st and Garcia on December 12th: such was the official version. According to the unofficial version, Giovanni and Garcia had both claimed credit for killing an animal, and so bitter was the contention that Garcia had slain Giovanni. Cosimo subsequently, in an access of rage, flung himself upon Garcia who had taken refuge in his mother's arms and stabbed him: 'Congratulate yourself', he cried, 'on losing your life by the hand of him who gave it you rather than with the ignominy of a felon.' It was added that Cosimo had become certain of Garcia's guilt on seeing the victim's blood boiling when placed near the presumed assassin.

Thus the story of pernicious fever was countered by a story of two murders. Was the latter version simply a legend invented by the exiles? The fact is that five days after Giovanni's death, his mother Eleonora also died.[1] She had been a good wife and business-woman, greedy of gain, and had amassed enough to buy the Pitti Palace; but she was not popular with the Florentines, who reproached her for her Spanish arrogance and took offence at seeing her always surrounded by ladies and gentlemen of her own nation. Did the Florentines merit such scorn?

Now that he was a widower, Cosimo grew unrestrained. He became enamoured first of a *giovinetta*, Eleonora degli Albizzi, who, with the assent of her father, went to bear him company in the villas where he rested. Involved when little more than a boy in the rough and tumble of existence, he now, at the age of forty-five, felt tired and even surfeited with public life; he therefore in

[1] Of tuberculosis, it was said. (If Giovanni had died on November the 21st, Eleonora on the 26th, and Don Garcia on December 12th, then the unofficial version cannot have been entirely accurate—Translator.)

June 1564 delegated the conduct of affairs to his eldest son Francesco, while retaining supreme authority in his own hands. But Francesco, who was now regent, feared that the liaison with the Albizzi girl might end in marriage and he was confirmed in this fear by Sforza Almeni, a gentleman of the Duke's bedchamber, who revealed to him 'the most secret particulars of this love-affair'. Francesco then ventured to remonstrate with his father. This was a perilous move, because Cosimo in a fury attacked Sforza for betraying his confidence and killed him. After that he lived in retirement with the Albizzi, by whom he had a son; but finding then that he had ceased to love her, he married her to a member of the Panciatichi family in 1567, and gave her a dowry.

But he had no talent for solitude or asceticism and, having provided for his former mistress, he chose as his companion Camilla Martelli, the daughter of a gentleman of modest condition, and a cousin of the Albizzi. People began to gossip, and the Holy Father, Pius V, advised his protégé to regularize this new connection. But Maximilian, Emperor of Austria, and Francesco, Regent of Tuscany, were not at all of that opinion, although indeed the Martelli could pretend to no formal title. 'You must be mad', said the Emperor, 'to think of marrying a woman of such low estate.' To which Cosimo replied: 'I took her to set my conscience at ease, and for that I owe account only to God.'

The Grand-Duke's second wife did not make life easy for him. He had become not mad, but prematurely paralysed in the legs, in the right hand and almost in his speech. Now, the Martelli, a tall woman, not beautiful, was cursed with an hysterical temperament and a vanity which made everyone dislike her; and she treated the poor invalid, who could not take his food unless he was assisted, without consideration. She made him weep with her violent language and ill-temper and sometimes seemed to abandon him. It was in this state of misery and fallen greatness that the Grand-Duke passed away, on April 25, 1574, at the age of fifty-five.

His enemies took care to blacken his memory. As if the murder of his son Don Garcia and of his gentleman of the bedchamber were not enough, condiments so to speak were added. He was alleged to have had his daughter Maria poisoned on her refusing to marry the Duke of Ferrara's son, because she was in love with a page at the court; and in fact Maria, an agreeable girl who was then sixteen, did die suddenly at the time when the marriage was being discussed. Cosimo was also said to have had incestuous relations with his other daughter, Isabella, and with the wife of his son Piero.

A tale of infamy is only too readily extended, and it is likely enough that the exiles and Cosimo's enemies in general did all they could to build up for him a fearful reputation; in certain respects he had himself provided the means.

But when all is said and done, this half-forgotten Medici had displayed remarkable qualities of statesmanship. He had enlarged the Florentine territory. Tuscany, when he died, was a well-organized and fairly powerful Duchy. It had a population of over 800,000, of whom 700,000 were in the Florentine domain proper; an army of 36,000, a navy of sixteen galleys, and State revenues amounting to over a million ducats, thanks to heavy taxation and forced loans which would have infuriated the old republicans, accustomed though they had been to being bled.

Morally speaking, there is little to be said for Cosimo; he was even something of a blackguard. And one can scarcely be surprised that his culture was mediocre. At the age of eighteen he had been plunged into a welter of politics which would have tried the virtue of a saint. On the other hand he had been interested to some extent in the natural sciences, in botany, for example, he had imported plants from America and established botanical gardens. For the rest he was a sober man and, when not in dread of the dagger, would indulge in a kind of gaiety.

His life, on the whole, had not been enviable. One has the impression of a painful rise to power, beset with pitfalls. But if Cosimo reached the top, the daily life of Florence did not gain either in joy or serenity. The days of the Republic, whether they had been days of real or only apparent freedom, had been less sombre.

CHAPTER XX

THE DECLINE: THE GALLERY OF MASKS

Decline of the population – The Florentines are excluded
from public life – Debility or indifference of public opinion –
Tragi-comedies of court life – The decadence becomes more
marked – An assassination in the Renaissance manner – The
years of comedy in Molière's manner – The last of the princes

Now that she had fallen under the Austro-Spanish hege-
mony, the decadence of Italy as a whole became more
pronounced as the years went by; and for several reasons.
The protective tariffs that were imposed, the excessive taxation,
the rage for luxury and the shifting of maritime trade-routes
consequent on the discovery of new lands, all had an unfavourable
effect. Between 1550 and 1600 the population declined from
11,165,000 to 10,080,000, that is, a loss of over a million souls;
while at the same time the proceeds of trade and agriculture
brought benefit only to the State and its representatives—
governors and viceroys—and to the nobility and clergy. From
this trend the Florentines themselves did not escape; and it was
an irony of fate that it was they who had taught their conquerors
the secrets of accountancy and the very terminology of commerce.
We shall now see them, under the last princes of the house of
Medici—picturesque enough persons in their way—sinking into
a life of dullness and mediocrity.[1]

* * * *

In the year 1574 Cosimo's successor Francesco was thirty-
three. His flattish physiognomy and large expressionless eyes did
not bespeak intelligence; but he had served his apprenticeship in
statecraft during his father's lifetime, he had travelled, had estab-

---

[1] The most recently discovered documents relating to this period have
been utilized by Antonio Panella and Umberto Dorini.

lished contact with the Spaniards and had been married to an Austrian Archduchess. The conditions necessary for a peaceful reign, namely alliance with the victor, seemed to have been achieved, but once again public and private tragedies complicated the situation and created a threatening atmosphere.

These tragedies began in 1575 with the plot of Orazio Pucci, a son of the Pandolfo whom Cosimo had had executed fifteen years before. Orazio wanted to avenge his father; but, as was almost bound to happen in a well 'administered' state, he was denounced. After trying to commit suicide, he was hanged from the same gallows as Pandolfo. Twenty of his accomplices were then condemned to see not only their personal property, but the property of their families, confiscated by virtue of the law known as the *Polverina*, which was most profitable to the Treasury. It brought in 300,000 ducats on this occasion; but the act involved Francesco and his government in great odium in Florence.

The following year was marked by a domestic drama. Francesco's youngest brother, Piero, was a vainglorious brute, a vagabond, idler, gamester, 'constitutionally immoral' and in fact half-mad. Cosimo had married him in 1571 to Dianora de Toledo, a niece of his wife, then a girl of eighteen. It was an unhappy union. On the night of July 9th to 10th, 1576, in the Medici villa at Cafaggiolo, Piero strangled his wife with a napkin and then wrote to the Grand-Duke to say that his unfortunate spouse had just succumbed to an attack of apoplexy. Francesco knew Piero too well to be taken in by this, and so the two brothers agreed to issue the following version of what had happened: a handsome Florentine named Bernardino Antinori had been Dianora's lover; her husband had simply avenged himself. This fiction convinced no one, but, though there was no proof of adultery, Antinori was made to pay. He was murdered in his prison; whether as Dianora's lover or as an accomplice of Orazio Pucci, the public was left to choose. But Piero's evil deed entailed at least one unpleasant consequence: it roused the fury of the Toledo and Alba families in Spain, and they spread the story far and wide.

We must now relate the story of Cosimo's elder daughter Isabella. This handsome, intelligent and cultured young lady, an excellent dancer, musician and horsewoman, represented the perfect type of a Renaissance princess. Her parents, however, had married her to Paolo Giordano Orsini, Duke of Bracciano, a loutish soldier who possessed none of the qualities of a nobleman and who passed most of his time in Rome. Isabella in these circumstances was left entirely to herself. But she was surrounded by admirers, and the example of her father with the Martelli, not to speak of similar cases, was probably not lost on her. She found consolation by taking as her lover Troilo Orsini, a cousin of Bracciano's. Informed of this situation, the Duke came in haste from Rome and, under pretext of going out to hunt, made his way to Cerreto Guidi, the villa where Isabella was living. Here at dawn on July 16th—six days after the murder of Dianora—Bracciano strangled her. The court did not trouble to invent an ingenious explanation. Isabella, it was said, had had an attack of apoplexy just when she was washing her hair and had expired in the arms of her women. Thus the month of July 1576 was marked with blood.

This time however it was a clear case of adultery; and in the following year the Grand-Duke sent his bravi on the tracks of his sister's lover. The latter had sought refuge in Paris under the wing of Catherine de Médicis, but he was duly stabbed to death all the same. As to Bracciano, he later fell in love with Vittoria Accoramboni, the wife of Francesco Peretti (a relative of the future Pope Sixtus V); and, as it was now almost a matter of habit, Bracciano had the husband murdered and then married the widow.[1]

* * * *

The historian has some difficulty in adapting his mind to the

[1] This Vittoria, whose behaviour was the scandal of Rome, was one of the most heartless and brazen sinners on record: a woman with nerves of steel and the courage of a she-wolf. Her deeds created a tremendous sensation in Europe, and furnished material for Webster's *The White Devil*, and more recently for one of Stendhal's *Chroniques italiennes*. (Translator)

K**

pitch of this period, which truly recalls the most savage days of the Quattrocento, the age of the condottieri and the adventurers all athirst to create some little duchy or tyranny for themselves, carved out of the living flesh of unhappy Italy. But history demands that we should not fight shy of the truth.

The Florentines, who were now excluded from any share in public life, made a bare living out of their various trades. They were sheep to be fleeced, to enable the Tuscan court to live in luxury. Gone now were the days of party strife, of those street brawls which imparted colour and movement to existence, maintained people in a perpetual state of excitement, stimulated the brain and produced new ideas as steel produces sparks from a flint. The only 'dramas' now were dramas of the palace, and it was the echo of these dramas, often distorted in the telling, that provided material for conversation behind closed doors; and of material there was no shortage.

The Grand-Duke Francesco was not merely the observer and commentator of the domestic tragedies in his family. He had his own affair, which in no way fell short of the others.

Towards the end of 1563, when Cosimo I was still Grand-Duke, there had arrived in Florence a certain Bianca, the daughter of a Venetian patrician named Bartolomeo Cappello. She was handsome,[1] energetic and, though still young, had a number of adventures to her credit, or rather, her discredit. She had been the mistress of a Florentine named Pietro Bonaventuri, who was employed in the Venetian branch-office of the Salviati Bank; and when this liaison was discovered, her lover, who had a practical turn of mind, married her and advised her to flee to Florence— after laying her hands on all she could in her father's house. This

---

[1] The portraits we have of Bianca date from the time of her high fortune and give no great impression of beauty. She was a fleshy, much-painted, Venetian type, with the beginnings of a double chin. Fine eyes, however, a well-marked mouth, rather thick-lipped, long fingers which look greedy and retentive. The hair, which is naturally of the reddish-blonde Venetian colouring, is set off by ear-rings and necklaces. There is little of the aristocrat about her. See the portraits by Bronzino in the Uffizi, and in the Pinacoteca of Lucca.

done, the couple decamped. In Venice Pietro's uncle and employer was arrested, and died in prison; and a reward was offered to anyone who should hand over the abductor.

This little romance, commonplace enough in its way, inspired great interest in Francesco, whose protection the lovers had come to seek. Bianca's beauty, wit and vivacity impressed him and he ordered the police to take measures for the security of the fugitives. He also tried, though in vain, to persuade Venice to raise the ban on them. But interest was soon followed by love; and one night, in defiance of the danger, Francesco made his way to Bianca's room. Her husband, a practical-minded man as we have said, connived with a good grace at these nocturnal visits. Now all this took place in secret, and for a very good reason. The negotiations for Francesco's marriage with the Archduchess Joanna of Austria were then in full swing. But once the marriage was concluded, Francesco ceased to conceal the affair. And as Bianca complained of being rather meanly lodged in the house of the Bonaventuri, who were very modest bourgeois, he gave her, near his own palace in the Via Maggio, a fine house (which is still standing), had it furnished and decorated; and appointed her husband as first gentleman of his wardrobe.

The Florentines and even the courtiers were scandalized. The thing was talked of all over Italy; and Cosimo, who made a point of keeping up appearances, tried to reason with his heir. But the latter refused to listen. His Austrian wife was the same age as Bianca; but she was slightly hump-backed, and moreover she was of a morose and melancholy disposition and of limited outlook. Distrusting the Italians, she surrounded herself with her own countrymen and women. How could one see any charm in this foreigner? With Bianca it was different. What lent a certain piquancy to the discussions between father and son was that the latter had posed as an austere moralist at the time of his father's liaison with the Albizzi. Florentines who knew about this must have smiled.

In any event the three-cornered establishment had been set up. But before long the ex-bank-employee who was now first gentleman of the wardrobe began to give himself airs and to affect an intolerable conceit; and it was perhaps to restore the balance of his situation in regard to Bianca that he took Alessandra Bonciani, the widow of a Ricci, for his mistress. He then went about proclaiming his good fortune so loudly that the Ricci family felt deeply insulted. The Castilian point of honour now reinforcing Italian susceptibility, Pietro Bonaventuri was assassinated on the night of August 26-27, 1572, in a street behind the Via Maggio. No one doubted the reason. The Ricci family had acted in agreement with Francesco, who had taken this opportunity for getting rid of the husband. A little later Alessandra Bonciani met her end, at the hands, or at the instigation, of her brothers. Neither of these crimes was punished.

The field was now clear. Bianca was free, and Francesco, who had become Grand-Duke after Cosimo's death, built a palace for his beloved in the once republican gardens of the Oricellari. The Grand-Duke cynically neglected the Archduchess, and it was in vain that she protested against the humiliation that was put upon her. Bianca the Venetian was the real sovereign and she led Francesco by the nose; perhaps, it was thought, by means of the magic spells she procured from a Jewish sorceress. The scandal provoked more gossip than ever; the Florentines had never loved what came from Venice.

The question of the succession arose about this time. The only surviving children of the Archduchess were girls, her son having died while still a baby; and Francesco was very anxious to have a male heir. Now it was that Bianca came on the scene. She had formerly had a daughter by Bonaventuri, but since that time 'her disorders' and maladies had left her sterile. No matter: as a woman without scruple she would pretend to be *enceinte*. So, during the night of August 29, 1576, she simulated a long and painful labour and then, having dismissed the persons in attendance, remained with her accomplices, who secretly introduced into the bedroom the *bambino* of a woman of the people, born the night before; the baby being concealed in a large lute. The pseudo-mother's room was then opened and Francesco, informed of the good news and weeping with joy, rushed in and clasped the *bambino* to his bosom. The child was to be called Antonio, Bianca affirming that she owed his arrival to the intercession of that Saint.

It now remained to remove any traces of the plot. First of all three women who had agreed in advance to hand over their babies disappeared one after the other, as if by chance. A year later Bianca, fearing the indiscretion of her Bolognese waiting-woman who had organized the whole affair, sent her back to her own country. Now, while crossing the mountains this woman was mortally wounded with a bolt from an arquebus, but she had recognized her assailant and before dying she confessed the whole story. And the story was immediately transmitted to the Grand-Duke's brother, Cardinal Ferdinand, in Rome. His relations with Francesco had not been cordial, and now he was still further edified.

Francesco for his part was enraptured at having little Antonio as his heir. When Bianca felt sure of her power over him and confessed the truth, he forgave her; his love even increased, and he bought a principate for his supposed son in the Kingdom of Naples.

Now on April 11, 1578, the poor Grand-Duchess quitted this valley of tears, leaving behind her only daughters,[1] one of whom was to be Marie, Queen of France. Her misfortunes had inspired pity and regret in the city; but for Francesco her death was a deliverance. At the same time he was tormented with scruples. In an attempt to detach himself from his bewitching mistress he undertook a long journey through parts of Tuscany; but at every halting-place he was harassed by desperate or threatening letters. In this situation his confessor, a *zoccolante* monk who had been well paid by Bianca, set the conscience of the penitent at ease and dismissed his scruples so effectually that when Francesco heard that his mistress was preparing to leave Tuscany for good, he held out no longer but returned post haste to Florence. And here, on June 2, 1578, less than two months after the Archduchess's death, he married Bianca in the Grand-Ducal Chapel. The marriage was

[1] A son born in 1577 died as a baby.

secret; even Cardinal Ferdinand did not know of it. Bianca was simply to be governess to the princesses.

But when the year of obligatory mourning was over, the mask was thrown off and the marriage proclaimed *urbi et orbi*. The Venetians, always good politicians, now judged it expedient to make themselves agreeable to the Grand-Duke. They solemnly declared Bianca to be a 'true and special daughter of the Republic by reason of her very rare qualities': festivities were organized, and Bianca's father and brother were knighted; after which the whole Cappello clan repaired to Florence, where amid new festivities they celebrated the triumph of the woman whom, fifteen years before, they had consigned to perdition. On October 12, 1579, the marriage-ceremony was solemnly renewed in the great hall of the Palazzo Vecchio. Francesco seated himself on the throne, Bianca took her place beside him and the ambassadors placed on her head the Grand-Ducal coronet. The Venetians returned home at the end of the month, the Cappello family being provided with handsome revenues, and Bianca herself receiving a dowry of 100,000 ducats. In spite of the dearth then prevailing, the Florentines paid the expenses. This series of rejoicings lightened their purses of a total of 300,000 ducats.

Bianca Cappello had now reached the zenith of her fortunes. There was, it is true, one dark cloud on the horizon—the animosity of Cardinal Ferdinand. But Bianca prudently worked to reconcile the two brothers and succeeded in persuading Francesco to send money to his brother—a thing he had previously refused to do. The effect was good, Ferdinand quietened down . . . for the moment.

The new Grand-Duchess had too much sense not to realize that her husband deeply regretted the absence of a legitimate heir. She saturated herself with drugs, had recourse to the artifices of quacks and sorcerers, but all in vain; and so, while awaiting better times, she persuaded Francesco to designate as his heir the young Antonio—who was neither a Cappello nor a Medici—and to give him a suitable portion including a palace in Florence and a villa.

Meanwhile the comedy continued. In 1585 the Florentines heard that their sovereign lady was expecting a child, then that her hopes had not this time been realized, but that she might be fortunate in the future and have sons. Cardinal Ferdinand took note of all this and kept a sharp look-out.

In 1586 it was again announced that Bianca was *enceinte*. The Grand-Duke was jubilant, and grave dignitaries including the Archbishop were invited to the palace to assure themselves regarding Bianca's condition and to bear witness to the imminence of the event. Was it simulation, or illusion, or merely a nervous condition, or autosuggestion?[1] The experts could argue on these points, but one thing was certain: no child made its appearance. And meanwhile the discord between the brothers became so violent that the Archbishop had to put his foot down.

Such were the relations between the members of this interesting family when, in October 1587, Francesco caught malaria while hunting near the villa of Poggio a Caiano. He died on the 19th, and Bianca succumbed to the same malady on the 20th. The post-mortem, it is recorded, left no doubt as to the origin of the trouble; but such an explanation appeared too simple, and the almost simultaneous disappearance of the couple, combined with the well-known hostility between the brothers, gave rise to the following story.

Bianca, who hated the Cardinal—a perpetual spoke in her wheels—invited him one day to lunch and offered him a slice of pie which had been carefully poisoned. Ferdinand declined, however, to be served before the Grand-Duke, not only out of courtesy and deference, but because a jewel he wore on his finger had suddenly changed colour from the emanations of the poison. Francesco ate his portion and Bianca, not daring to give a hint of her sinister design, ate hers. She was counting on taking an antedote to save herself and her husband, but the Cardinal was on the watch. He prevented any help from coming and presided over their death agonies with an air of cold satisfaction. This is a story

[1] Mary Tudor had gone through similar miseries when hoping to have an heir by her husband Philip II.

quite in the Renaissance vein, and of the Borgia pattern; but there is no likelihood of its being authentic.

The Florentines received the news of Francesco's death without the least regret, and even with a certain pleasure. He had confirmed their servitude by consenting to become the liege-man of the Austro-Spanish coalition, and the latter had rewarded him by recognizing his title as Grand-Duke. Furthermore, he had inspired the antipathy of the French by refusing any financial assistance to Catherine de Médicis, whereas he was generous in his subsidies to the Italian tyrants; and by having one of the accomplices in the Pucci conspiracy assassinated in Paris where he had taken refuge.

Melancholy and uncommunicative, puffed up also with vanity and pride, he had no contact or spiritual community with his subjects or even his familiars, except with Bianca, to whom he had remained attached for twenty-four years. His only distractions appear to have consisted in dabbling in chemistry and alchemy, in poisons and counter-poisons, in searching for gold and rock-crystal, and sometimes in the manufacture of Indian porcelain. His activities in the laboratory were mostly those of a moron. It must however be added—for there was still a spark of the Medici in him—that he began the reconditioning of the upper rooms of the Uffizi as a gallery in which he exhibited his art-treasures. For the rest, he was a despicable creature; although one can understand why the imagination of the Romanticists was so unduly excited by a life at once gloomy and tragic, highly coloured, scarlet and black in the manner of Stendhal.

*   *   *   *

Under Ferdinand I Florentine life resumed a more normal, if much less colourful, tone. He had been a Cardinal from the age of fourteen, and being disgusted by the intrigues of Bianca Cappello, had been living for a long time in Rome, where, in Vatican circles, he had become an adept in politics. As soon as he heard of his brother's death he left for Florence; and here he was received with gladness, as people knew him to be agreeable and benevolent. He had the good taste not to indulge in any reprisals against his enemies at court, the former partisans of his brother; but, on the other hand, he could not agree that 'the very evil' Bianca should repose in San Lorenzo, beside the other Medici, and he had her coffin removed to some secret spot in the Basilica which has never been discovered.

The question of the succession now came up again. That Francesco should have died without a male heir was a precedent of ill omen. It was desirable that Ferdinand should marry as soon as possible, but he was a Cardinal. Fortunately Pope Sixtus V understood the importance of State interests; he authorized Ferdinand to lay down the purple; and in 1589 Ferdinand married Christine de Lorraine, a granddaughter of Catherine de Médicis. By her, in the following year, he had a son and successor, the future Cosimo II.

This rapprochement between Tuscany and France very much annoyed the Spaniards who feared that their vassal was slipping out of their grasp. But Ferdinand was not to be intimidated.[1] He played an important part in the conversion of Henri IV to Catholicism, and then arranged for the king's marriage with his own niece Maria, a daughter of Francesco and poor Joanna of Austria. The banns were published in the great hall of the Ducal

[1] Ferdinand I, one of the most far-sighted statesmen of the age, was fully alive to the need for checking the increase of Austro-Spanish power. When in 1600 it was thought that Elizabeth I was near her end, the best Protestant claimant to the throne was James VI of Scotland; the best Catholic claimant, the Infanta Isabella. If the Infanta succeeded, England might well move into the Spanish orbit, France would be overawed, the United Provinces overrun, and the independent Italian states would then share the fate of Milan and Naples. Now Ferdinand had just had wind of a plot to murder the Scottish king by poison, and he entrusted young Henry Wotton, who happened to be in Florence at the time, with a secret dispatch to James and an antedote to poison to be used in case of need. Izaak Walton in his *Life of Sir Henry Wotton* describes how successfully the Englishman, disguised as an Italian, carried out his mission. Thus it is not impossible that Ferdinand averted what would have been for England and Scotland a crisis of the first magnitude —Ferdinand was no creature of the Pope, but a tolerant prince, and Protestants, who were not at that time very safe in Rome, could always find a refuge in Tuscany. (Translator)

Palace, Maria was recognized as queen, and on October 5, 1600, the marriage itself was celebrated in Santa Maria del Fiore by proxy, Ferdinand on behalf of Henri IV placing the wedding-ring on the bride's finger.

Marie de Médicis, who had been born in 1573, was twenty-seven at this time. She was a handsome woman but rather stupid and vainglorious, and she did not for long retain her husband's affection. Although Ferdinand had desired her not to take with her to France a large retinue of Florentines, Marie refused to be separated from her foster-sister and confidante, Leonora Dori, the daughter of a joiner and a woman of ill fame who pretended to belong to the noble family of the Galigaï. Another adventurer who figured among the attendants of the new Queen of France was Concino Concini, a grandson of Cosimo's first secretary. Now Leonora and Concino soon discovered that their characters were very much in harmony, as also were their interests. So they married (Leonora not being an ill-favoured person, whatever has been said to the contrary), and they were to play a conspicuous role in history.

If Ferdinand did not abolish despotism, he tempered it, establishing a *Consulta* of which the business was to receive and examine his subjects' petitions and suggest means of dealing with them. Life in Florence now became less distrustful and more agreeable. Ferdinand ruled without rigour, he strove to diminish the suffering consequent on the dearth, he founded a convalescent home and, to improve the state economy, undertook important public works such as the dredging and extension of the harbour at Livorno.[1] This was a free port where many Protestants could live at ease; the former Cardinal being a naturally tolerant prince.

[1] This was the work of Sir Robert Dudley, a son of the Earl of Leicester and Lady Sheffield. He was a skilled mathematician, engineer and ocean-ographer. Being in trouble in England, he had fled to Tuscany, where he became naturalized, and was rewarded with a handsome pension, a town house in Florence and a villa in the country. He had also drained the maremma of Pisa. One might add that official relations with England were also parti-cularly close and cordial during the seventeenth century.   (Translator)

Although not a man of outstanding culture, Ferdinand remained true to the Medici tradition. It was he who, while still a Cardinal, had built the famous villa on the Pincian hill in Rome. The family sanctuary in San Lorenzo, that *campo santo* which glows perhaps too brightly with gilt and marble, was raised in his time. And finally he recognized the merit of that genius Galileo who, at the age of twenty-five, became lecturer in mathematics at the University of Pisa.

Ferdinand died in February 1609. Everyone regretted him. The funeral was simple, as it had been decided to use the money which might have been spent on it in providing dowries for the daughters of poor families. Apart from this, however, he left a comfortable fortune. A good business-man like his ancestors, he had made considerable profits in banking and in the corn-trade.

*   *   *   *

The historian Umberto Dorini writes that Ferdinand I was the last of the Medici who deserves to be remembered. Decadence set in once more, after his death, with princes who were incompetent, odious or absurd.

When Cosimo II came to the throne, he was an indolent and weakly youth of nineteen, without a will of his own. He was dominated by his mother, Christine de Lorraine, and his wife Maria Maddalena of Austria, a lusty German who fatigued him a good deal. He had little notion of how to govern and, being very devout, surrounded himself with priests and monks who mixed with the nobles of the court, exploited him and hedged him in. The other classes of society considered their exclusion intolerable, and Cosimo did not gain in popularity. Life was difficult in other ways, owing to a succession of wars, epidemics and famine. Agriculture, stifled by taxation and governmental restrictions, hardly held its own. The population declined, labour became scarce, and Cosimo—a *minus habens* and suffering from consumption—was not the man to cure these evils. One may perhaps place to his credit the protection which he, like his father, accorded to Galileo, who received the title of 'mathematician extraordinary' and 'philosopher to his most Serene Highness the Grand-Duke.'

On the death of Cosimo II in 1621, his successor, Ferdinand II, was only eleven, and under his reign calamities descended on Florence in even greater numbers. In 1630 the plague claimed 7,000 victims out of a population of 70,000, and still more three years later. The woollen and silk industries, which had been the ancient source of wealth, suffered severely from English and Dutch competition; while the wars, which were a result of the explosive international situation, added the final touch to the miseries of Florence. It was not until 1644 that peace dawned on the horizon, and from that moment indeed Tuscany had the privilege of being exempt from wars and armies until 1799.

The new Grand-Duke, though somewhat grotesque in person and of mediocre abilities, was a gentle and simple creature whose great desire was for peace. He had to spend a lot of money to maintain himself more or less tolerably amid the tempests then rocking Europe. Nor did he enjoy domestic happiness. Vittoria della Rovere, to whom he had been married as a very young man, was terribly haughty, 'cold too in her affections', and life with her proved so unendurable that the Grand-Duke and his consort lived separately for eighteen years. Like her, however, he was severely and strictly pious, and blindly obedient to his director of conscience. This was perhaps why he did not oppose Galileo's being sent to Rome to face the Inquisitors; but he did at least try to have him freed after his condemnation.[1]

Ferdinand II died of apoplexy in 1670 after a reign of forty-nine years which were in no way distinguished or memorable. One may simply note a few minor circumstances which recall the names of his relatives but with which he had nothing to do. Cardinal Giovan Carlo, a *bon vivant* who was very assiduous in his attentions to handsome women, presided over the Academy of

---

[1] Galileo passed his last days in the beautiful villa he owned at Arcetri, a village on the hills to the south of Florence. Although under house-arrest, it is doubtful whether this made much difference to him as he had lost his sight and was near his end.   (Translator)

the *Immobili* in the Via del Cocomero (now the Via Ricasoli) and also over the colloquies in the Oricellari gardens. Prince Leopold, a man of considerably greater capacity, helped to found the first of the scientific academies, that of the *Cimento*, which was the heir to the work of Galileo.[1] The collection of artists' self-portraits which one can see in the Uffizi was also due to Prince Leopold whose 'pastimes and interests were of a studious nature'.

*   *   *   *

The somewhat dull and monotonous reign of Ferdinand II witnessed a drama in which Florence recognized the savour and colour of the Renaissance, of the great days of her history.

Veronica Cibo belonged to an old family which had counted among its members a Pope, a number of Cardinals, some remarkable women, lords and assassins. She was not very beautiful, and yet not displeasing, but a woman of unfathomable pride, energetic too and vindictive. This Veronica had been married to Jacopo Salviati, Duke of San Giuliano, a Florentine noble descended from wealthy bankers. The couple did not get on very well, and as the Duke was wearied of his wife's moods and temper, he sought distraction elsewhere. One evening when surprised by a rainstorm, away from home, he was sheltering under the portico of a palace when a maid came to invite him in, on behalf of the master of the house, old Giustino Canacci. Jacopo accepted the invitation and on entering the salon he was almost rooted to the ground in admiration of Caterina Canacci, a young person whom his host had taken as his second wife. Grace, charm, *morbidezza*, the whole vocabulary of aesthetics was inadequate to describe her. Compared with such splendour, Veronica hardly seemed to count.

Jacopo was completely bewitched. He paid further visits; and Caterina, although surrounded with gallants, let herself in the end be seduced by this noble gentleman. Veronica, however, had

---

[1] And of Torricelli. Tuscany at this time was playing a very notable part in the advance of the natural sciences. The State University at Pisa had on its staff a number of distinguished professors and was a centre of important research, particularly in microscopic biology.   (Translator)

doubtless been warned of what was happening by some unfortunate wooer of the Canacci. She had Jacopo watched and, once
certain of his infidelity, she ruminated the means of vengeance.

At the end of December 1638, at the time of the year when it
was customary for a wife to present her husband with a basket of
fine linen—shirts, handkerchiefs, lace and collars—Veronica
secretly hired some *bravi*[1] of the Scoroncocolo type, who were to
kill Caterina, cut off her head and bring it to the San Giuliano
palace. The assassins accordingly entered Canacci's house, found
Caterina alone—Veronica having foreseen and planned everything—and duly executed the orders they had received. Veronica
now, with a smile of triumph, placed the head at the bottom of
the basket, carefully hiding it under the linen which was still
immaculate. On December 31st she handed to her husband the
customary gift, and then swiftly departed. A little later, when he
was dressing, Jacopo discovered under the lace and handkerchiefs
the livid head of his beloved.

This seems to have been what really happened. But in order to
heighten the story and give it a more artistic turn, currency was
given to the following version:

When Veronica had been advised of her husband's faithlessness, she purchased an enamelled vase from the Della Robbia
workshops. On this she painted in Gothic letters the word *Tradi-
mento*—betrayal—and arranged in the vase a bouquet of rare
flowers to which she pinned a paper with the word *Sorpresa*—
surprise—on it. When the Duke said he was puzzled by these two
words she answered: 'In a few days I will give a merry party and
you will understand.'[2] On the appointed day, when the murder
had been carried out, Veronica concealed the head among the

[1] According to Guerrazzi's *Veronica Cibo*, Ferdinand II himself maintained *bravi*, among whom was the famous Tiberio Squiletti, commonly
known as Fra Diavolo or Fra Paolo because he was an apostate monk.
Squiletti however went too far and ended up in the Bargello dungeons.—
Veronica is said to have assured herself of the complicity of old Canacci's
two sons who were poor and one of whom, Bartolomeo, was in love with his
stepmother Veronica.

[2] What made the crime more atrocious was that Caterina was *enceinte*.

flowers. Jacopo expressed surprise that no guests had arrived and asked his wife what mysterious visit she was expecting. 'Can't you guess, my friend? It is your beloved Caterina.' And she displayed the head, hidden among the flowers. 'My dear friend', she murmured in Jacopo's ear, 'I loved you, and you have betrayed me. I have taken vengeance.'

Whether there was a basket or a vase, linen or flowers, the fact is that Veronica had time to make good her escape, that she was seen again in Rome, that those who paid the penalty were minor actors in the drama and not the most guilty one[1]; and that the Florentines who had long been deprived of any sensational news,[2] could now discuss the case, and express pity, approval or indignation at their leisure.

*   *   *   *

Coming now to the reigns of the last members of the Medici family, we find ourselves in a world that reminds us of Molière. There was to be no more effusion of blood; what came now was conjugal discord and the accession to power of a society of Tartuffes.

Ferdinand II's son, Cosimo III, was a big fellow, much attached to court etiquette and pompous titles, fond of luxury and exotic fashions. At the same time he was an extreme bigot; and his whole existence was to be tormented by the wife to whom he had been married while still a very young man, namely, Marguerite-Louise d'Orléans, a cousin of Louis XIV.

This marriage, which had been planned by Mazarin, acquired the proportions of a catastrophe. Marguerite, a young, brilliant, witty and capricious person, was in love with Charles, Duke of Lorraine; she detested everything Italian, and especially did she

[1] A contemporary observed in this connexion that the laws are like those spider's webs which catch flies and other small insects, but which are broken by stronger creatures.

[2] It may be of interest to recall that Milton after visiting Florence in 1638, when he apparently stayed at the Palazzo Gaddi, paid a second visit to the Tuscan capital in 1639, and that he very likely then heard of the Cibo affair; though of course he does not mention it in his writings. (Translator)

despise and detest her husband. She was constantly telling him she wished to return to her own country and when, in order to tame her, there was a question of removing her French attendants, she entered into such a fury that she had to be confined in the villa of Poggio a Caiano. The method was not good. When Cosimo—not yet Grand-Duke by the way—came to see her and try to calm her, for he entertained only kindly feelings for his wife, she threatened to hurl at him the first object she could lay hand on.

There were some intermissions of quietness which allowed of the birth of a few children, but then her violence was renewed. Once, although she was with child at the time, she tried to escape with a French groom, on another occasion she planned to go to Pisa with a gipsy. Poor Cosimo was reduced to seeking distraction in military parades and foreign travel.[1]

When he succeeded his father, Marguerite, who was now Grand-Duchess, a circumstance flattering to her pride, displayed a milder temper, and in 1671 another child was born. He was to become the absurd Giangastone. But the respite was of short duration. Marguerite's aversion for her husband broke out once more, she complained that he treated her badly and wrote to him, not without reason: 'You make me wretched and I make you.' Her dearest wish now was to devote her life to God; and so, after twelve years of conjugal hell, the couple separated with the assent of Louis XIV.

Marguerite was received into the convent of Montmartre; but feelings of piety soon evaporated. She began to haunt the Court: and, what was far more unseemly for a nun, she associated with the royal guardsmen and the stable-hands. This made the Sun King really angry. He sent her back to the convent; she tried to set it

[1] In 1668 he went to Spain and Portugal, and thence early in 1669 to England, where he visited the southern counties, was royally entertained in London by Charles II and taken to Newmarket. The two Universities received him with distinguished honours. On his return homeward by way of Paris, he was entertained in the Luxembourg by Mademoiselle de Montpensier—la Grande Mademoiselle—who on this occasion engaged Molière and his company to give a performance. The play they presented was *Tartuffe*! (Translator)

on fire; and turning her wrath against her husband, albeit from a distance, she wrote to him: 'I swear, by all that I most hate, that is yourself, that I enter into a compact with the devil to drive you mad.' Her favourite at this time was an ostler. The king now decided to confine this ungovernable fury in the convent at Saint-Mandé; and here she was to die in 1721, a wiser woman, at the age of seventy-six.

Cosimo, in the meantime, as he grew older, had come more and more under the influence of a company of calculating Tartuffes, pious hypocrites. In the previous century the spirit of the Counter Reformation had restored the purity of the faith and the greatness of the Catholic Church; but here it was degraded. In this Tuscan court, closed as it was to any noble or intelligent influence, money was spent like water on such illusory projects as the conversion of Protestants, Jews and heretics in general. Speculating on their ruler's piety, these persons drew pensions designed to maintain them in the right path, allowances which the Florentines described cynically as 'pensions on the Creed'.

One could have wished for a more enlightened sort of charity, for the people as a whole were poor and very heavily taxed. The country districts were becoming depopulated owing to the ravages caused by thieves and starving vagabonds. But the Grand-Duke was unaware of all this; he seems not even to have realized the extent of his extravagance, and in fact he exhausted his revenues to the extent of lacking funds to pay the militia and the civil service. On the other hand the Florentines were subjected to a régime of austerity which, from a certain angle, recalled the distant times of Savonarola. The police proceeded severely against debauchery and illicit love. Young girls were not even allowed to sing in the street. A hush descended on Florence.

Cosimo's main anxiety was to assure the permanence of his house on the throne. But this was not easy. His elder son was a fast liver who, even when he married, did not change his ways an iota, and had no desire for children. The second son, Giangastone, had been married to a German and, as we shall see, this person was a sort of repetition of Marguerite-Louise, after a somewhat different pattern. Cosimo now in despair turned to his brother, Cardinal Francesco-Maria. The Cardinal, now fifty years of age, was physically finished. Nevertheless Cosimo forced him to discard the purple and, lured on by the hope of a successor, chose as his wife Eleonora Gonzaga, a very young princess. But when after the marriage ceremony Eleonora found herself in the presence of a husband as ugly, obese and repulsive as the ex-Cardinal, she refused to live with him. And so at last, after occupying the throne for more than half a century, Cosimo III, now an octogenarian and still a prey to the fixed idea of the succession, was gathered to his fathers.

We now come to the last specimen of the Medici dynasty. The bust of Giangastone which has been preserved conveys the impression of a half-wit and even of a candidate for Bedlam: the eyes are large, wild and threatening, the moustache bristling like that of a musketeer; the whole face is the face of a grotesque who is trying to look terrible. The man was in fact a degenerate and a drunkard. His father had supposed he was doing the right thing by giving him as his companion, and for breeding, a wealthy Saxon woman, Anna Maria, the widow of the Prince of Neuburg. Now this rough, graceless and intractable person had a mania for hunting and, after the marriage which took place at Dusseldorf, she obstinately refused to leave her castle of Reichstadt and her hunting-grounds in the Bohemian Forest. She preferred the society of wild beasts to that of human beings.

Although there was a touch of the wild beast in Giangastone himself, he could not persuade his wife to follow him to Italy. After ten years he gave up the attempt and left the Teutonic Diana to her stags and wild boars. He was seen in Paris with his mother—another crazy eccentric: then in Prague. And throughout all these wanderings he was pursued by his father's appeals: 'Give me a grandson.' But Giangastone was disgusted with women. He cottoned on to students, caroused, got drunk and gambled.

Once in a while, however, a certain homesickness for the hills of Tuscany came upon him. In 1705 he reappeared in Florence, but soon wearied of the austerities of the Court. He returned to

Bohemia and tried to cajole the formidable huntress; then came back. And now the Florentines saw a species of old man who was not yet forty, a solitary figure, dead drunk, stumbling along the streets.

In 1723 when he was over fifty this wreck of a human being mounted the throne. He was now independent: no longer would he have to listen to the eternal refrain of 'Give me a grandson.' Surrounded as he was by widows—a sister, a sister-in-law and an aunt—he had before his eyes the very picture of his family's dissolution. He could be under no illusion now as to his destiny. The sovereigns of Europe had already decided what was to be done with Tuscany. By virtue of the treaty between Louis XV and Charles VI, Emperor of Austria, Tuscany was assigned to François, Duke of Lorraine, to compensate him for the loss of his own dominions which had been ceded to Stanislas Leczinski on the latter's having surrendered his rights to Poland.

In Tuscany Spanish garrisons were now replaced by German, and Giangastone stood by, accepting the degradation without protest. Having become a complete materialist, a thing which would have shocked his father, he abandoned himself to his vices in the midst of a sort of sham court composed of women, men of mean estate and a few nobles to whom he gave a *ruspo*[1] a week, whence their name of *ruspanti*. Giuliano Dami, the major-domo, who was head of this clique, became the dispenser of favours; he helped himself in the first instance, and succeeded in keeping his master under his exclusive control.

Amid such Bacchanalia dwelt Giangastone, worn out with debauchery and sunk in decrepitude. One day in 1732 when staggering along in his usual manner he put his foot out of joint, then took to his bed and in an atmosphere of alcohol and evil odours finally passed away on July 9, 1737. Many dynasties have come to an ignominious end, but none as ignominious as that of the Medici.

One might cite as conclusion to this sketch of life in Florence the remarkably lucid comments of Bernardo Segni, a Florentine

[1] A Florentine sequin.   (Translator)

historian of the sixteenth century. Florence would have been great and powerful, had she been governed by good laws; but to obtain them she never contrived. She was never able to set up a really stable constitution, whether princely or republican, which would have made her strong. Weakened by internal discord, she was content with a limited sort of dignity instead of uniting with other states in order to augment her reputation and dominions. Hence the bad popular régimes, the very bad régimes of little potentates, the tyrannies,[1] which continually afflicted and choked her, so that she was never able to flourish and spread far and wide the glory that animates the men of this country.[2]

In the judgment of political philosophers, Florence might have prospered as a notable State, had she possessed an orderly government and an army which would have invested her with real power. Unhappily, it was not her lot to increase but to decrease and, as a state, to perish.

This may be true in the political sense. Intelligence and brilliant constitutions are not enough to make a people happy. And yet the influences that radiated from Florence, with her wonderful gift for initiating and propagating new ideas and beautiful art-forms, have none the less rendered her immortal.

[1] It is not clear whether he is speaking here of Florence herself, or Tuscany, or Italy as a whole. Apparently all of them.   (Translator)

[2] Among the vicissitudes of Florence, writes Symonds in *The Age of the Despots*, p. 175, one meets with the intrigues of factions and exiles, the skill of demagogues, the selfishness of party-leaders, the learning of scholars, the cupidity of inferior employees, the ingenuity of theorists, the malice of traitors . . . and all this put into action by burghers who regard the State as something they can mould to their own desire.

INDEX